Decision-Making for Value Creation

BUSINESS LEADERSHIP
IN TURBULENT TIMES

MICHAEL LAWRIE AND
GEORGE TSETSEKOS

ARCHWAY
PUBLISHING

Archway Publishing books may be ordered through booksellers or by contacting:

Archway Publishing
1663 Liberty Drive
Bloomington, IN 47403
www.archwaypublishing.com
844-669-3957

ISBN: 978-1-6657-0878-4 (sc)
ISBN: 978-1-6657-0877-7 (hc)
ISBN: 978-1-6657-0876-0 (e)

Library of Congress Control Number: 2021913065

Print information available on the last page.

Archway Publishing rev. date: 09/15/2021

This book benefited from numerous discussions with fellow executives and many leaders who shared views and constructive suggestions in creating corporate value and navigating change during crises. Our interactions with academics provided insights from plethora of research findings on strategy, culture, and finance and offered the intellectual foundation for developing a unified theme, bringing together theory and practice for business leadership. We are grateful to our colleagues for their support and often criticisms for shaping our experiences in leadership roles in business and academia. We are especially thankful to many Drexel University business students who attended the Lawrie Leadership Development program and the LeBow MBA program at Vanguard; discussions and debates provided comments on the pedagogy and refined our methodology for decision making. We also express our gratitude to several speakers who shared their deep professional knowledge and subject matter expertise during our lectures and presentations. While not an exhaustive list, we are grateful to Alyse Bodine, partner at Heidrick & Struggles, Will Forrest, Senior Partner at McKinsey, Ed Nelling, Professor of Finance and Head of the Finance Department at Drexel, Krishnan Rajagopalan, President & CEO at Heidrick & Struggles, Jo Mason, former Chief HR Officer at DXC, Dave Kurz, Professor of Business at Drexel University, Jo Gupta, Partner at McKinsey, Joseph May, Managing Partner Adelphi Capital Partners, Paul Saleh, President & CEO of Gainwell Technologies, Dustin Semach, CFO of Rackspace Inc., Jonathan Ziegert, Professor of Management at Drexel University, and Pallav Jain, Senior Partner at McKinsey, for sharing with our students their experiences. Special thanks to Teresa Harrison, Professor and Associate Dean of the LeBow College of Business for reviewing early parts of the manuscript, and introducing innovations in delivering our lectures and presentations to Drexel's MBA students. John Papadopoulos, Justin Luu and Jeanne Ruane offered fantastic research support during earlier drafts of the book. We recognize Linda Pancari and Angel Hogan for their assistance in managing our demanding schedules and often reminding us of important deadlines. Finally, we appreciate the tolerance of our families for taking precious quality time away from them while being involved in countless hours of zoom conversations and absorbed in writing the manuscript.

CONTENTS

Theory and Practice:
Polarities and Contradictions

This book is intended to help leaders navigate the differences, the polarities, and sometimes the contradictions between the theory of how things are done and the practicality of what must be done, the what and the how. When you are leading an organization, it is important to have a theory and a framework to guide your thoughts about issues and challenges. Based on simplifications and abstractions from reality, the theory provides a foundation for the development of a rational hypothesis, which invariably leads to solutions and gives a sense of how things should be done.

In this regard, having a good generalizable theory to confront business management and strategic challenges helps leaders frame problems and make decisions. However, a theory can never consume the ability to respond, act based on the situation, and adapt to your environment. It is the unique circumstances that make leaders deviate from a theory to present practical solutions. Indeed, while a theory offers a general approach to solving problems, every situation is unique. Applying only theory may lead to misguided answers. Relying exclusively on the world of practice weighs heavily on uniqueness and exceptional or perhaps extreme circumstances. In short, one must always hold two contradictory thoughts in mind while leading and should reconcile both thoughts in a rational way. There are times when the theory provides clarity and guides decision-making to a path of certainty and success. There are other times when practicality forces you to deviate from a straightforward path or to confront unexpected issues and circumstances that will eventually let you complete the work successfully.

Therefore, business leadership and strategy are all about holding two seemingly contradictory views. A metaphor for strategy is the behaviors of the hedgehog and the fox.[1] The hedgehog has a comfortable routine and follows a determined path well-planned ahead, methodically with precision. The behavior of the fox is different. By developing quick thinking with increased awareness and great adoptability when faced with tricky and difficult situations, the fox is responsive and finds ways out of tricky circumstances. Business leadership and strategy are not fully based on the behaviors of these two animals. It is not a straightforward plan (that is, the behavior of the hedgehog) that moves in a methodical way toward a goal where the leader stays absolutely focused, straight ahead. Nor does it reflect the behavior of a fox because while the fox has set on a well-thought-out plan, it capitalizes on unexpected opportunities by changing the course of action. A strategy reflects the balance between these two allegories of behavior. On one hand, insights, intuition, analysis, and the process and then the ability to make the strategy work require the ability to maneuver the strategy itself. Business leadership and strategy are therefore not a linear process but a very dynamic, complex, and chaotic process.

The purpose of this book is to provide a framework and a methodology to support leaders in balancing these opposing forces and contradictions as they move forward. We advance the notion that business success leading to value creation is based on five fundamental drivers: (1) strategy formulation, (2) asset deployment, (3) a financial model that supports the strategy while it creates profits, (4) leadership of the CEO and its team, and (5) organizational culture. While these drivers, components, or elements of our framework independently are well understood as key components to a plan, their management is paramount for value creation. All these elements are interdependent; however, they should be considered in an integrated way.

---

[1] We attribute these words to the historian Thucydides, who described the different military tactics Persians and Greeks used during the Persian invasion in Greece in 485 BC. In a similar fashion, Dr. John Gaddis, a Yale professor of military and naval history, used these words in his research and writings about diplomacy in the book *On Grand Strategy* (New York: Penguin Press, 2018).

Conventional wisdom and theory suggest that strategy is the only element that defines the success of a business. We believe the contradiction is that, in practice, strategy is an important facet but not the only determinant for success. While strategy provides a road map, it remains an aspirational plan unless it is supported by strong leadership, a robust asset-deployment program, a financial model that aligns investments with profits, and an inspiring culture with the support of teams allowed to execute the strategy. All these considerations taken together represent concepts that deliver a powerful perspective and offer an implementable framework for managing a company. It is a paradigm based on the idea that two possible contradictory views, the theory, and the practice, can provide answers to adapt to unique circumstances. While it is intuitive to think about the paradigm for companies with cash flows and profitability, the paradigm is equally applicable for nonprofits, where key drivers, such as assets, a financial model, leadership, and culture, are present.

Each chapter presents a synopsis of key theoretical views with emphasis on what we know about strategy formulation, asset deployment, financial model, leadership team, and organizational culture. Many years of research on these subjects and teaching students in business and management fields provided the basis for the key components of theory and of what we know. The theory is then contrasted with or assessed against how we do things and how things must be done in a complex organization with exposure to an ever-changing and often turbulent environment. The presentation of how we do things draws on long experience in the practice of leading organizations, irrespective if they are large multinational New York Stock Exchange (NYSE)-traded firms or small nonprofit higher education institutions. Apparently both theory and practice seem to provide different recommendations and often contradictory views. However, they represent complementary approaches for leaders to navigate the difficulties and challenges in decision-making.

ORGANIZATION OF THE BOOK

In chapter 1, "Decision-Making for Value Creation: The New Paradigm," we present key considerations of a methodology that we believe, when considered in an integrative way, leads to business success. We propose a new approach for decision-making based on an alignment of vital business functions and outline the need for integration between strategy, an asset deployment program, a financial model that supports the strategy and the asset acquisition plan, a strong leadership team, and the organization culture. This integrative view of handling the business activities of a company, when backed by a strong execution by management, offers the greatest high probability of success. In chapter 2, "Strategy: An Aspirational Road Map," we present the process of strategy formulation from both the academic and pragmatic approaches. In chapter 3, "Asset Deployment: Building Capabilities and Competitive Advantage," we outline the meaning of asset deployment and the process by which a firm identifies its required assets to enhance its capabilities for a successful strategy. The success of strategy and asset deployment depends to a certain extent on the implementation of a financial and business model that will provide profits to generate sustainable value. In chapter 4, "Financial Model for Value Creation," we outline the process for developing a viable financial and business model in support of the firm's strategy. The financial model creates sustainable profits with a well-thought-out capital allocation plan and operating budgets, all supported by a robust benchmark measures of performance. In addition to the creation of a financial and business model, the firm's competitive advantage requires internal capabilities and human capital. In chapter 5, "Leadership," we outline those necessary leadership traits and characteristics. However, it is not only the traits, the style and energy of a CEO, that drive results. It is also the relationships between the leader and the employees that form an environment that allows the smooth execution of a strategy. In chapter 6, "The Role of Organizational Culture," we write about the role of culture in support of the success of the company. Like an ecosystem, the culture contains "software components" and "firmware components," both important in the decision-making process. In chapter 7, "Corporate Governance and the Role of the Board of Directors," we pay attention to the work of board directors as their participation in ratifying corporate decisions impacts decision-making and influences outcomes.

While each of these five drivers or components in our methodology (that is, strategy formulation, asset deployment, financial model for value creation, leadership team, and organizational culture) is an important ingredient for value, they do not guarantee success in creating value. Our framework presents the context within which decisions are made. However, without effective management of these components, business success is in doubt. Certainly, the business environment is very complex, fluid, and dynamic. In modern business history, we cannot identify any other time with so much turbulence in the world as today. In chapter 8, "Execution and Strategy Implementation," we outline the execution process and associated challenges when gaps arise from deviations between actual and expected outcomes, or when new opportunities for value creation are discovered as the market evolves. In chapter 9, "Globalization 2.0," we report recent societal and transformational changes that will most likely transcend cultures and nations. The new type of globalization—globalization 2.0—will most certainly challenge the Anglo-American model of capitalism and indirectly impact corporate decision-making. While our methodology is intact, future changes, if they are realized, should be considered as given in decision-making process. Chapter 10, "Leadership in Turbulent Times," concludes our book with a discussion of the challenges placed on executives to provide leadership in an environment with complexity in decision-making, expectations for impact and ESG investing, and high hopes for equality. Business leaders in such turbulent times will be expected to tolerate ambiguity, place emphasis on dynamics, not mechanics of decision-making, and deliver alignment of incentives among competing constituencies. Our proposed methodology will help guide business leaders through these difficult times. In the "Appendix" we provide insights and predictions about the impact of COVID-19 on business leadership. The crisis has implications on CEO's shifting priorities, on the pace of innovations in technology and on the Board's traditional roles as directors assess the tradeoffs between closing revenue gaps in the short-term with strategic long-term priorities.

Through the chapters we strive to demonstrate the practicality and yet the academic foundation of our approach. We present possible contradictions and polarities between theory and practice and offer a unified approach in moving business decisions forward. We believe both executives and students of business and management programs will benefit from our approach and our framework, whose appropriate implementation will lead to business success. We hope our work will help both executives and students to rethink, reconceptualize, and reorient their critical thinking about business leadership in an environment of change.

CHAPTER ONE

Decision-Making for Value Creation: A New Paradigm

INTRODUCTION

During our careers in academia and in business, many things have changed. First, in academia, over time the pedagogical emphasis has changed, reflecting some of the spectacular successes or failures in businesses. Leadership and ethics, along with accountability and auditing, were introduced during the Enron collapse. Globalization and internationalization, which are familiar economic concepts, were introduced as a result of the successful integration of China's new open economy. Following the 2008–2009 financial crisis and the emergence of big data, business analytics came to the front stage. Strategy was always part of the standard tool set in the MBA curriculum, either as a case study course or a course with emphasis on the process of developing and formulating a strategy. Value creation was and still is a constant part of the pedagogy and is discussed in many ways as part of various functional areas of business, including finance, accounting, marketing, and strategy. Academic research has produced an incredible number of findings, all offering normative recommendations to executives in decision-making. Bringing their academic research into the classroom, professors provide details on what matters in functional business areas and offer to MBAs tools and techniques to impact value.

Entire industries have been transformed, and many companies that were once at the top of the list of the most admired companies in the United States fell out of favor. By 2019, almost 70 percent of the companies listed on the NYSE in 1970 have disappeared via merges and reorganizations and bankruptcies.[2] [3]The dot-com area provided humble experiences of shaky strategies, and the industry followed a steep consolidation. Advances in the internet and information technology that led to the digital transformation of businesses have changed customers' purchasing behaviors. In addition, the COVID-19 pandemic in 2020 has provided new challenges and opportunities for revenue generation.

While all these changes took place in the background, the notion of winning in business and creating value has been a central focal point for both executives and academics. Naturally, executives are interested in winning the war of competition and adding value to the firm they lead. Many CEOs believe that leadership is the precondition for success, and the so-called level-5 leaders described by Jim Collins are those who will make organizations move from good to great.[4] However, anecdotal evidence suggests only a few firms go from good to great. Once stars, many firms fall behind and occasionally disappear through mergers and reorganizations instead of maintaining their prominent roles in an industry. Others when observing a successful firm attribute positive qualities and behaviors to its CEO. Yet many CEOs believe that a differentiated strategy makes a firm successful. In short, in practice, stories of firms' successes tend to emphasize leadership skills or strategic foresight. While these success stories impute high qualities to firms' CEOs, they offer no insights as to how things are done in the real work, where leaders make decisions.

In academia, faculty focus on empirical research to answer questions on how firms develop strategies to compete and win, and on how executives make investment and financing decisions to solidify profitability and ultimately add value to their firms. The logic of this type of academic work is

---

[2] J. Resett and R. Smith. Are Public Markets Declining in Importance? Journal of Applied Finance, Vol 24, No1 2014 pgs. 6-13

[3] *Where Have All the Public Companies Gone?* (New York: Bloomberg, April 9, 2019); Jay Ritter University of Florida IPOs Database.

[4] Jim Collins. *Good to Great: Why Some Companies Make the Leap and Others Don't* (New York: Harper Collins, 2001).

based on the law of large numbers. If someone collects much information and data about companies and analyzes historical performance for a large sample of companies, linkages and fundamental relationships between strategy, leadership behavior, and performance will be uncovered. Using the same logic, key figures and characteristics of firms, such as assets, leverage, and operating margins are correlated to the performance and valuation of firms.

Using this methodological approach and relaying on historical data, academics analyze ex-post strategic moves and conclude that leadership behaviors and developing a perfect strategy are factors that have predictive power for future success. In fact, in order to educate future business leaders, faculty use simplified paradigms to outline key considerations in strategic decisions that eventually create value. While this approach captures simple elements of business decision-making, it is often simplistic in explaining a complex set of parameters that impact success. In addition, missing from discussions are caveats and cautionary notes about the conclusions reached. Typical limitations for the simplified methodologies used in academia in explaining business success include the following:

- The interdependence of key drivers for success. While there is always consideration for several key drivers of success, rarely there is an evaluation of possible interdependence of these factors that, when considered holistically, will lead to value creation.

- Confusion between correlation and causation. Correlation is simply the observation that two or more parameters are linked via a relationship that constitutes a positive or negative association. For example, success and profitability are correlated to a strategy of differentiation. In this respect, a strategy of differentiation explains why firms in a large sample perform better than other firms that lack strategy differentiation. However, it cannot be argued that strategy differentiation exclusively causes profitability. Profitability may be caused by other factors, such as types of assets employed, the culture of the organization, its financial model, and other characteristics that are separate from the strategy of differentiation. Similar concerns are placed when great leadership is presented as a cause of performance.

While there is a clear correlation between good leadership and performance, in a similar fashion, performance may explained by other considerations as well, one of which may be the company's strategy.

+ Failures are difficult to be explained. Many suggest that companies fail because their strategies are wrong. Others stipulate that while the strategy may be correct, the tactics and the execution are not aligned with the organizational capabilities. Academic studies cannot possibly differentiate the reasons for failures, despite efforts to control for firm characteristics and economic variables. Often business failures are attributed either to the wrong strategy with the right execution or the wrong execution of the right strategy.

+ Successes are also difficult to attributed to a singular contributing factor. The idea that leadership contributes to the success of the firm cannot be verified as there is a large number of parameters that explain a company's success. The nature of competition in an industry, asset structure and leverage may be key elements that influence success along with leadership.

The academic world offers limited recommendations for a unified approach for making a company successful. Certainly, these topics are important, but what is needed is a conceptual framework that will provide future aspiring CEOs with the most critical components for business success.

A NEW APPROACH

Reflecting on our diverse experiences in business and academia, we contemplate answering several key questions confronting practicing corporate managers while adding context for students of management and business programs to gain an appreciation of what means to manage a company. First, what enables some firms to be winners in their respective sectors and others to be losers? Why do some firms create and sustain value and others steadily lose value? What do firms need to gain and then sustain value over time? Why do once-great firms fail, and others succeed in creating value? Most important, how senior executives approach decision-making under conditions of uncertainty facing constraints from multiple constituencies outside and insider the company?

While many believe what matters is a good strategy, we postulate that a good strategy is certainly necessary but not sufficient for a firm to succeed and create value. A host of several other elements, when managed and integrated appropriately, creates preconditions for success. In an analogous example, we wonder: What does it take to win a war? In our view, a good strategy by itself is not sufficient for winning a war. Identifying the right capabilities, deploying the appropriate human assets, creating the required intelligence, and providing logistical support are all key considerations.

With practicality, we provide a framework for decision-making to understand companies' successes and advocate a process executives follow to create value. The central thesis of our work advances the notion that success and value creation are based on executive decisions that integrate five fundamental components or drivers: (1) strategy formulation, (2) asset deployment, (3) a financial model that supports the strategy while it creates profits, (4) leadership team, and (5) organizational culture. While these elements independently are well understood as key components to a plan, their management is paramount for business success and value creation. When executives make decisions, they consider in an integrated way the interdependence of these five components. Conventional wisdom suggests that strategy is the only element that determines the success of a business. To the contrary, while we believe decisions about strategy are important, they are not, nevertheless, the only determinant for success. While strategy provides a road map, it remains an aspirational plan unless it is supported by strong leadership, a robust asset deployment program, a financial model that aligns investments with profits, and an inspiring culture that facilitates the execution of the strategy. We therefore advance a new paradigm in decision-making by integrating these five components and advocating responsive management of the process to create corporate value (see figure 1).

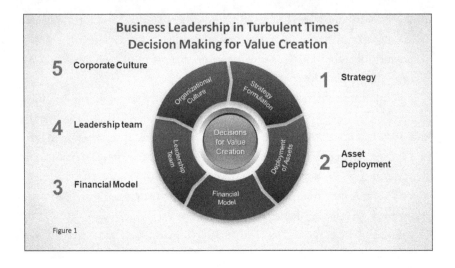

Figure 1

The old paradigm suggests that strategy is the key driver in creating value. While value creation is synonymous with shareholders' wealth, stakeholders can affect or be affected by the firm's actions, and stakeholders' value is impacted.

Our thesis is that strategy is just one component of the decision-making framework that allows for the creation of corporate value and success. The framework includes strategy formulation, asset deployment, a value-enhancing financial model, leadership team, and organizational culture. When all components are considered simultaneously in an integrative manner, the corporation succeeds in creating value. Corporate decisions should be guided by creating value, all leading to competitive advantage.

BUILDING BLOCKS OF A NEW FRAMEWORK

Frameworks present a convenient structure to allow executives to think about challenges in their corporate worlds and make good decisions. Interactive forces inside and outside of the company influence the type of decisions and the modality of decision-making. A framework provides a basic structure and a conceptual context within which decisions are made. Our decision-making framework includes five components as follows.

Strategy. Both practitioners and academics have attributed the success of any organization to a variety of reasons, but all agree that a well-thought-out strategy is a precondition. Academic theorists, under simplified assumptions, have developed models depicting how firms could win in the competitive landscape and highlight the role of a CEO as a perfectionist in implementing a well-thought strategic plan.

Asset Deployment. Physical, tangible, and intangible assets constitute the basis for establishing a corporate entity. Asset acquisition helps companies to position themselves in the competitive marketplace and seek profits. When acquired, assets provide unique resources and often develop product or service capabilities that establish under certain circumstances a differentiated advantage for the firm. While there are many types of assets that a company may consider acquiring, only a subset of these assets satisfy two important constraints. The first constraint is the financial resources required for the purchase of assets. Companies, while they have options, also face constraints in financing asset acquisitions with internally generated cash flows, debt, or equity issuance of securities. The second constraint is based on the strategic choices of the firm. Not all assets provide support in advancing the firm's strategy, and only a careful choice of specific assets required to develop capabilities will help the firm improve its strategic posture.

Financial Model. The financing model illustrates the cash flow and financial implications from the execution of a strategy that creates sustainable profits and value. It serves as a constraint as well as a benchmark for the firm. It is a constraint in developing a strategy in that it balances projected sources and uses of cash flows. Also, it serves as a benchmark since it allows the comparison of a company's resources relative to industry competitors. When the leadership of the firm assumes the responsibility to deploy assets based on a well-developed strategy, the financial model incorporates the outcome of the firm's operations; it depicts the company's resources, transactions, and value.

Leadership. Successful executives with sound experience in managing corporate assets have developed their own philosophies as to how to win the game of competition and create corporate value. In fact, CEOs, especially successful ones, from Lee Iacocca to Jack Welch, have developed recipes for success based on their own experiences. The CEOs leadership involved among other things the development of a team to support initiatives and the execution of the company's strategy. Professional books about leadership justify great profits and success to executive style and emotional attributes. Academic research has also offered meaningful insights into the contributing factors for leaders to make good decisions, all enhancing the value of the organization that they lead.

Corporate culture. The role of human capital in any organization cannot be overstated. Employees with the leadership of the organization are involved in strategy, and they manage and deploy assets. The firm's employees become key contributors to the utilization of acquired assets that will advance the company's strategy. The collective habits of these employees, their shared values, and behaviors create a culture that, when interfacing with the leadership, the assets and the prerequisite financial resources, produces conditions for operational excellence.

Our framework focuses on each of these five components. We advocate that a leadership team in any organization will be successful in generating profitable outcomes only when decisions consider all five elements simultaneously and holistically.

CHAPTER TWO

Strategy: An Aspirational Road Map

One of the contradictions between academics and practitioners is around the concept and workings of strategy. Every organization requires strategy to attain certain objectives. Faculty talk about what strategy is and what we know about strategy. Executives and practitioners talk about how to make strategy. Academics often cite as gold standard theories and evidence-based outcomes of strategy that produce outstanding performance and profitability. CEOs and practitioners point to a design of a thoughtful course of action that creates sustainable advantage reflected in the firm's value or performance. Naturally, while the vocabulary is the same, the teaching of strategy by academics and the practice of strategy by executives represent two frameworks that are not necessarily linked to each other. Often contradictory, these approaches create learning gaps in MBAs and students of management who eventually will become operating executives or heads of a division of a firm.

The teaching of business strategy is based on a top-down approach. Students learn of a process that involves several steps, first setting the company's mission and vision, then performing an internal assessment, followed by an evaluation of the external environment for opportunities. As a result, the theoretical models suggest a strategy analysis and choice that match the company's strengths with the needs of the external environment. The strategic choice becomes a road map that requires implementation and support from the functional areas of business, such as finance, marketing, operations, and accounting. At the end of the process, after its implementation, the strategy is evaluated in terms of desirable outcomes, and any potential deviations are bridged with the appropriate future corrective action. Certainly, the learning of strategy is based on a mechanical framework that describes what we know about strategy, while it offers limited insights into how we make strategy.

In contrast, executives make strategy based on a different framework that requires the design of an aspiring plan that involves three elements:

1. The firm's position in the marketplace to serve customers by offering a valuable proposition. Typical questions to identify the firm's position are: Who are we serving? How can we augment the scope of customers? What kind of service or product are we offering that competes effectively in the marketplace?

2. The operating or business model that will deliver value to the consumer. This may be a combination of practices and choices that answer the questions: How can the company deliver? What kind of processes and organizational assets are required?

3. The sources of uniqueness or competitive advantages that will capture and sustain value in the long term. How distinctive is the product or service offered, how rare is it, and why will it not be copied or replicated?

The interdependence among value creation, value delivery, and value capture creates a unique aspiring road map for the firm, which practitioners call strategy.

To provide a road map for strategy formulation, we follow figure 2.1 and first address what strategy is followed by practical discussion of how an executive goes about formulating a strategy. Part of this exercise is to blend academic tools with practical solutions and analyze the external competitive environment of a company while assessing its internal capabilities. Various tools and techniques offer insights to identify the firm's competitive advantage in terms of resources and capabilities as well the nature of the competition in its industry. The formulation of a strategy is the outcome of the alignment between the firm's external opportunities for growth and profits and its internal capabilities that create value.

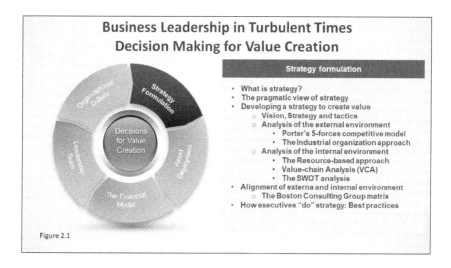

Figure 2.1

However, a strategy formulated based on this alignment, when executed, may not result in desirable outcomes for value and profits. Possible shifts in the competitive environment and/or erosion of the firm's competitive advantage may lead to the wrong path for success. Corrective action requires executives to acquire or deploy assets and partnerships to execute its strategy. A financial model provides requisite resources to further boost the firm's capabilities, and a supportive culture incentivizes and rewards employees when meeting goals and targets. In following chapters, discussions focus on decisions that create value after a strategy is formulated and management attention is shifted to the execution or implementation of the strategy.

WHAT IS STRATEGY?

"Strategy" is the most widely used word in business. Not a day goes by without reading in headlines the word "strategy." It means different things to different people, and it applies both in functional areas of business (for example, marketing strategy, supply chain strategy, and financial strategy) and the overall business organization.[5]

---

[5] "Strategy" is a Greek word that appeared in Homer's work. The word "strategy" is derived from *strategea*, which is comprised of the two words *stratos*, meaning army, and *egea*, meaning to command, guide, and lead with the explicit goal to win a war. The related derived word

Academics have defined "strategy" as follows:

+ "Strategy can be defined as the determination of the basic long-term goals and objective of the enterprise, and the adoption of courses of action and the allocation of resources necessary for carrying out these goals."[6]
+ "Competitive strategy means deliberately choosing a different set of activities to deliver a unique mix of value."[7]

At the macro-level, strategy fundamentally is answering two related questions: (1) What are the enablers for firms to gain and then sustain a competitive advantage over time? (2) How can executives influence firm's performance?

Academics have convincedly positioned strategy as a cluster of goal-oriented actions a firm takes to gain and sustain competitive advantage leading to superior performance in its industry. Executives and practicing managers refer to strategy as an aspirational plan that uses the firm's capabilities to turn them into competitive advantage over rivals with the explicit purpose of creating value.

Strategy may be perceived as a set of activities or actions aimed at creating a unique and valuable position in the industry or a segment of the industry with the following alternatives: (a) serving few needs of many customers in a broad market; (b) serving broad needs of a few customers; (c) serving broad needs of many customers in a narrow market. This requires trade-offs that involve competing with some firms but not with others, and involves decisions regarding investing and financing and decisions on what to do and not to do.

The required ingredients to develop a successful strategy include three

---

strategos refers to an army general who follows a strategea (strategy). Strategos is the leader who oversees the army, devises a grand strategia or strategy, and makes decisions with the objective of winning a war. Sometimes the word is misused; indeed, it has been applied to operational matters, political events, and even everyday life situations. However, strategy is not an idea or a technique.

[6] A. D. Chandler. *Scale and Scope: The Dynamics of Industrial Capitalism* (Cambridge, MA: Belknap, 1970).

[7] M. E. Porter. *Competitive Strategy: Techniques for Analyzing Industries and Competitors* (New York, NY: The Free Press, 1980).

critical elements: (1) identification of the competitive challenges facing the organization; (2) an action plan to deal with the competitive challenges identified; (3) effective execution of the plan through a series of tactical actions, all implemented based on a set of performance metrics. In this context, the management should identify the firm's competitive advantage that, under certain conditions, its competitors will be unable to imitate. Competitive advantage comes from performing different activities or performing the same activities much differently from the way competitors do. The competitive advantage is established and measured in relation to industry rivals rather than in absolute terms.

THE PRAGMATIC VIEW OF STRATEGY

A core concept in strategy is value creation for stakeholders. While in any organization stakeholders include groups, constituencies, and individuals that can affect or be affected by a firm's actions, the Anglo-American model of stakeholders emphasizes their roles, that is, individuals who have contributed capital at risk to create a corporation with a business model and primary economic objective to maximize profits.

Clearly, strategy is central to the prosperity of any organization. It is the plan that allows organizations to win by creating value. Studying a strategy requires an understanding of the context and an analysis of the environment within which an organization operates.

In our view, strategy is an *aspirational* action plan an organization develops with the explicit purpose to win over rivals. Winning in the world of business creates value for stakeholders by developing capabilities that lead to competitive advantages. Strategy is an aspirational plan in the sense that it is bold, audacious, and risky with targeted, expected outcomes. As in the case of a military engagement, strategy is the general's plan to win the battle. In order to execute the strategy, the general relies on capabilities and perceived advantages over the enemy, and during the engagement, the aspirational strategy becomes a pragmatic action plot considering the enemy's moves and capabilities. In addition, the general adjusts the strategic "plot" to take into account the dynamic interaction of the environment with the enemy and his or her troops, such as changing weather conditions. In a similar fashion, in business, executives convert their strategies into pragmatic action plans by leveraging resources and competencies, capabilities, and human capital with the objective of winning the war of creating more value than their rivals.

Therefore, when strategy is contextualized, it represents a set of activities or actions aimed at creating a unique and valuable position in the industry (or segment of the industry) with the following alternatives: (a) serving the needs of as many customers as possible; (b) serving broad needs of few customers; (c) serving broad needs of many customers in a narrow market. Customer scope is a key element in determining the strategy.

As an aspirational road map, strategy requires trade-offs. First, it forces executives to identify in which markets the company should participate, which firms are direct rivals within the selected market, and why the company should participate in some markets and not in others. Then and most important, strategy allows a firm to determine which actions not to undertake, in which markets not to participate and against which firm not to compete, which decisions to avoid, and which investment and financing decisions to undertake to create competitive advantages.

As an aspiration ploy, strategy is a firm's hypothesis about converting capabilities into competitive advantages. It will require coordinated actions within the firm to derive competitive advantage over time. As aspirational strategies vary, a particular strategy is suitable to a particular firm in a particular set of circumstances. As circumstances change, a strategy reflects the ability of the firm to adopt to the external environment while deploying its internal capabilities to achieve unique advantages over competitors.

If follows that strategy is an alignment between a company's internal capabilities with the external environment based on the firm's vision and goals. In this respect, executives use tools and techniques to analyze threats, opportunities, or even features of the external environment that may impact the firm's success. They also analyze the firm's internal environment to determine available resources, differentiated strengths, or even explore how unique values may help the company address the competitive pressures of the external environment.

In the following sections we present a methodology founded on both academic research and practical experiences that allows for formulating a strategy. The methodology outlines the mission, vision, and goals of a firm, and provides tools suitable in analyzing the external and the internal environments of any business through which the company will effectively align capabilities and strengths with its competitive landscape. After presenting drivers for change in the external environment, we explore how Porter's 5 forces competitive model and the industrial organizational model (approach) help in understanding the dynamics of competition. We proceed with the analysis of the internal environment of the firm and present useful techniques that help executives determine the firm's capabilities and unique strengths. When employed, the resource-based analysis (RBA), the value-chain analysis (VCA), and the SWOT analysis provide recommendations of sources of differentiation and competitive advantage, all leading to profitability and value creation. Finally, the firm's strategy is nothing more than an equilibrium point with an alignment of the firm's internal capabilities with its external environment. We present the Boston Consulting Group (BGG) matrix as a tool to aim in the process of developing a company's strategy.

DEVELOPING A STRATEGY TO CREATE VALUE

Students of business and management programs learn that formulating a strategy is a top-down approach that is based on the assumption that strategy development is a linear process. According to this prescriptive approach, to formulate a strategy, executives work with stakeholders to develop a vision and mission for the organization. The firm's mission, in turn, informs and provides a guide to goals to be achieved after evaluating the internal and external environments of the business. In essence, the organization's mission drives strategy formulation. When strategy is developed, its implementation should pass the test of supporting the firm's mission. At the end, when a strategy is formulated in a prescriptive way, it should create competitive advantages aligned with the firm's mission. This linear approach to strategy formulation includes key elements that we now examine.

VISION, STRATEGY, AND TACTICS

The first step in developing a strategy is to consider an organization's vision. The vision answers the question of the organization's purpose. More specifically, the vision is about the aspirational future that the organization wants to create. Since the firm participates in markets and serves customers, naturally a vision statement can be either customer-oriented or product-oriented. The aspirational future of the organization should contain elements of logic and motivation. Typically, a vision statement is usually short, memorable, and inspiring, reflecting choices about what the organization does. Vision looks into the future and inspires the constituencies of the organization to think about the contributions and successes of the firm five to ten years from today. The vision is linked to the mission in that the mission of the firm answers the question of how the organization fulfills its vision. A mission statement often expresses aspiring goals that motivate employees to develop unique capabilities to achieve competitive advantage. The mission is the sole purpose of existence of a firm.

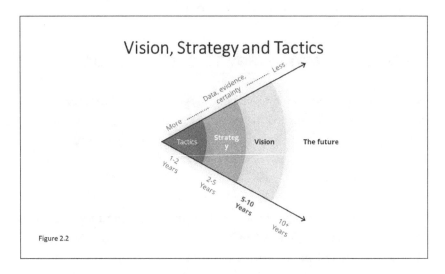

Figure 2.2

A strategy has a shorter horizon perhaps, three to five years, as it focuses on current competencies of the firm. A strategy is supported by tactical plans, a short-term operating initiative required for the execution of the strategy (one to two years). Figure 2.2 shows indicative horizons for a company's tactics, strategy, and vision along with corresponding uncertainty associated with information, markets, and products. The firm's vision is guided to a certain extent by its core values, which present the boundaries of social and moral tolerance that governs the firm's mission and vision. This is in essence the firm's culture. Leaders representing the firm should set the example by living their firm's culture and exhibit behaviors with core values consistent with customers' and employees' values aligned with the firm's strategy.

To better understand the strategy formulation process, it is necessary to evaluate and analyze the firm's external environment, which offers opportunities and threats, and its internal capabilities and competences.

A. ANALYSIS OF THE EXTERNAL ENVIRONMENT

The next steps in the prescriptive approach of strategy formulation is analysis of the external environment within which the firm operates. External analysis involves a methodical examination of the context in which the firm operates. In fact, the external analysis identifies opportunities and threats that will affect how an organization pursues its mission. It involves examination of the industry environment in which the company operates, country or national environment, and socioeconomic or microenvironment. The external environment, a reflection of competitive forces, allows the firm to make choices and undertake financing and investment decisions to develop suitable plans in servicing the market. Primarily, external analysis enables managers to think about how to develop capabilities. If these capabilities are cultivated appropriately, they will become sources of competitive advantage and fulfill unmet needs or offerings in underserved segments in the market.

One significant contribution of external analysis is developing a clear understanding of the threats and opportunities that exist in the firm's competitive environment. A good grasp of these threats and opportunities guides the firm in what it should do and provides strategic choices. Without a thorough external analysis, firms face the risk of encountering threats that they had not foreseen when they implemented their strategies. Likewise, such firms may also miss out on opportunities. Of course external analysis cannot identify every possible threat and opportunity, but it can greatly increase the probability that a firm's strategy will be able to neutralize threats and exploit opportunities. Firms that take a disciplined approach to external analysis will likely have an advantage over those that embark on strategies without taking the time to understand the external environment.

An important dimension of strategy is timing. A good analysis of the external environment may allow a firm to face threats and opportunities at a point in time when the firm does not have resources committed to a strategy. For example, a firm contemplating entry into a new business may discover a significant threat through its external analysis prior to entering the new business. Such a discovery would allow the firm to either abandon the idea or adopt a strategy that would neutralize that specific threat.

External analysis focuses on two levels, namely (a) the general environment, and (b) the industry environment.

First, the general environment is the environment in which all firms in an economy operate, regardless of a firm's specific industry. Macroeconomic and societal changes provide systemic risks to the environment. These changes have a potential effect on every firm in an economy, albeit with different intensity. In the general environment, the following six drivers influence changes and, therefore, have systemic impact on the context of the firm:

1. Technological change
2. Demographic trends
3. Cultural trends
4. Economic climate
5. Legal and political conditions
6. International events (crises, wars, or pandemics)

Many disciplines (including political science, sociology, government and international affairs, and international economics) offer several frameworks in analyzing the firm's environment.

Second, the industry environment consists of elements or forces that the focal firm faces directly. Drivers influence the general environment, whereas interest rates in the general environment may have an indirect effect on a firm. The firm's customers have a more direct effect. Considerations about competition and supply chain, among others, influence the firm's environment.

Two tools are widely used for the analysis of a firm's external environment:

1. Porter's competitive 5-forces framework allows for searching the company's environment to identify drivers that impact performance and profitability.

2. The structure-conduct-performance (SCP) model, an economics-based framework, analyzes the conditions in an industry under which a firm can differentiate itself or compete to achieve performance.

a1. Porter's 5-Forces Competitive Model8

The central theme is that if a company is to survive and prosper, its management must understand the implications environmental forces have on strategic opportunities and threats. We will discuss the forces that shape competition in a company's industry environment using Porter's 5 forces model as an overall framework.[9]

The thesis of Porter's 5-forces competitive model is that each of these forces grows stronger and limits the ability of established companies to raise prices and earn greater profits. Within this framework, a strong competitive force can be regarded as a threat because it depresses profits. We will present these forces in the following.

1. The First Force of Porter's 5-Forces Competitive Model

The first force involves the conditions under which a firm, given the environment, risks its current position and profitability due to a new competitor entering the industry. The risk is small only when an established firm has developed brand loyalty for its products, has an absolute cost advantage over potential competitors, has significant scale economies, benefits from high switching costs, or enjoys regulatory protection. Under these conditions, established companies can charge higher prices, and industry profits are therefore higher. Evidence from academic research suggests that the height of barriers to entry is one of the most important determinants of profit rates

[8] Michael E. Porter. "How Competitive Forces Shape Strategy," *Harvard Business Review*, vol. 57, no. 2, May 1979, pp. 137–145.
[9] Michael E. Porter. "The Five Competitive Forces that Shape Strategy." *Harvard Business Review*, vol. 88, no. 1, January 2008, pp. 78–93.

within an industry. More specifically, the first force includes the following elements:

a) *Risk of entry by potential competitors.* A high risk of entry by potential competitors represents a threat to the profitability of an established firm. If the risk of new entry is low, established companies can take advantage of this opportunity, raise prices, and earn greater returns. The risk of entry by potential competitors is a function of the intensity of the barriers to entry; that is, factors that make it costly for companies to enter an industry. The greater the costs potential competitors must bear to enter an industry, the greater the barriers to entry and the weaker this competitive force. High entry barriers may keep potential competitors out of an industry even when industry profits are high. Important barriers to entry include economies of scale, brand loyalty, absolute cost advantages, customer switching costs, and government regulation.

b) *Economies of scale.* Sources of economies of scale include:

- Cost reductions gained through mass-producing a standardized product
- Discounts on large purchases of raw materials or other inputs of production
- The advantages gained by spreading fixed production costs over a large production volume
- The cost savings associated with distributing, marketing, and advertising costs over a large volume of output

c) *Brand loyalty.* Brand loyalty is based on consumers' preferences for products or services of established firms. Examples of a firm's actions to create brand loyalty include continuously advertising its brand-name products or services, patent protection and product innovation achieved through company research and development programs, focus on high-quality products, and exceptional service. Significant brand loyalty makes it difficult for a new competitor to entry the market and challenge established firms' market shares.

d) *Absolute cost advantages.* An absolute cost advantage of a company relative to potential entrants allows established firms with low costs to have a competitive advantage over new companies. An absolute cost advantage arises from one or all of the following sources:

- Production costs: Superior production operations and processes due to accumulated experience, patents, or trade secrets.
- Input costs: Control of inputs required for production, such as labor, materials, equipment, or management skills that are limited in supply.
- Financing costs: Access to cheaper funds because existing companies represent lower risks than new entrants.

e) *Customer switching costs.* Switching costs arise when a customer invests time, energy, and money switching from the products offered by an established company to the products offered by a new entrant. When switching costs are high, customers can be locked into the product offerings of established companies, even if new entrants offer better products.

f) *Regulations.* Government regulations and the associated costs of regulations create barriers for many firms to enter an industry. When the government deregulates an industry, many more firms will enter the industry. As a result, this increases the intensity of industry competition and results in lower profitability.

2. The Second Force of Porter's 5-Forces Competitive Model

The second force in Porter's 5-forces competitive framework involves the intensity of rivalry among established companies within an industry. Rivalry refers to the competitive struggle between companies within an industry to gain market share from each other. Four factors have a major impact on the intensity of rivalry among established companies within an industry: (1)

Industry competitive structure; (2) industry demand conditions; (3) cost conditions; (4) the height of exit barriers in the industry.

Industry competitive structure. The competitive structure of an industry refers to the number and size distribution of companies in it, something that strategic managers determine at the beginning of an industry analysis. Industry structures vary, and different structures have different implications for the intensity of rivalry. A fragmented industry consists of a large number of small or medium-sized companies. A consolidated industry is dominated by a small number of large companies (an oligopoly), or in extreme cases, by just one company (a monopoly), and companies are often in positions to determine industry prices.

Low-entry barriers and commodity-type products that are difficult to differentiate characterize many fragmented industries. This combination tends to result in boom-and-bust cycles as industry profits rapidly rise and fall. Low-entry barriers imply that new entrants will flood the market, hoping to profit from the boom that occurs when demand is strong and profits are high. Often, the flood of new entrants into a booming, fragmented industry creates excess capacity, and companies start to cut prices in order to use their spare capacity. The difficulty companies face when trying to differentiate their products from those of competitors can exacerbate this tendency. The result is a price war, which depresses industry profits, forces some companies out of business, and deters potential new entrants.

Then, a fragmented industry structure constitutes a threat rather than an opportunity. Economic boom times in fragmented industries are often relatively short-lived because the ease of new entry can soon result in excess capacity, which in turn leads to intense price competition and the failure of less-efficient enterprises.

In consolidated industries, companies are interdependent because one company's competitive actions (for example, changes in price and quality) directly affect the market share of its rivals and thus their profitability. When one company makes a move, this generally "forces" a response from its rivals, and the consequence of such competitive interdependence can be a dangerous competitive reaction with feed-back loops.

Companies in consolidated industries sometimes seek to reduce this threat by following the prices set by the dominant company in the industry. However, companies must be careful about explicit, face-to-face, and price-fixing agreements which are illegal.

Industry demand conditions. The level of industry demand is another determinant of the intensity of rivalry among established companies. Growing demand tends to reduce rivalry because all companies can sell more without taking market shares away from other companies. Demand declines when customers exit the marketplace, or when each customer purchases less.

Cost conditions. The cost structure of firms in an industry is a third determinant of rivalry. In industries where fixed costs are high, profitability tends to be highly leveraged to sales volume, and the desire to grow volume can spark intense rivalry. In situations where demand is not growing fast enough and too many companies are simultaneously engaged in the same actions, the result can be intense rivalry and lower profits.

Exit barriers. Exit barriers are economic, strategic, and emotional factors that prevent companies from leaving an industry. If exit barriers are high, companies become locked into an unprofitable industry where overall demand is static or declining. The result is often excess productive capacity, leading to even more intense rivalry and price competition as companies cut prices, attempting to obtain the customer orders needed to use their idle capacities and cover their fixed costs. Common exit barriers include,

- Investments in assets such as specific machines, equipment, or operating facilities that are of little or no value in alternative uses or cannot be later sold.
- High fixed costs of exit, such as severance pay, health benefits, or pensions that must be paid to workers who are being laid off when a company ceases to operate.
- Emotional attachments to an industry, such as when a company's owners or employees are unwilling to exit an industry for sentimental reasons or because of pride.
- Economic dependence because a company relies on a single industry for its entire revenue and all profits.
- The need to maintain an expensive collection of assets at or above a minimum level to participate effectively in the industry.

Bankruptcy regulations—particularly in the United States, where Chapter 11 bankruptcy provisions allow insolvent enterprises to continue operating—can keep unprofitable assets in the industry, result in persistent excess capacity, and lengthen the time required to bring industry supply in line with demand.

3. The Third Force of Porter's 5-Forces Competitive Model

The third competitive force is the bargaining power of buyers. An industry's buyers may be the individual customers who consume its products (end users) or the companies that distribute an industry's products to end users, such as retailers and wholesalers. The bargaining power of buyers refers to the ability of buyers to bargain down prices charged by companies in the industry or to raise the costs of companies in the industry by demanding better product quality and service. Powerful buyers, therefore, should be viewed as threats. Buyers are most powerful in the following circumstances:

- When the buyers have choice of whom to buy from.
- When buyers purchase in large quantities and use their purchasing power as leverage to bargain for price reductions.
- When the supply industry depends on buyers for a large percentage of its total orders.
- When switching costs are low and buyers can pit the supplying companies against each other to force down prices.
- When it is economically feasible for buyers to purchase an input from several companies at once so that buyers can pit one company in the industry against another.
- When buyers can threaten to enter the industry and independently produce the product, thus supplying their own needs and potentially force down industry prices.

4. The Fourth Force of Porter's 5-Forces Competitive Model

The fourth competitive force is the bargaining power of suppliers, the organizations that provide inputs into the industry such as materials, services, and labor (which may be individuals, organizations such as labor unions, or companies that supply contract labor). The bargaining power of suppliers refers to the ability of suppliers to raise input prices or to raise the costs of the industry in other ways, for example, by providing poor-quality inputs or poor service. Powerful suppliers squeeze profits out of an industry by raising the costs of companies in the industry. Thus, powerful suppliers are a threat. As with buyers, the ability of suppliers to make demands on a company depends on their power relative to that of the company. Suppliers are most powerful in these situations:

- The product that suppliers sell has few substitutes and is vital to the companies in an industry.

- The profitability of suppliers is not significantly affected by the purchases of companies in a particular industry; in other words when the industry is not an important customer to the supplier.
- Companies in an industry would experience significant switching costs if they move to the product of a different supplier because a particular supplier's product is unique.
- Suppliers can threaten to enter their customers' industries and use their inputs to produce products that would compete directly with those of companies already in the industry. Companies in the industry cannot threaten to enter their suppliers' industry and make their own inputs as a tactic for lowering the price of inputs.

5. The Fifth Force of Porter's 5-Forces Competitive Model

The final force in Porter's model is the threat of substitute products, the products of different businesses or industries that can satisfy similar customer needs. The existence of close substitutes is a strong competitive threat because this limits the price that companies in one industry can charge for their products, which also limits industry profitability.

The analysis of forces in the industry environment using Porter's competitive forces framework is a powerful tool that helps managers think systematically about strategic alternatives (see Figure 2.3). However, each competitive force may affect the rest, and all forces need to be considered when performing industry analysis. The interdependence of all these forces may lead to complicated scenarios for strategy formulation. What is clear is that analyzing the industry environment to identify opportunities and threats leads logically to a discussion of what strategies should be adopted to exploit opportunities and counter threats.

Certainly, there are limitations in analyzing the nature of competition within an industry to identify opportunities and threats. One important consideration is the role of innovation and change. Over any reasonable length of time, in many industries competition can be viewed as a process driven by innovation. Innovation is frequently the major factor in industry evolution and propels a company's movement through the industry life cycle. Innovation is attractive because companies that pioneer new products, processes, or strategies can often earn enormous profits. Successful innovation can transform the nature of industry competition. In recent decades, one frequent consequence of innovation has been to lower the fixed costs of production, thereby reducing barriers to entry and allowing new, smaller enterprises to compete with large, established organizations.

Michael Porter talks of innovations as "unfreezing" and "reshaping" industry structure. He argues that, after a period of turbulence triggered by innovation, the structure of an industry once more settles into a stable pattern, and the five forces and strategic group concepts can once more be applied. This view of the evolution of industry structure is often referred to as "punctuated equilibrium." The punctuated equilibrium view holds that long periods of equilibrium (refreezing), when an industry's structure is stable are punctuated by periods of rapid change (unfreezing) when the industry structure is revolutionized by innovation.

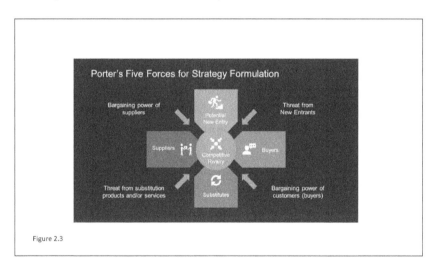

Figure 2.3

a2. The Industrial Organization Approach

Another approach to the firm's external analysis involves the assessment of competitive dynamics within an industry. The industrial organization (IO) approach utilizes a well-established economic model that describes the dynamic competitive interactions of firms in an industry and the performance of firms. It is known as, "the structure-conduct-performance (SCP) model," and when it is utilized, the CEO implicitly receives an answer to the question, Is this the right industry environment for the firm to be involved in and develop a successful strategy? Capitalizing on the so-called SCP model in economics, the IO approach contributes to the understanding of what makes the industry suitable for the firm to operate. It also explains why some companies may perform better in certain industries while companies with similar structures may perform poorly in other industries. The result of this analysis provides insights on missing resources or capabilities that prevent the firm to operate in the right industry.

More specifically, the IO approach focuses on the economics of competition in a market or an industry where rival firms compete for market share and profits. According to this approach, to understand the firm's internal capabilities and differentiated advantages, someone should examine the industry structure within which the firm operates and explore the interdependence of structure and firm's performance. The word "structure" describes the characteristics and composition of the market and industries in the economy and refers to the range (or distribution) of numbers and sizes of firms in the economy. Essentially the structure describes the environment within which firms operate in a market or industry. The environment may be characterized as highly competitive, with many small firms, or oligopolistic, with a handful of large firms. The word "conduct" refers to the behavior and actions of the firms in a market and to the decisions these firms make to compete effectively against rivals. For example, conduct means how firms set prices, how they expense resources for R&D, how they develop innovations, and how efficiently they produce goods. The word "performance" refers to the firm's profitability and how prices and costs are linked.

The market or industry structure has a direct impact on the firm's economic conduct and its ability to determine prices for its goods or services. In turn, this impacts the firm's performance in the marketplace and consequently, its profits. Via feedback loops, a firm's performance may impact conduct and structure as more profitable entities may undertake decisions to price services below those of the competitors to gain oligopolistic advantages, thus impacting the industry structure. Also, the structure of the industry and the type of rivalry among firms will determine the firm's performance as a highly competitive industry with a large number of rival firms produces marginal profits for all participants.

The SCP framework was originally developed with the intent of helping economists and policy makers understand when an industry was likely *not* to be competitive. Competitive industries were the ideal—social welfare was maximized and there were no monopoly profits being extracted from markets. Management scholars who were more interested in individual firms began to see that the SCP framework was useful for identifying market imperfections that would possibly allow firms to make above normal economic profits. Based on the SCP model, scholars have developed models of environmental threats that are highly applicable in identifying threats facing a firm. Industry analysis is based on well-established economic theory, even though in strategic management it is used for a nearly opposite purpose than that for which it was originally developed. Students need to understand that the model of environmental threats is deeply rooted in sound theory.

The internal analysis of a company based on the SCP model from IO economics brings attention to the interdependencies of the firm's actions, the type of competition, and the firm's performance. The key drives of the firm's performance are industry structure and conduct or form of rivalry among competitors in the industry. An internal analysis of a firm's resources and capabilities from the lens of the SCP model provides insights on the success of a strategy in the long term. In addition, at the macro level, the model explains why some firms are more profitable than others in the same industry and why a particular industry is more attractive than another in terms of profitability.

B. ANALYSIS OF THE INTERNAL ENVIRONMENT

While the analysis of the industry is important and the available models are based on good economic analysis, critics contend that the industry models overemphasize the importance of industry structure as a determinant of company performance and underemphasize the importance of differences among companies within an industry or a strategic group. In fact, Richard Rumelt's research, for example, suggests that industry structure explains only about 10 percent of the variance in profit rates across companies. This implies that individual company differences explain much of the remainder.[10] Other studies have estimated the explained variance at about 20 percent, which is still not a large figure.

These findings and criticisms of relying on industry structure to explain performance led many to suggest that a company's individual resources and capabilities may be more important determinants of its profitability than the industry or strategic group of which the company is a member. As a result, the analysis of the firm's internal environment focuses on reviewing the resources, capabilities, and competences of a company with the objective of identifying strengths and weaknesses explaining a firm's performance.

The analysis of the internal environment involves a systematic evaluation of a firm's resources and capabilities. This evaluation enables executives to recognize capabilities and sources of possible competitive advantages and the firm's abilities to meet those needs.

The idea behind internal analysis is to assess critically the firm and uncover capabilities leading to potential sources of competitive advantage. The analysis is not comparable in identifying capabilities relative to other firms. Rather, it is focused on identifying if a firm possesses capabilities that could be deployed in such a way that competitive advantage could be achieved. A strategy that is informed of internal analysis will allow a firm to implement an action plan based on building capabilities and competitive advantages. Without a thorough internal analysis, a firm would just be guessing as to whether a chosen strategy would result in competitive advantage.

Executives often use three approaches to develop the internal analysis in a systematic fashion:

1. A resource-based analysis (RBA), which places emphasis on available capabilities for the firm and aligns its strategy with the environment.
2. The value-chain analysis (VCA), which is based on the notion that the firm's activities are divided into a series of value-creating steps.

---

[10] Richard Rumelt. "Diversification Strategy and Profitability." *Strategic Management Journal*, December 2012.

Both individual activities as well as the interrelationships among activities within the firm—and between the firm and its suppliers, customers, and alliance partners—add value to the firm.
3. SWOT analysis.

B1. The Resource-Based Analysis (RBA)

The RBA suggests that internal resources are more important for a firm than external factors in achieving a competitive advantage. It is stipulated that a firm's performance is determined by internal assets, which could be categorized into tangible and intangible assets. The key to the sustainability of advantages is the creation of bundles of activities and processes leading to products or services that satisfy four criteria: They are rare, valuable, difficult to imitate, and difficult to substitute. These characteristics of resources enable a firm to implement strategies that improve efficiency and effectiveness, and lead to a sustainable competitive advantage. Distinctive competences are a firm's strengths that competitors cannot easily match or imitate. Building competitive advantage involves taking advantage of distinctive competencies.

The RBA determines to what extent the firm has chosen the right resources or portfolio of assets to compete in its industry. In academia, scholars have presented evidence that when considering a large cross-section of firms, performance is agnostic to the industry in which the firms operate, but it is explained primary by internal resources utilized by the firms. In essence, primary drivers of a firm's performance and profitability are attributed to internal resources available to the firm, such as human capital, intangible assets, capital structure, and pricing flexibility. This shifts the analysis from the industry level to the firm's level. While an industry may offer a fertile ground for a firm to prosper, investment choices in the right resources create capabilities to produce value for the firm. Therefore, the formulation of a strategy becomes critical in developing resources that yield capabilities.

Resources a firm possesses or controls include the following portfolio of potential assets, tangible or intangible:

- *Financial resources:* The firm's capital structure and generally money available to the firm from whatever source, including cash flow and retained earnings.
- *Physical resources:* Typically, fixed assets, such as machinery, plant, offices, raw materials, and tangible technology.
- *Human resources:* Human capital, experiences from learning by doing, teamwork, training, individual intelligence, judgment, and work ethic.
- *Organizational resources:* Including reporting structures, reward systems, management structures and coordinating systems.
- *Relationship resources:* Such as supply chain and customer relationships.

Each firm's portfolio may have different allocations of resources across assets. In fact, assets may be heterogeneous across firms. Also, some assets may not be transferable from one firm to another. For example, a firm may be endowed with unique fixed assets compared to its competitors. Firms do not hold the same asset portfolios, and the composition of the portfolios may vary. Therefore, differences in the portfolios of assets or resources explains why one firm performs better than another, and why one firm has competitive advantage over another, even though both firms operate in the confines of the same industry. In essence, a firm may have developed an asset portfolio with a composition that yields capabilities with enduring impact on a long-term competitive advantage of the firm.

The conclusion from an RBA of the firm's internal environment is that an assessment of a firm's assets helps a company compete in its industry. Strategy formulation then is infused with input for acquiring or even enhancing exposure to assets that create unique competitive advantages for the firm.

A way to make the RBA operational is to use the value-rarity-imitability-organization (VRIO) framework, which helps firms anticipate the responses of other firms and solidifies the sources of competitive advantage. Sometimes it may be in the firm's interest possessing the resource advantage to signal to competitors that it would be extremely costly to imitate the resource.

The VRIO framework (see Figure 2.4) is a very effective tool for managers to use as they attempt to position or "bundle" the resources of the firm in the pursuit of competitive advantage. The VRIO framework allows the drawing of conclusions about competitive advantage based on four criteria:

1. *Value:* If the resource enables the firm to exploit an opportunity and neutralize a threat, the resource potentially increases revenues and decreases costs. A valuable resource is strategic. If the firm receives a benefit that outweighs the carrying cost of the resource, then we would conclude that the resource is valuable and could, therefore, be a potential source of competitive advantage. Some firm resources that are valuable but not rare are still important to the firm (for example, computer systems). A resource can still be rare even if more than one firm possesses it. The real question is this: Is the resource rare enough that the firm derives some advantage from having the resource? A resource is considered rare if so few firms possess the resource that nearly perfect competition is not observed.

2. *Rarity:* If the resource is scarce or unique in the marketplace, most likely this resource leads to advantages over competitors. A resource is rare enough that it creates a difference between the firm and its competitors such that the firm realizes some advantage from the difference. This question is tied to the assumption of resource heterogeneity. If there is to be any advantage in having a resource, it must create differences between firms. Maintaining the rareness of a resource is the key to having a sustained competitive advantage. If competing firms can acquire a valuable and rare resource, then the advantage of possessing that resource will quickly dissipate. The big issue here is the cost of imitation. A firm can expect to sustain its competitive advantage if other firms face a cost disadvantage in acquiring the valuable and rare resource. For example, ntellectual property that is protected by patents, or trademarks is by definition rare and valuable.

3. *Imitability:* The resource is protected from possible imitations by rivals. Rivals will face cost disadvantages attempting to imitate resources. For example, it is difficult to imitate a video-sharing network like the one developed by Tik Tok. A competitive disadvantage means that a competing firm would face such a high cost that acquiring the resource would not be worth the cost.

The rivals attempting to imitate a resource face two types of cost disadvantages: (1) Mover advantages, such as brand loyalty and market share as these are difficult to overcome and require time and expenses; (2) path dependency as a resource to be imitated depends on expenses and knowledge of previous stages of development of the resource, and this dependency of the past experience is prohibitively expensive to a rival firm.

4. *Organization:* It refers to the firm's organization suitability to exploiting a resource. A well-organized firm has better chance of developing a resource, and this is a function of learning and experience that a rival firm may lack. The logic behind the question of organization is simply that a firm must be appropriately organized to be able to exploit the potential competitive advantage stemming from valuable, rare, and resources and capabilities that are cost-prohibitive to imitate. Conceivably, a firm could have a valuable, rare, and prohibitively costly to imitate resource and never realize a competitive advantage because of an inadequate organization.

The VRIO framework allows the assessment of the probabilities for a firm's competitive advantage. However, there are several caveats in place. First, the VRIO framework is to be applied on a resource-by-resource basis, not to the resources or capabilities of the firm as a whole. For example, if a firm sought help in analyzing its proposed introduction of a new product (for example, personal digital music device), the VRIO framework might be applied to the firm's design capability, marketing capability, distribution capability, or proposed product per se. This helps to highlight which of these resources, if any, might be sources of competitive advantage. Second, the framework can be used to assess what a firm is currently doing relative to its competitors. Or it can be used to help a firm craft a strategy using its resources and capabilities. It can be used to answer the question, Is this resource likely to be a source of competitive advantage? Finally, the VRIO framework can be applied in a descriptive and prescriptive sense. It can help firms analyze their current sets of resources and capabilities (descriptive). Further, the framework can be applied to help firms formulate strategy (prescriptive).

A resource may be found not to be valuable. The implication is that the resource, not the firm, is at competitive disadvantage. The resource may be valuable but not rare. In this case, the implication is that this resource is at competitive parity. Indeed, another possibility may be a resource that is valuable and rare but not costly to imitate. This means that the resource is a temporary competitive advantage. The last alternative is a resource is valuable, rare, and costly to imitate. In this case, the resource creates a sustained competitive advantage.

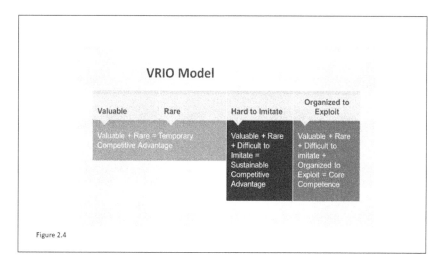

Figure 2.4

B2. Value-Chain Analysis (VCA)

The term "value chain" refers to the idea that a company is a chain of activities that transforms inputs into outputs that customers value (see Figure 2.5). The transformation process involves both primary activities and support activities that add value to the final product. A VCA analysis helps identify the key contributors to profit margins and profitability of the firm. Primary activities involve the entire process, from designing to producing a product or a service. Primary activities require input from support activities that provide inputs, and critical support activities are linked and require efficiency in executing strategy. These support activities involve logistics, human resources, control and auditing systems, information technology, and intangible contributors such as managerial processes and culture. All provide inputs for the primary activities to take place.

Each activity adds incrementally to revenues and profits but also to costs. The VCA helps managers analyze those activities and processes that contribute to strengthening profit margins, but also highlights costs.

VCA is a useful tool that helps managers identify the company's strengths and weaknesses and profit margins. In order to be operational requires the following actions:

- Performing a quantitative assessment of the efficiency and effectiveness of each activity in the process.
- Measuring and benchmarking each activity with the activities of rival firms.
- Benchmarking each activity against best-in-class in other industries.
- Analyzing how well value-creation activities are performing and identifying opportunities for improving the efficiency and effectiveness of those activities through process improvement methodologies. One of the most famous process improvement tools is Six Sigma.

The VCA helps understand the sources of profit margins and profitability of a firm. When looking for potential for improvement within a value-chain activity, leaders within the company need to (a) empower managers to take the necessary actions, (b) measure performance improvements against goals over time, (c) reward managers for meeting or exceeding improvement goals, and (d) analyze why goals are not met and take corrective action if necessary.

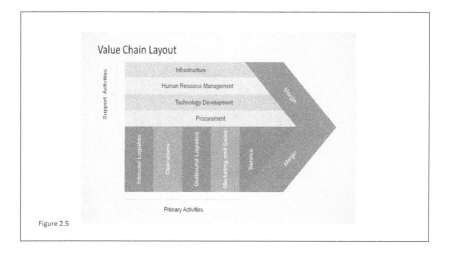

Figure 2.5

External analysis only tells part of the story. A firm would be hard-pressed to formulate an effective strategy using only external analysis. In most cases, there is little the firm can do to change the threats that have been described. However, firms can respond by avoiding the industry (choosing not to enter or choosing to exit) or making strategic choices that may neutralize the threats. Strategic choices that may neutralize threats are typically a matter of changing the incentives of other players—rivals, suppliers, buyers, substitutors, and complementors. In a sense, many of the possible strategic choices basically consist in turning a threat into an opportunity.

In brief, internal and external analyses, taken together, allow executives to think about *positioning* firm resources in a way that is likely to lead to competitive advantage and achieve above-normal returns. Internal analysis helps to sharpen attention on the role of assets, the financial model, and the leadership of the CEO. If we accept that CEOs are responsible for the economic performance of a firm, then the role of a CEO must be to bundle the firm's resources. External analysis is a necessary precursor to strategic choice. CEOs must understand the external environments in which they operate before they can make effective choices. The analysis of the general external environment helps firms identify conditions and trends that may create threats and opportunities.

B3. The SWOT Analysis

A frequently used model for strategic analysis is the SWOT analysis, which is a comparison of strengths, weaknesses, opportunities, and threats for a firm. The central purpose of the SWOT analysis is to identify a strategy to exploit external opportunities, counter threats, build on and protect company strengths, and remove weaknesses. The analysis places emphasis on products and services the firm offers and the external markets.

The goal of a SWOT analysis is to create, affirm or fine-tune a company-specific business model that will best align, fit, or match a company's resources and capabilities to the demands of the environment in which it operates. Managers compare and contrast various alternative possible strategies and then identify the set of strategies that will create and sustain a competitive advantage (figure 2.6).

The strategies identified through a SWOT analysis should be congruent with each other. Thus functional-level strategies should be consistent with or support the company's business-level strategies and global strategies.

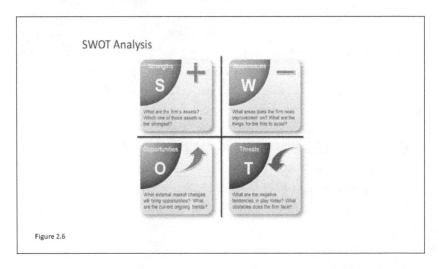

Figure 2.6

C. ALIGNMENT OF EXTERNAL AND INTERNAL ENVIRONMENTS

A widely held view suggests that a strategy is the equilibrium point where a perfect alignment between the external environment and the firm's internal capabilities takes place. The most widely used tools to assess this equilibrium point is the Boston Consulting Group matrix.[11]

C1. The Boston Consulting Group (BCG) Matrix

This matrix maps out the relative market share of a firm's products relative to market growth rates. It categorizes products or services into *stars*, with high growth and high market share growth potential; *question marks*, with low market share and high market share; *cash cows*, low market growth rates and high market share, and *dogs*, with low market share and low market growth rate. The reason for presenting this taxonomy of growth versus market share is to devise a strategy for migrating products or services to a star category while discontinuing products in the dog category. The matrix also serves as an indirect mechanism of internal financing for the firm as cash cows products serve to support investment and funding gaps to further help products move to the star category (figure 2.7).

---

[11] Other tools include the internal-external matrix and the Strategic Positioning and Action Evaluation (SPACE) tool.

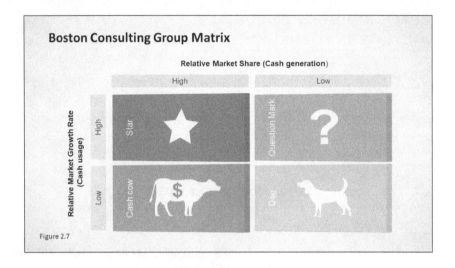

Figure 2.7

How Executives "Do" Strategy: Best Practices

CEOs are big believers in vision. This is appears to be a common theme from interviews in the popular business press of CEOs regardless of firm size and industry classification. Indeed, a credible leader must paint a picture of what the company is trying to become. It may be called a true North, but it guides the broad activities of the company toward a well-articulated inspirational story of how the company may look like in the future. While vision may be perceived as a story with lofty statements or ideas that tend to be difficult to be executed, it brings about the key question of, "What do you want to be known for?" The strategy should be the vehicle that will allow the company to achieve its aspirational vision that ensures that the firm will be known for it. Vision is stable; it never changes. It is aspirational because it is much more than what the company is today.

To formulate a strategy, a CEO may follow many of the analytical tools described in the prescriptive approach. In fact, the actual formulation of the strategy is very closely aligned with the academic approach. The tools and the analysis that helps put the strategy together are well-known, and there is agreement on their contribution in formulating strategy. For example, looking at strengths, weaknesses, opportunities, and threats is an absolute must. In addition, the firm needs to look at competition and take an inventory of its capabilities, of the markets in which it is competing, and of adjacent markets in which it can compete. The structure of the market and the nature of the competition are key considerations requiring detailed analysis and assessment. Thus, strategy is important to positioning the company so that it can create a clear value proposition in the market while competing effectively through differential and based on internally fostered capabilities.

However, the question has always been how to make the "correct" strategy and then convert it into a series of tactical or executional initiatives. Several considerations are necessary in this regard:

1. *Clarity.* The strategy should be clearly communicated. While the priority is sharing the strategy with employees, it should also be communicated to clients, customers, and partners of the organization. If management cannot present the strategy intuitively to their employees, or if it requires time to explain the complexities of a strategy, the strategy lacks clarity.

2. *Strategy evolves, grows, and advances.* The strategy should not be rigid; it should evolve and grow with refinements over time. However, the strategy itself should not change in a radical way over time. Frequent changes in strategy signify unclear and sketchy assessment of market trends and consequently, lack of company focus. A good strategy considers changes in the marketplace and is tweaked and evolved gradually over time, but without radical or sweeping changes. Making drastic changes to the strategy means the organization is in search of a strategy. The strategy shows in what the firm wants to compete and where it can add value, where it has strengths, and where it can overcome weaknesses.

3. *Strategy may be adjusted, corrected, and modified.* Changing strategy requires changes in asset deployment plans and adjustments to the firm's business and financial model. The case of Airbus and Boeing 777 is instructive of the contrast between a successful strategy and a strategy that required adjustments. About twenty five years ago, these two well-run companies came up with diametrically different strategies based on different views of the industry. One view, based on the hub-and-spoke system, assumed that passengers would be flying into a hub, one of many in large regional areas, and then the

hub would consolidate passengers prior to arriving at the final destination. The other view was based on the conjecture that passengers would prefer to fly point to point and with a nonstop flight; they had no desire to go to a hub. These two views led to two different strategies. Airbus, the largest commercial airplane ever built, was based on the economics of a hub-and-spoke system, while Boeing 777 was based on the point-to-point assumption. Boeing 777's vision of the industry was completely right. The big hubs got congested, they could not build more runways, passengers did not like to go to those big hubs, and they wanted to go point to point. Airbus then had to readjust its strategy and execute a different product development plan. As a result, rather than continue to invest in the Airbus 380, they began to invest in a series of airplanes that could go point to point, such as the Airbus 350. Within that strategy and execution elements, all kinds of things happen. The SARS epidemic happened, oil prices increased substantially, as well as regulations. Manufacturers went from four engines to two engines, and from small engines to much bigger engines. Those are all adjustments to the strategy, but the strategy was put in place to compete in an industry that, at that stage, was much more point to point rather than a hub and spoke. This is a real-life example of a strategy that was persistent for twenty years but had to be adjusted based on the realities of the marketplace, what consumers valued, and what they were willing to pay for.

Complete reset of a strategy is expected if outcomes are not consistent with expectations and if there are dramatic market changes. For example, Kodak, a well-managed company, did not change strategy at the time of digital camera revolution. Kodak knew digital cameras were coming on the market, but the CEO could never get the company readjusted to that change in the market. This then dictated a different strategy, which produced a whole different set of technologies that they needed to compete. It was a different financial model. Thus, if the industry does shift, then it is necessary to shift every piece of our five-components model in order to remain on the market. It may take time, but this is the process of creative destruction in our economy. In addition, the way a firm manages creative destruction implies the company has to be aware of those technologies that can really disrupt the end and its industry. Then the firm has to acquire or build this organically, or it ends up not surviving over a long period of time. It is important to highlight the failures, spectacular failures of not working within the framework. On one hand, we advocate a new paradigm in value creation or value enhancement for a company. However, on the other hand, we should consider what kind of failures would a company experience by not following this paradigm. The landscape is littered with examples, and Kodak was certainly a great one. Another example is General Motors, which had a real rough time adjusting. Not recognizing shifts in the marketplace may result in bankruptcy. IBM had experienced similar problem as well. The company following several crises was able to recreate itself around the services business, but it is struggling again because of difficulties in adjusting to dramatic shifts in the marketplace.

Other examples that demonstrate how market shifts may require adjustments, corrections or modification of a strategy include:

- The effects of the internet on the hotel industry and on big retailers.
- The devastating impact of the COVID-19 on almost all retailers. Whether it be Macy's or the rental car market, Hertz clearly did not adjust to the fact that Uber and Lyft were going to disrupt that market, and they have never realigned themselves.
- Blockbuster video is a company that came into the entertainment industry and completely disrupted the market. Yet it was disrupted when the technology changed. Indeed, it was completely disintermediated by its lack of ability to stream videos.
- Telecommunication carriers and the ongoing change with cable are finding difficulties in these hanging times. In the past, television networks such CBS, NBC, and ABC were pillars, while now they are just small segments. Viewers watch very little television nowadays. They may watch the news, but for entertainment, they rely on platforms like

HBO, Netflix, Showtime, or Amazon Prime. Everything has completely changed. While these technologies were known for a while, and there were companies that were building this capability, not too many firms adjusted their strategies to reflect upcoming changes.

4. *The challenge of strategy execution.* Breaking down the strategy into operating and tactical steps that require careful execution is by itself a challenge. While it seems to be an easy task, this dividing into pieces that require tactics for execution is an activity that has multiple solutions. It is uncertain which tactics should be used to achieve desirable outputs that validate the strategy. These actions can be taken in the short or medium term to create the traction needed for the strategy. A financial model that makes the strategy come to life in terms of cash flows is needed. A CEO while may be visionary, without focusing on details of execution may fail in moving the company forward.

5. *The role of the management team.* It is important to have a team that understands and buys into the strategy. If the team does not agree with the strategy, either the strategy requires review and uplifting, or the team does not have the right people to execute the strategy. Either way, this calls for change in an effort to find the management team that can drive the strategy.

6. *The ownership and accountability of a strategy.* Often the strategy is delegated to the head of a corporate department that reports to the CEO. However, such delegation creates ambiguity and certainly establishes the impression that strategy is a linear process with inputs and outputs. The owner of the strategy should be the CEO with the corresponding responsibility. Undoubtedly, the senior management team should be involved in the strategy preparation, but the ownership and accountability for the outcome should lie with the CEO. During the strategy formulation process, he or she should lead the process but should not dominate the process. Input should be from people who understand the industry and the trends in the industry to help formulate that strategy. Nevertheless, the management team should be part of the strategy because it has to execute the strategy.

It is hard to get people to execute something in which they have not been part of the formulation.

7. *Interdependencies.* If the assets do not fit the strategy, the firm may discard them. If the firm does not have some assets that it needs to compete, then it may need to acquire these resources. In addition, it is crucial that the company considers its human resources and the skills to execute the strategy. Assets are about companies' resources, especially about the competencies that are required. A company can acquire these competencies in several ways, such as partnerships, acquisitions, or internal investments.

8. *Strategy and outcomes.* When execution elements are in place, a measurement system is also used to assess results. When results are not consistent with expectations, this requires examination of what are the root causes of the variance. The explanation of the variance may be based on lack of good execution, lack of skills required for the execution, or lack of assets. Or the strategy that we thought we had the capacity to execute is no longer suitable. This requires adjustment to the strategy. As the firm executes an aspirational plan, it needs to change the components of the plan.

9. *The role of people cannot be overestimated.* Persistence and change are key in strategy development and execution. Managers occasionally run into a bump, an obstacle, and often change both strategy and tactics. Much more persistence to stick to the goals of the strategy is necessary. Perseverance, persistence, and stick-to-itiveness are keys to successful outcomes.

10. *Strategy and goals.* Translating strategy to a coherent set of goals is part of a successful execution. In fact, the selection of goals makes the organization follow a good or a bad strategy. When goals are either ambiguous or unachievable or contain every possible suggestion, the firm will eventually follow a bad strategy.[12] Instead, goals characterized by clarity and involve informed assessment of the markets and the firm's capabilities lead to a good strategy consequently to great outcomes.

---

[12] Richard Rumelt. *Good Strategy/Bad Strategy: The Difference and Why It Matters* (New York: Crown Business, 2011).

11. *A practical view of the strategy.* On one hand, strategy is presented as a linear process, with analysis of the external and internal environments and development of competencies for value creation. On the other hand, the pragmatic approach suggests that strategy is a combination of insights, intuition, some analysis, some process, input from many different sources, and ability and desired flexibility to maneuver within that strategy. While one approach is not "better" than the other, in essence, the two approaches to strategy should be reconciled and selected elements from each approach should be utilized in practice.

12. *A metaphor for strategy: Hedgehogs and foxes.* Strategy is not based on the behavior of the hedgehog or the fox. It is not a straightforward plan that moves in a methodical way toward a goal straight ahead. Nor does it reflect the behavior of a fox that, while has set on a well-thought-out plan, capitalizes on unexpected opportunities by changing the course of action. The hedgehog has a comfortable routine and follows a determined, well-planned path methodically and with precision. The behavior of a fox is different. By developing quick thinking with increased awareness and great adoptability when faced with tricky and difficult situations, the fox is responsive and finds ways out of tricky circumstances. Strategy reflects the balance between these two allegories of behavior of the hedgehog and the fox. On one hand, insights, intuition, analysis, and then the ability to make the strategy work require talent to maneuver within the strategy. On the other hand, following the process, especial its intellectual components such formulation, continuous assessment of strengths and opportunities, and evaluation of the competition require attention to follow a disciplined process. Indeed, the polarity here is clear as strategy is a process considered dynamic and occasionally chaotic, yet it includes elements of a linear and well-disciplined process.

CHAPTER THREE

Asset Deployment: Building Competencies and Competitive Advantage

OVERVIEW

A company with a product or service portfolio has established boundaries in the marketplace. The boundaries outline what the firm does, how large the firm is, and the business it is in. Boundaries may be extended when a new strategy is implemented.[13] To support the strategy, the company may acquire, organically build, or deploy assets that extend the firm's boundaries. Therefore, asset deployment becomes a key consideration in decision-making as the firm expands its boundaries. Executives follow a process of deploying assets suitable to creating value and sustaining profits.

"Asset deployment" is a term used to describe a variety of alternatives in utilizing assets that extend the boundaries of the firm. These alternatives include acquiring new assets and/or organically increasing the asset

---

[13] B. Holmström and J. Roberts. "The Boundaries of the Firm Revisited," *Journal of Economic Perspectives*, 12, 1998, pp. 73–94.

base of the company; having access to assets via leasing, joint ventures, or partnerships; and/or outsourcing to a third-party a portion of the operating or service processes of the firm. For example, the firm can deploy assets by purchasing another firm, through building more manufacturing plans with internally generated funds or outsourcing part of its production, or event engage in a joint venture with another firm to offer a service or product that was costly to offer it along.

Since there are alternatives to asset deployment, there are many types of assets that fit into a strategy. However, there are two conditions that make assets fit a chosen strategy. First, a firm must select the types of assets that when deployed maximize its competitive advantage. This in turn is a function of the markets in which the firm competes and the na-ture of the competition among all firms in the industry. Determining and deploying the right assets that fit the strategy allow the firm to establish a position in the industry with the long-term objective to achieve sustainable advantage. Second, the deployment of assets should be consistent with the financial model of the company which outlines the sources of funds required for the purchase of assets. In addition, asset deployment should be aligned with the leadership and culture of the organization to ensure compatibility in executing a strategy. To present the diverse views and perspectives and the practice in asset deployment we follow the outline that appears in figure 3.1.

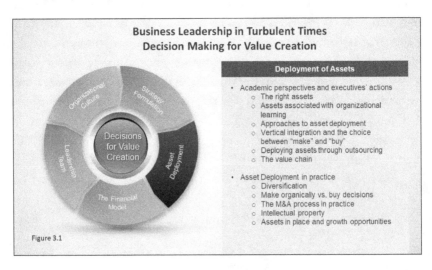

Figure 3.1

ACADEMIC PERSPECTIVES AND EXECUTIVE ACTIONS

Academics and executives approach the acquisition or deployment of assets from two different perspectives.

Academics focus discussions on the type and characteristics of assets that expand the boundaries of the corporation. The boundaries of the firm may be expanded horizontally or vertically. A horizontal expansion of the firm from newly deployed assets yields economies of scale, reduction in average unit costs, and produces possible diversification of product offerings.[14] An example may be the Marriott's 2016 acquisition of Starwood Hotels and Resorts or Facebook's 2015 acquisition of Instagram. Vertical expansion of the firm involves acquisition of assets that strengthen the supply chain, reduce production costs, and capture upstream and downstream profits. An example may be the 2015 Ikea purchase of forests in Romania to supply the firm's own raw material or Google's 2012 acquisition of smartphone producer Motorola.

How the firm expands its boundaries hinges on the structure of the market where the company offers products or services.[15] Therefore, academics search for types of assets that assist in expanding the boundaries of the firm while at the same time address the competitive conditions in the market. More specifically, academics try to address the question: "Given a certain structure of the competition, what type of assets helps the firm shape its boundaries to advance its goals of achieving competitive advantage?"

Executives' attention is on assets that create capabilities and uniqueness to allow for a chosen strategy to be executed. Executives answer the practical question: "Which type of assets produce capabilities that when achieved allow the firm to implement a strategy leading to competitive advantage?"

The apparently different approaches between academics and practicing executives show the different perspectives. Academics address the question, "For a given market structure, what assets create competitive advantages?" while executives address the question, "What assets are required to be deployed to implement a strategy?"

---

[14] Milgrom, P., and J. Roberts. *Economics, Organization, and Management* (Englewood Cliffs, NJ: Prentice-Hall, 1992).

[15] A. D. Chandler Jr. *Scale and Scope: The Dynamics of Industrial Capitalism* (Cambridge, MA: Belknap, 1990).

Executives strive to develop capabilities to execute a strategy. A strategy requires resources and deployment of assets to be used for its implementation. It is expected that assets in support of the strategy are used in a productive and effective manner. Highly productive assets create efficiencies and yield returns to all stakeholders, including employees and shareholders. Assets used effectively produce competitive advantage as their utilization enhances strategic positioning of the firm.

There are two related questions. First, what kind of assets are required for a firm to support the strategy for creating value and competitive advantage? Second, how do executives go about deploying assets to support the strategy? The first question deals with the mix of assets that will create a competitive advantage. The markets in which the firm competes and the nature of competitive interactions among firms in the industry will determine the mix of assets. The second question deals with the process of executing a series of actions to bring about assets needed in support of an agreed-upon strategy. The process allows the firm to develop capabilities to position itself to compete but also allows it to adjust over time to account for tactical adjustments required for success.

THE "RIGHT" ASSETS

All assets are not created equally. As they are used for different purposes, a firm may deploy any combination of tangible assets, human capital assets, relationship assets, intellectual capital, or intangible assets. Tangible assets involve assets with physical characteristics, for example, plant, equipment, and the like. Human capital assets reflect specialized and/or experienced human resources with managerial and skill-specific expertise. Relationship assets are based on customer and other revenue-producing relationships because of contractual agreements of the firm. Relationship assets enhance the company's reputation and expand the customer and investor base. Finally, intellectual capital is a set of patents or proprietary processes or information vital to the business activities for products/services of the firm. Intellectual capital may be the result of the company's organizational structure that advances innovation and discovery. In a broader category, intellectual capital is part of intangible assets that include proprietary processes, intellectual property (IP), copyrights, clinical processes, and so on.

Assets vary in terms of their usefulness and duration; some may be depleted over time (for example, equipment), and yet certain assets may increase in value over time (for example, mining). Assets may also be highly liquid in the sense they can be sold in an active secondary market and redeployed to other, higher-value uses. Other assets may be highly illiquid and highly unlikely to be sold to others at the end of their useful lives.

Yet another way of asset categorization is based on the future strategic orientation of an investment associate with the acquisition of assets. Assets-in-place represent assets required for the continuity of business. Assets in growth opportunities represent acquisition of assets that create upstream growth in cash flow and opportunities for profitable diversification.

ASSETS ASSOCIATED WITH ORGANIZATIONAL LEARNING

One important asset category not well articulated by executives is organizational learning assets. Typically, employees improve production processes and efficiencies with experience. Incremental improvements in skills, processes, and services by the employees of a firm lead to organizational learning. Essentially, improvements in performance of human capital through learning by doing represent unique know-how. Therefore, learning achieved from experience, if protected, can create reduced costs and improved quality.

More specifically, organizational learning is attributed to (a) general ability of employees to plan, organize, and control the output of a process; (b) specific knowledge developed based on industry standards and norms; and (c) skill levels of workers as their skills will improve through learning by doing. As a result, organizational capital is accumulated through experiences within the firm and involves (a) specialized knowledge and information possessed by employees, (b) jobs that require employee teamwork, and (c) creative collaboration of employees to produce innovation and discovery. The *combination* of organizational learning and organizational capital create firm-specific human capital which is unique to a company and cannot be transferred to others. Only when another firm acquires the human capital can the firm-specific human capital be deployed for the benefit of the acquiring firm.

Organizational leaning is different than economies of scale. Economies of scale is the outcome of deployment of more assets in the same process with the goal of reducing the average cost. Scale economies that lead to cost efficiencies are suitable for capital-intensive firms. As a contrast, organizational learning is the deployment of human capital that through learning by doing and experience results in decreasing average costs and increasing quality of output. Organizational learning is a key consideration for human capital–intensive firms with service orientations, such as consulting firms and service-oriented companies.

APPROACHES TO ASSET DEPLOYMENT

A strategy to be successful should be supported by the capabilities arising from the unique mix of assets. When brought together, the right mix of assets generate an optimum mix of resources that produce distinctive capabilities for the firm, thus allowing it to create favorable conditions to support its strategy. Asset mix becomes an important determinant in positioning the firm to compete in its industry.

Depending on the firm's strategy, assets may be deployed to expand the boundaries of the firm in three distinct ways.[16] First, assets may be deployed to support a strategy that aims in dominance in product markets. In this case the firm is building capacity, and by expanding its asset base, it creates economies of scale. Because of its size, economies of scale allows the firm to compete effectively on costs. The size creates market-power, and this may allow a firm to exercise monopoly power or dominance in pricing products or services or even determine the terms of competition in the industry.

Second, assets may be deployed to expand the company's boundaries to support a strategy that focuses on offering a variety of related products in the marketplace. The firm is building a collection of related assets to support a strategy that allows the scope of activities to create a competitive product or services portfolio. The scope of assets creates capabilities in support of the strategy. Typically, the cost of producing two or more different but related products or services is lower when just one firm produces them instead of two firms. Costs saving create a competitive advantage for the firm in the marketplace.

---

[16] B. Klein. "Vertical Integration as Organizational Ownership," *Journal of Law, Economics, and Organization*, 1989, pp. 199–213.

These two ways of asset deployment are mostly realized in capital-intensive production processes where assets that build scale or scope display efficiencies and create opportunities for developing capabilities helpful in implementing a strategy. Strategic outcomes are realized more readily when the deployment of assets offer cost advantages of economies of scale and scope as they affect the sizes of firms and the economics of markets. A company can achieve long-term advantage in the market through expansion and building of capacity in a cost-effective way.[17]

Yet there is a third way that assets may be deployed to expand the company's boundaries and support a strategy.[18] Assets may be deployed with the objective to provide integration in the production process. In any typical business that involves production of goods, the process begins with the acquisition of raw materials and ends with the distribution and sale of finished goods and services. The firm may want to pursue a strategy of organizing all activities internally instead of relying on other firms in purchasing components of its final product. The strategy requires deployment of assets that will essentially vertically integrate all activities from raw material to the final product. The firm performs the activity itself and does not rely on an outside entity to perform the activity under contract. Developing its own source of materials instead of outsourcing or purchasing it from another company is an expensive proposition. However, it has merits when the decision to integrate products and/or services vertically offers a competitive advantage that helps the strategy succeed.

VERTICAL INTEGRATION AND THE CHOICE BETWEEN MAKE OR BUY

The decision to deploy assets to integrate vertically production processes or services represents an executive decision to either make internally or buy a part of the process. In some instances, a strategy may require building capabilities by deploying assets useful in making parts of a production

[17] O. Williamson. "Strategizing, Economizing and Economic Organization," *Strategic Management Journal*, 12, 1991, pp. 75–94.
[18] S. Grossman, S., and O. Hart. "The Costs and Benefits of Ownership: A Theory of Vertical and Lateral Integration," *Journal of Political Economy*, 94, 1986, pp. 691–719.

process or service. In other instances, however, a strategy may be based on building capabilities that require buying assets already available in the marketplace. The meaning of making or buying products or services is used broadly to indicate the deployment of assets (indirectly investments) to make them internally or to purchase a firm or part of a firm that offers these products.

When considering deploying assets, often the question confronting executives is under what conditions the decision of making a production process internally dominates the decision of buying from others to achieve competitive advantage. The following key considerations help in evaluating the make decision:[19]

+ If the product is a source of competitive advantage for the firm and it is inefficient for the firm to obtain it from the marketplace, the firm should always deploy assets, that is, invest to produce it or make it internally.

+ A company should always deploy assets to produce or make internally goods or services to contain associated costs only if the returns on investment are superior relative to similar risk returns made for the acquisition of the same product from an outside entity.

+ A firm should deploy assets that help make parts of the process rather than buying to solidify a distribution channel. The firm will gain market share by fending off rivals and competitors. This holds true when the costs of integration are less than the costs associated with buying the same part from an independent entity.

+ A firm should make rather than buy a part of the process to avoid incurring associated costs if those costs are lower from those incurred by an outside firm.

+ Often a product/service is part of lineup of activities in a vertically integrated process. Fitting the product into the vertical integration process requires coordination that involves features such as time, size, and sequence. When the costs of coordination to fit a product/service in a vertically integrated process is higher from an outside

---

[19] C. Avery, J. C. Chevalier, and S. Schaefer. "Why Do Managers Undertake Acquisitions? Analysis on Internal and External Rewards," *Journal of Law, Economics and Organization*, 1998, 14, pp. 24–43.

vendor, the company should deploy assets to make a product or service internally.[20]

The above conditions create competitive advantage in investing internally to expand assets or processes relative to buying them from the marketplace. Conversely, the reasons for executives to buy a firm (or assets) in the marketplace that offers a product or process include the following:

- Capture tangible benefits. Often making an input in a vertically integrated firm is unattainable, and an outside firm may be able to achieve economies of scale in production of the same input. It is therefore more economical to invest and buy this input instead of developing internally. Thus the integrated firm captures immediate tangible benefits. Also, outside firms possessing the desired input must survive the discipline of the market competition without hiding inefficiencies as may be the case of an integrated company. This encourages productive efficiency and innovation for firms operating outside the vertically integrated structure.
- Capture intangible benefits. Vertically integrated firms can try to replicate market incentives but may encounter problems associated with human capital and proprietary processes.

Ultimately, the make or buy decision depends on which decision leads to the most efficient production. This is determined by assessing the benefits and costs of using the market to outsource production.

DEPLOYING ASSETS THROUGH OUTSOURCING

Vertical integration creates competitive advantage by deploying assets that are made internally or could be purchased externally. An alternative for expanding the boundaries of the firm is to deploy assets that allow outsourcing products or services. Outsourcing takes place when a company instead of building assets internally or buying them from the marketplace invests in

---

[20] P. Milgrom, and J. Roberts. "Limit Pricing and Entry under Incomplete Information," *Econometrica*, 50, 1982, pp. 443–460.

a contractual relationship with another firm. Outsourcing provides a good solution for implementing a strategy that requires parts of a product or service to be developed quickly and efficiently.[21]

The most difficult part of a contract for an outsourced production is associated with the development of a relationship between a company that seeks vertical integration and the entity that provides the outsourcing. The asset (product or service) that is outsourced is a relationship-specific asset and supports a given transaction. It cannot be redeployed to another transaction without some sacrifice in productivity or some additional cost. Firms that have invested in relationship-specific assets cannot switch trading partners without seeing a decline in the value of specific assets.

The costs of outsourcing stem from the possibility of accepting an incomplete contract with a trading partner. An incomplete contract involves some ambiguity or open-endedness about the rights and responsibilities of each trading party in the relationship. A contract may be incomplete for several reasons: bounded rationality of parties involved, difficulties in specifying or measuring performance, and asymmetric information. As a result, incomplete contracts potentially create inefficiencies and failures to the firm that seeks outsourcing. Typical problems involve the following:

- Outsourcing often presents coordination problems. This is especially problematic for inputs with design attributes that require a careful fit between different components. Many times there are misfits that result from outsourcing relative to outcomes when the firm internally coordinates production or processes. To be avoided these misfits may involve time, size, color, and R&D.
- Outsourcing might result in leakage of private information. When a firm outsources a process or production, the outside entity often learns about sales, strategy, and growth plans, all important considerations that involve private information not to be disclosed to industry competitors.
- Outsourcing generates transactions costs. Transaction costs include the cost of negotiating, writing, and enforcing contracts. These

---

[21] G. Stigler, and R. Sherwin. "The Extent of the Market," *Journal of Law and Economics*, 28, 1985, pp. 555–585.

costs, while not immediately estimated, may be sizable as they involve management time and opportunity costs.

+ Outsourcing cannot eliminate opportunism on behalf of both entities involved. Contracting parties may be rational, but their rationality is constrained by experience and past knowledge. As a result,
bounded rationality makes parties seek their own agendas, and this
may be one of the difficulties in outsourcing production or services.
Since the outsourcing relationship is product- or service-specific,
a partner may exhibit opportunistic behavior to exploit the other
partner's vulnerability. This behavior may produce a hold up in
the relationship between the trading partners and raises the costs
of outsourcing. Typical increased costs include time and money
spent in negotiations, possible distrust, and expenses in inducing
the parties to safeguard their positions through investing in standby
facilities or other suppliers. All these costs as a result of hold ups
threaten outsourcing and relationship-specific investments.

While outsourcing offers advantages, the disadvantages make asset
deployment for vertical integration more beneficial to outsourcing, especially when the company designs a contract that is incomplete and involves
relationship-specific assets. In fact, there are three reasons that make vertical
integration a good alternative for asset deployment. Vertical integration (a)
may result in avoiding conflicts with external parties, (b) reduces uncertainty
and makes relationship-specific investments more profitable, and (c) allows
organizational culture to promote an atmosphere of cooperation.[22]

THE VALUE CHAIN

Asset deployment aims at supporting a strategy for the firm to create value.
If we consider a company as a collection of activities requiring inputs and
providing outputs, an asset deployment converts inputs into business outputs in a way that outputs (product or services) have a greater value than
the original cost of creating those outputs. A useful tool in determining

---

[22] F. Fisher. *Industrial Organization, Economics and the Law* (Cambridge, MA: MIT Press,
1991).

when to deploy assets is the firm's value chain. Pioneered by Michael Porter, value chain is a set of activities arranged in a way that a vertical process of producing a product or service has dollar values.[23] The value chain helps to identify those parts in the vertical chain where the most value is added. Porter's value chain has five primary activities: (a) purchasing/inventory and logistics, (b) operations/production, (c) distribution, (d) sales and marketing, and (e) customer services. In addition, there are four support activities: (a) human resources, (b) research and development, (c) design, (d) systems and infrastructure, and (e) procurement.

The value chain tool is important in pointing out for a firm the value-added proposition relative to its industry competitors. Differentiation relative to competitors is attributed to the part of the activities that come from converting inputs to outputs that create value. The value chain is a useful way of systematically thinking about the various ways in which the firm creates value. Value added depends on consumer value, cost/efficiency, and the ability of the firm to extract some of the difference between the two.

ASSET DEPLOYMENT IN PRACTICE: THE CASE OF DXC TECHNOLOGY[24] [25]

While the previous discussion focused on alternative ways to deploy assets, the following case study demonstrates how asset deployment works in practice.

DXC Technology corporation is a NYSE-listed firm that was created by the merger of Computer Science Corporation (CSC) and the Enterprise Services business of Hewlett Packard Enterprise. Established in 1959 by two computer analysts Roy Nutt and Fletcher Jones, CSC provided computer manufacturers with complex programs known as assemblers,

---

[23] M.Porter. *Competitive Advantage* (New York: Free Press, 1985).

[24] Information about DXC's history was obtained from internet search of the company's official site. Details about DXC's asset deployment program in 2017 are based on insights from Michael Lawrie the President and CEO of the company at that time. In addition, Dustin Semach, DXC's former VP Global operations and Director of Corporate Financial Planning and Analysis provided additional information about DXC's financials.

[25] This case captures the deployment of all types of assets, including physical assets, site-specific assets, and human capital assets.

operating systems and compilers. In 1962, Electronic Data Systems was founded in Dallas, Texas, by Ross Perot. EDS, a pioneer in IT outsourcing, grew from Perot's initial $1,000 investment to a global enterprise that helped 500 million passengers board planes, processed 13 billion credit card transactions and performed 2.4 billion healthcare transactions. Hewlett Packard acquired Electronic Data Systems in 2008, and soon created HP Enterprise Services, focused on transforming enterprises and achieving measurable business outcomes. In November 2015, Hewlett Packard Company split into HP Inc. and Hewlett Packard Enterprise, and the Enterprise Services business became part of HPE. Through their histories, both CSC and HPE Enterprise Services were known for evolving to keep pace with the ever-changing world of technology — and for offering customers a fresh perspective built on a rich heritage of innovation and industry-leading services.

One of the key value drivers for the company is its asset size and mix that helped generate in 2020 approximately $21 billion. Assets have been deployed to create scale, agile delivery, strong digital capabilities, compelling offerings to clients all leading to a diverse client mix. Scale economies were created from investments in diverse geographic areas including the Americas, North Europe, South Europe, Asian, and Australia and New Zealand. The firm has active presence in more than 100 countries with more than 130,000 employees.

DXC offers agile delivery to drive automation, reduce human interactions, and enhance service levels. With AI and other technologies DXC's provides analytics and lean automation through process simplification, standardization, and automation. Investments in assets have delivered over time a compelling portfolio of services which includes cloud and platform services, workplace and mobility, security, application services, enterprise and cloud applications, analytics, business process services and industry software solutions. Assets were also deployed to create strong digital capabilities and differentiated advantages that provide clients with deep industry expertise, standardized offerings at scale, industry leading partners all leading to integrated solutions.

With more than 6,000 clients worldwide, including 200 Fortune 500 firms, the company serves a truly diverse client mix. The vertical industry expertise reported as a percentage of total revenues includes manufacturing

(20%) International public sector (14%) Healthcare (13%) Insurance (11%), Banking (15%) Travel and transportation (7%) Retail (8%) and Energy (12%).

While today the firm enjoys a comfortable leadership role in global IT services, it took several years to implement a new strategy that required deployment of assets across geographic regions that led to the introduction of new services. In late 2017, DXC decided to follow a strategy toward digital IT space, helping companies digitally transform their business processes. Helping companies transition their processes to digital format coincided with broad market trends of the growth in the IT market; the significant profit pools available at that time, including profit margins; and the value-added prospects in all company processes that require input to produce outputs. To identify the potential, DXC took an inventory of the skills of approximately 130,000 employees and compared it to the skills needed to be successful with that strategy. The firm needed experienced professionals like data scientists and staff with advanced analytic skills, business intelligence skills, deep process reengineering skills, as well as traditional IT skills. Following the inventory of the skills, DXC realized it had fewer than a thousand employees who had advanced Amazon Web Services (AWS) skills, Microsoft Cloud skills, or business analytics skills. With only one thousand employees with these types of skills, the firm was unable to build capabilities to produce meaningful an annual revenue stream in perpetuity. Only significant perpetual revenue would have added value to shareholders. As a result, the leadership team determined that the execution of the strategy of providing services to IT space, helping companies digitally transforming their business processes, was at risk due to lack of capabilities. To bridge the gap of current and required capabilities, assets should have been acquired. The firm then bought a digital IT company with a couple thousand employees. The firm was in Eastern Europe and had fantastic access to Eastern European universities and a significant STEM-training program in Eastern Europe. The acquired firm had locations in Ukraine, Poland, and Russia, but also had operations in Romania and Bulgaria. While the firm had added considerable human skilled labor, it still was not enough to make a big difference in establishing an annual stream of revenues monetizable. The firm went to its key partner, Amazon, and asked if they would put a training course in place, and they would send their employees through it to receive certifications. As a result, thousands of employees went through the AWS-certified program so employees could demonstrate and validate technical cloud knowledge and skills. A similar approach was used with Microsoft for several thousand employees to be certified in Microsoft products. In addition, a decision was made to retool/reskill people coming to work from traditional business entities. As a result, the DXC University was established. An inventory of online digital training for employees was developed, and all employees received certifications by taking these courses.

Over a short period of two to three years, DXC went from around one thousand employees who had the skills necessary to execute the strategy of offering digital transformation to clients to about forty thousand employees. In addition, the firm decided to change all its hiring practices. Rather than hiring professionals with traditional skills, where after a period people left the company following a usual attrition, the company had to redo its hiring and hired people with the skills necessary for the future. The results were spectacular. Within a period of two years, DXC transformed about a third of its labor force to serve the market, and digital revenues were growing at 40 percent annually, while the traditional business was declining at 4 or 5 percent a year.

This is an example of the process used to develop capabilities required to deploy assets in support of a strategy. A strategy was developed, while aspirational, and a process was implemented to evaluate the skills and capabilities. To support the strategy, a series of actions and executable tactical plans were devised. To evaluate progress, executives on a very regular basis used key metrics to make possible adjustments of plans versus desirable outcomes. Among others, metrics measured the number of people who were retooled, the increasing skill level of employees, and the revenue and profit per person after retraining and redeployed to serve customers' needs.

DIVERSIFICATION

Often DXC took a physical asset, augmented with it with intellectual capital, in this case people with skills to be able to scale it, after starting out small. The firm decided to hire people with different skills, which meant basically hiring millennials, and it also meant they had to understand how millennials work. It was concluded that it made no sense to hire inexperience professionals and then put them on existing teams with the firm's clients because they would be overshadowed by the people who were already there and would not have enough visibility to make a difference. To build scale it was decided to build on existing delivery centers around the world, the United States, India, China, Malaysia, Australia, Germany, France, and the United Kingdom. It was decided to create a physical digital transformation center, place a manager in the center, and accumulate corresponding performance metrics. When hiring people locally, those people went to that physical facility, so they were working with people who were very similar to themselves. That creates this nexus between individuals and creativity, and then they would be assigned to projects with customers out of that digital delivery.

Then DXC established partnerships with the universities LSU, Tulane University, and New Orleans Louisiana Tech, committing to hire several undergraduates from the STEM program to honor the commitment for hiring four hundred new employees. That was a combination of IP, physical assets, and partners to achieve scale.

When DXC acquired leading digital innovator Luxoft in January 2019, almost thirteen thousand people had produced lot of IP. In several cases, DXC filed patents, copyrights, or other ways of protecting that IP.

DXC was able to leverage some of the assets because it maintained facilities around the world and was able to reuse some of those facilities. Instead of having 100,000 square feet dedicated to just one activity, 80,000 square feet dedicated to one activity and 20,000 dedicated to another activity. One of DXC's assets was recruiting because it recruited everywhere in the world. However, recruiters were not trained to adequately hire the type of new skills that DXC needed, so it outsourced the recruiting process.[26] The firm went to a third-party company that did have those recruiting skills and used them while at the same time building DXC's own internal recruiting capability. DXC also built an online system where people could post skills on the Web, and people who had those skills could bid against the work. DXC called it their talent cloud. It was a way to hire people who did not want to work for a big company, who were part of the gig economy. They wanted to work on

---

[26] The advantages and disadvantages of outsourcing a service or product were presented in the previous section.

some specified contracts, and when that contract was completed, they could go do something else.

DXC build a mechanism to attract people who matched performance and experiences and paid them accordingly. But the big thing was the redeployment of human assets. Almost 30 percent of DXC's employees had the ambition to retrain themselves. DXC provided the training and the curriculum for them to get the skills necessary to participate in these new markets of growth potential with great opportunities. While not all employees were interested, the focus was only on those who had a great interest and wanted to be retrained. Those are examples of physical assets and human assets, and how they can either be utilized differently in some cases, partnering to get the skills while you're building the skills, and retraining and transforming the human assets that you already have.

MAKE INTERNALLY VERSUS BUY DECISIONS

Whenever you are acquiring different assets, you must go through a make versus buy decision process. The decision to make products or services supported by investments is often the least expensive, but it takes the longest period to implement it. Buying products or services allows the company to access markets quickly and serve emerging customer needs faster, but it requires availability of financial resources as searching for suitable acquisitions hinges on extensive due diligence. Also, executives must be willing to take on the task of integrating new employees and making them a part of the larger corpus of the company.

Are there other constraints to buying and deploying assets? The answer to the question depends on size of the firm. For large firms, a corporate office institutionalizes methods for searching for suitable acquisitions and merger candidates and devises procedures for assessing market opportunities. The office usually determines criteria and scans emerging developments in the produce and service markets. In smaller firms, the approach of considering buying assets or merging with other companies is ad hoc and typically controlled by the CEO. Relationships with private equity funds and investment bankers help to explore candidates with a good strategic fit.

THE MERGERS AND ACQUISITIONS PROCESS IN PRACTICE AT DXC

At DXC a mergers and acquisitions (M&A) process was utilized that focused attention on several parameters, including the following:

1. Financials of the company to be acquired and the ability of the bidder to pay the target price.
2. Evaluation of the asset portfolio of the target firm that includes physical, human capital, and organizational assets. Particular attention was placed on the examination of these assets and if they matched the capabilities of the acquiring firm that would help implement the strategy.
3. Evaluation of management and technology systems in place and costs associated with the integration of those systems with DXC. Cost and benefits analysis was performed to evaluate the extent to which systems can stand alone. Simple examples include e-mail system, cybersecurity, Enterprise Resource Planning (ERP), human resource systems, sales force systems. For example, DXC spent $200 million just on cybersecurity when it took over the assets from Hewlett Packard.
4. Culture fit and leadership style. Does the acquiring firm believe that the CEO will be able to add value to the new environment, or are the skills of senior management more important and need to be retained? What is the cost of retaining those skills versus the cost of recruiting those people?
5. Integration costs tend to create additional expenses for bringing together assets and operating processes.

Buying companies, however, must be consistent with the firm's strategy. An internal team of M&A professionals routinely performs due diligence, and the CEO looks at ten or fifteen deals in the pipeline monthly. At DXC, once a decision is made to go ahead, a deal team is assigned to work with the company to try to put together the technical details of a merger or acquisition. The process to acquire or dispose assets is an integral part of the management system.

However, the fundamental question regarding asset acquisition is related to what extent the acquired assets are consistent with the strategy. If they are not consistent with the strategy, why does the firm want to buy the assets? What are the financial implications? Some businesses generate a lot of profit and decide to keep that business even though it is not consistent with the strategy. These questions bring to the attention of the company's leadership the BCG's four-quadrant approach, where star companies require such investments and others to be cash cows. DXC's approach was to consider carefully which businesses and assets fit into its strategy. There are companies considered cows that sometimes offer "milk" for profit, and other times, target acquisitions are sort of in-between things with ambiguous operational and strategic direction requiring close monitoring and oversight. Finally, dogs are slow-growth and unprofitable businesses that are good candidates for disposition and prune the corporate asset base.

INTELLECTUAL PROPERTY (IP)

An evaluation of the IP is required at the time of considering a buyout. The firm should evaluate not only the IP in its portfolio but also the IP it might be creating by some of its ongoing development work. This is particularly the case in some of software businesses. Typically, an outside law firm helps evaluate some of that IP. Prioritizing the IP allows the firm to identify the most value and obtain some sort of IP. Obviously, a patent is the most extreme way of protecting IP, but it is also the most expensive and takes the longest. It is often customary to license a technology for a period.

OTHER ASPECTS

Asset deployment should be linked to the company's strategy. Unfortunately, many businesses develop grand strategies and outline detailed tactical plans, but they never focus attention on the type of assets required to develop needed capabilities to execute that strategy.

While the linkage between asset deployment and strategy is clear, executives should also pay attention to the financial model. For example, if margins are 20 percent and the firm wants to acquire a business that fits into its strategy but has a projected 10 percent margin, management must be careful to evaluate the implications from a possible reduction of company-wide overall margins. The justification for a reduced post-acquisition profit margin may be explained by skills and competitive advantages acquired on a bulk basis instead of a piecemeal basis; buying in bulk would overall costs in the long term. Alternatively, the reduction can be justified by the extraordinary synergistic advantages because the acquisition would lead to improved medium-term profitability of the overall company.

When DXC purchased Luxoft, the cost was about $8,000 per person to acquire, train, and deploy the skills. For approximately $1 billion, DXC was acquiring human capital of four thousand people. After considering a normal attrition rate, it was less costly to buy the entire company's human capital and receive access to their skills. Those decisions are linked to the financial model. Growth assets, then, are linked to an overall financial model, and the financial model is linked to the firm's strategy. Accepting an acquisition that generates a financial return inconsistent with the financial model breaks the linkage between strategy, assets, and financial model.

After the decision for an acquisition has been finalized as part of the overall asset deployment program that links strategy and the financial model, the next step is working with the leadership team that understands the business the firm has acquired. Invariably, the senior management team of the acquiring firm is only used to the current business they have been running for a long time without considering expanding the asset base. There is limited confidence that the same senior management team will acquire the capability, insights, intuition, and instinct to be able to run the newly acquired business. This suggests that the CEO should evaluate the leadership skills and potentially bring new talent to manage the new acquisition.

Following a decision about leadership, the next step is reviewing the company's culture. In fact, when DXC considered several buyouts, the CEO reviewed very carefully the culture of the potential target company to make sure it would be a reasonable fit with the dominant culture of DXC.

ASSETS IN PLACE AND GROWTH OPPORTUNITIES

Assets in place help with the continuity of business, while growth opportunities provide assets with potential for market disruption and abnormal growth, albeit risky for the firm. To select assets in place and growth opportunities, the BCG four-quadrant chart is helpful. The star assets or businesses consistent with the strategy that they grow and do well are ones to be maintained. If additional assets like those could be added to the portfolio, overall performance will be improved. Problematic assets or business(es) should be disposed and or deployed to a third party, a higher-value user. Assets or businesses with characteristics of cash cows should be treated differently. While valuable to the overall performance of the company, they often do not fit the strategy and should be considered for a possible sale or disposition. One example instructive from the experience of DXC is the case of a federal government business. The business was generating enormous profits, was stable, and had a perpetual profit margin. But the leadership had decided not to invest in it anymore as it did not fit DXC's overall strategy. It was decided rather than selling it to another concern to spin it off into its own company, thus rewarding existing shareholders with additional shares of an independent company. In turn, investors could decide whether they wanted to hold the newly distributed shares as an investment or to sell them in the market. Generally, cash cows mostly representing assets in place may create funding for other investments or be disposed if they do not fit the strategy. Companies or assets with characteristics of dogs are simple in that they should be disposed, especially if they do not fit with the overall asset portfolio that supports the firm's strategy. Finally, a different approach is required when assets, while consistent with the strategy, may produce marginal performance and perhaps do not live up to their potentials or specific metrics of performance. These assets may generate businesses that have not been growing as fast as is anticipated, they may not be as profitable, and they may be slightly off in terms of the strategy. As a result, assets falling into this category are more difficult to handle and require the attention of the company's leadership. Regardless, the process of evaluating assets and categorizing them as assets in place and growth opportunities while assessing strategic fit should be continuous and on annual base.

THE BALANCE

The competitive conditions within which the company operates—that is, the structure of the market and the nature of the competition—guide an asset deployment program that adds to the company's long-term competitive advantage. Broadly, attractive assets include those that enhance the firm's intellectual portfolio, create unique relationships, improve organizational learning, facilitate vertical or horizontal integration, and generate economies of scale and/or scope. The theory and teaching of asset deployment and allocation also provide insights on the trade-offs involved in building assets internally or in an organic fashion, that is making or producing products or services, versus acquiring assets, that is buying products or services through a merger or acquisition from the marketplace. Extensive volume of knowledge acquired from academic research outlines the profile of assets, their characteristics, attributes, and features that create competitive, differentiated advantages and, therefore, when acquired or developed add value to the company.

Notwithstanding this evidence, the focus of executive leaders is on identifying how a company is competitively positioned in its industry. This is done by adopting an asset deployment plan that ensures requisite assets, services, and partnerships are available to execute its strategy. This focus requires striking a balance between an asset allocation plan, the firm's financial resources (model), and the company's culture. Executive leadership ensures that management systems are in place to build an asset portfolio vital to the firm's quest for competitive advantage. The asset portfolio with the right profile of assets should be financed with internally generated cash flows, or with external capital while an inclusive and transparent culture is engaged in improving performance to execute the firm's strategy. When all these elements are aligned and balanced, the probability for the company to achieve its upside potential for value, returns, and profitability is measurably improved.

CHAPTER FOUR

The Financial Model for Value Creation

DIVERSE VIEWS

One area where practice and theory diverge is in the development of models to assist in decision-making. A model is a simple representation of a relationship. Academics use models to teach business students insightful lessons on how companies operate and to display critical relationships that influence outcomes. Past data are often used as input parameters to fit models that provide normative recommendations for these relationships. Practicing executives use models to operate companies; they use them to benchmark outcomes and measure performance against peer industry groups or self-imposed measures.

Academic research has produced findings leading to a better understanding of how businesses operate or compete. To convey these findings to business students, faculty have developed simplified abstractions of reality that isolate parameters or characteristics to show how businesses can prosper. A typical abstraction is that the firm is considered a "black box." While unrealistic, conceptually it is appealing to present an input–output relationship for the firm and convey to students the message that the firm, the black box, is susceptible to external competitive and economic factors.

And if the internal workings of the black box do not adapt to changes, its output, such as profits or value, will change as well.

Practicing executives use models differently; their models answer tangible, pressing questions. Is the firm building more capital or destroying capital? Is the firm making enough returns comparable to returns that would have been made were it investing capital in financial markets with a similar risk profile? Does the firm's business model generate enough profits? Executives also focus on developing models to assess how the company's asset portfolio supports the strategy and measures of firm's performance. Models measure profits, not only in terms of returns and accounting profits, but also returns that surpass or exceed opportunity costs.

The differences in the design of models for academics and executives stems from the distinct needs of their audiences. Faculty focus on using research and empirical findings to design models to teach the dynamics of a broad set of parameters on the output for every business as they are agnostic when it comes to industry. Their models present a holistic view of how a company operates. Executives, on the other hand, are tasked with running a business based on objectives; for example, maximizing stock prices or profits. They design models to measure how their decisions impact or deviate from targeted outputs. Both approaches are complementary yet often incompatible. Academic models tend to be conceptual, addressing the posture of a firm relative to the industry's competitive structure and the broad economic trends. They tend to add value to understanding the big picture, helping to navigate the firm considering competitive forces. Models developed by executives address pressing needs for meeting cash flow and profitability benchmarks and tend to be firm-specific, not holistic. Academic models can benefit from executives' insights and practicality, while executives can better understand the theory of how things work under ideal conditions. The academic and practical worlds sometimes offer seemingly contradictory models. Our approach in presenting the theory and practice regarding financial models follows figure 4.1.

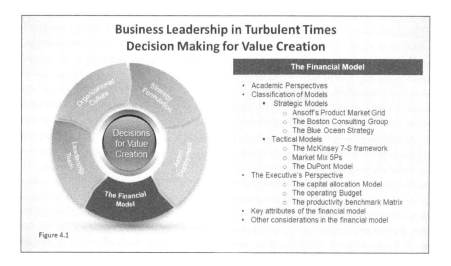

Figure 4.1

ACADEMIC PERSPECTIVES

For faculty teaching business courses, a model is a representation or depiction of the economics and the business activities of a company. The model approach to teaching the workings of the company is very appealing as it directs attention to relationships among key firm resources and outputs. In designing models, academics identify the impact of possible changes in the environment on business operations, cash flows, and profitability. Depending on the scope of a firm's activity, models may apply strategically, tactically, or operationally. Several models serve as problem-solving tools designed to improve efficiency and firm effectiveness in handling competitive pressures. Others are descriptive and capture the essence of a simplified business process. Yet many models presented by academics are designed to solve specific problems because of particular economic or business conditions or situations.

Models are certainly valuable tools in offering insights and providing a sound framework for making appropriate business choices. As tools, they may be employed to enhance the daily functioning of the business by improving both performance and outcomes. As conceptual frameworks, they can identify possible innovations and improvements helpful to business.

Models may differ in terms of functioning and scope. Models may stand up to a high degree of scientific rigor supported by research findings. But many are simply a descriptive map of a process. Other models provide useful ways of ordering reality. They are often a common language with which to compare performances and challenges as well as solve problems. Models contain inspiring characterizations and offer practical value when it comes to analyzing situations and identifying possible courses of action. The financial model describes the rationale of how an organization creates, delivers, and captures value in an economic context considering stakeholders' interests.

CLASSIFICATION OF MODELS

There are many ways in which models could be categorized. Models could be classified into two broad categories in terms of their use and function.

Strategic Models

Strategic models are helpful when analyzing and planning the strategic position of a company and assist in answering strategic questions. Examples of strategic models include Ansoff's product market grid, the BCG, and the Blue Ocean Strategy. There are many other models, including SWOT analysis, but Ansoff's, the BCG, and the Blue Ocean Strategy are covered in the following section.

Ansoff's Product Market Grid

Ansoff's product market grid offers a framework for strategic planning and strategy formulation. It helps understand how to devise strategies for business growth as the foundational knowledge provides important insight into the core features of the model. Known also as a product/market expansion grid, Ansoff's model depicts major growth alternatives for businesses.[27]

---

[27] H. I. Ansoff. "Strategies for Diversification," *Harvard Business Review,* Sept.–Oct, 1957, pp. 113–124.

Alternatives, appeared in Figure 4.2, may be clustered into the following categories across two broad dimensions: product markets and customers:

1. *Market penetration* involves the growth of a company relying primarily on expanding its existing products and services, increasing product value from the customer's perspective. For example, the firm may increase the actual or perceived value of its product by making price adjustments, increase promotion and distribution support, and/or develop product refinements. All these actions lead to product market penetration.

2. *Market development.* This involves business expansion into new markets using the company's existing offerings. For example, through the development of different customer segments, a company may use product technology to create leverage in the new market or diversify the target market.

3. *Product development.* This involves the reinvention or creation of new goods and services for the existing markets to achieve growth.

4. *Diversification* This occurs when the business introduces new offerings in new markets. However, this is the riskiest strategy because both product and market development are required. Basically, this means launching unproven goods and services into an entirely new market.

As there is a continuum between the states of market penetration and product development, an intermediate step of product extension may appeal to a focused clientele of customers by extending the life cycle of a product through enhancements and/or modifications. In a similar fashion, modifications or alternatives in a current market provide opportunities for expansion. All these are alternatives of clusters of markets and customers with distinct characteristics. When plotted on a two-dimensional map of markets and customers, the cluster of alternatives helps to analyze risks associated with every quadrant. When business focus shifts into a new quadrant (horizontally or vertically), the risk increases. Therefore, careful planning, testing, reevaluation, and reinvention are required.

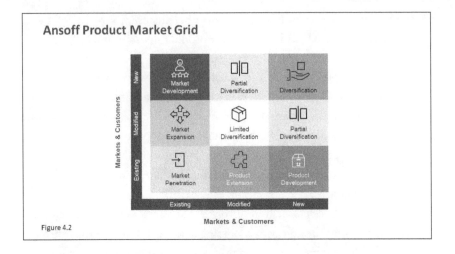

Figure 4.2

The Boston Consulting Group (BCG)

The BCG which depicts business activities across the dimensions of growth and market share, shows cross-financing opportunities for a diversified firm (Figure 4.3). Cash cow businesses with low growth potentials and high market shares are used to finance high-growth business units with high market share potentials. Businesses that experience low growth potentials and low market shares may be phased out or discontinued.

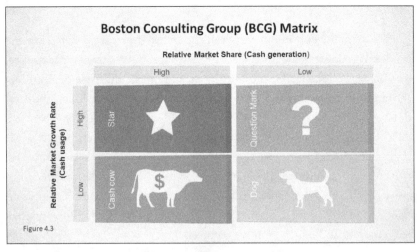

Figure 4.3

The Blue Ocean Strategy

The core idea of the Blue Ocean Strategy[28] is based on the notion that to make the competition irrelevant and exploit opportunities for products the company must create new market segments. The traditional competitive markets represent a hostile, highly competitive environment, and the metaphor of blood in the water (red ocean) represents them. Competitors fight to increase their market shares with traditional competitive techniques like differentiation and low cost. On the other hand, the new markets, where competition still does not exist (thus the metaphor of blue oceans), is where the company strategy needs to focus, where the market is fruitful, and customer demand is fulfilled by the first arrival. The interesting side of the story is that blue oceans and indirectly markets to be discovered require an innovation to take place or disruption to appear (Figure 4.4).

The Blue Ocean Strategy is based on a model that helps companies explore, create, and exploit new markets, and afterward, generate barriers to maintain them. Key considerations in Blue Ocean Strategy include answers to questions such as:

+ How do you create uncontested market segments?
+ How do you make the competition irrelevant?
+ How do you create and capture new demand?
+ What ways can you break the value-cost trade-off?
+ How do you align company activities to become low-cost differentiators?

---

[28] W. Chan Kim and Renee Mauborgne. *Blue Ocean Strategy: How to Create Uncontested Market Space and Make the Competition Irrelevant* (Cambridge, MA: Harvard Business School Press, 2004).

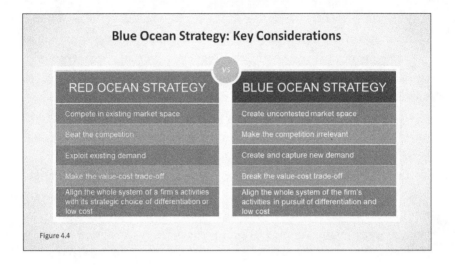

Figure 4.4

Tactical Models

These models are used to organize a firm's processes, resources, and people. They provide insights in analyzing the operations and design of a company and may focus on finances, marketing, or general operating concepts. While there are many models, we cover only the McKinsey 7-S framework, the 5 Ps marketing mix, and the DuPont model.

The McKinsey 7-S Framework

When using this framework, executives can assess the status of a tactical plan as part of different stages of goal attainment. These can be used to determine the effects of past events, the current state of the company, and the future consequences and benefits that may be gained from the various activities in which the company is engaged.

The 7-S structure uses seven principal elements to analyze the company's business model.[29] Elements include structure, system, style, staff, skills, strategy, and shared values. Utilizing these elements, management

---

[29] Thomas Peters and Robert Waterman developed the McKinsey 7-S model while serving as consultants in the later 1970s.

can then evaluate the business strategy in accordance with the company's vision. (Figure 4.5)

The first element in the McKinsey 7-S framework is *strategy*, a focus on the business's initial plan to focus on markets and customers. The second element is *structure*, which refers to streamlining the structure of the organization itself to support the strategy. The third, *systems*, involves the development of the methodology, management processes and procedures involved in executing the strategy. This is followed by *staff*, which refers to the demographics, diversity, and the composition of human capital. Also included in the framework are *skills* and *style*. These refer to the abilities of the employees and the leadership styles that are implemented to optimize these abilities. The last element in the framework is *shared values*. These are the driving or guiding principles found in the company culture.

Ideal for analyzing and restructuring the company procedures, the 7-S framework can be utilized in comprehensive and holistic discussions about the company. The seven success factors may be further categorized into soft factors (skills, staff, and style) and *hard factors* (strategy, structure, and systems).

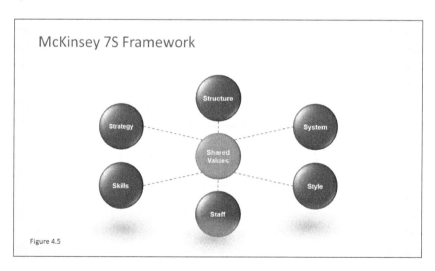

McKinsey 7S Framework

Figure 4.5

MARKETING MIX 5 PS

The 5 Ps is a conceptual model that represents the key factors in marketing strategy. Also known as marketing mix, the model include product, price, promotion, place, process, and people. *Product* refers to the product and services offered by a firm. While developing a marketing strategy, the firm should provide differentiating characteristics of the product or services offered to consumers that should include, among others, the features, advantages, benefits, and functionality that can be enjoyed by the consumer when buying the product or services. *Price* refers to the cost incurred by the consumer to purchase the products or services. Typically it is the nex price as discounts, payment arrangements, price-matching services offered, and competitive credit terms are several factors that determine the cost to the consumer. *Promotion* refers to the activities and programs that improve consumer awareness and increase the visibility of the product or services. Advertising makes a product more well known to consumers, but when making decisions, it is important to factor in the value assigned by the firm to a customer and to what extent it is worth conducting promotions to convert a prospective consumer to a buyer. *Place* refers to where the product/service is made available for sale or is distributed. Indirectly it denotes accessibility of the product and availability to customers at the right time and right place and in the right quantities. *People* refer to the human resources required to provide service and support to potential and actual buyers of the product or services.

The 5 P model offers a conceptual framework within which a marketing strategy yields a committed and loyal customer base that generates revenues and profits for the firm.

The DuPont Model

The model provides insights into the company's returns on equity expressed as a measure of profitability to shareholders and investors. The model, popularized by the DuPont company, which used it extensively in the 1960s, identifies three components of returns on equity: (a) a company's operating efficiency expressed by net profit margin, (b) asset turnover, expressed by the company's ability to utilize assets to produce higher levels of sales, and (c) leverage expressed by the portion of total assets financed by equity. The mathematical expression is stated as:

$$ROE = (\text{Net income} / \text{Sales}) \times (\text{Sales} / \text{Total assets})$$
$$\times (\text{Total assets} / \text{Book value of equity})$$

The practicality of the DuPont model is its simplistic composition yet powerful representation of a company's overall performance. Additionally, the model brings together measurements of a company's operational efficiency and asset structure in one formula. The ratio of net income to sales reflects profit margins and indicates how the firm transforms sales to net income through cost-containment measures. The ratio of sales to total assets reflects the firm's turnover, which measures the firm's efficiency to convert, or turn, assets into sales. Finally, the ratio of total assets-to-book value of equity reflects the amount of equity used to finance total assets. The reciprocal of this ratio is a measure of the firm's leverage and indirectly shows the capital mix or capital structure of the firm required for financing its assets. Over the years the DuPont model has provided a pragmatic approach to measuring returns to equity holders or shareholders in very succinct and easy way to implement.

THE EXECUTIVE PRACTICE

A financial model is very important because it is the primary metric by which the board and investors evaluate the performance of the company. Also, the financial model becomes important to the perceptions of others, including industry competitors, regarding the status of the company. Additionally, the model is useful to employees who assess their efforts and evaluate the firm, and to some extent, helps customers develop perceptions about the company's long-term viability.

The board plays a pivotal role in a company. As agents of the company's investors, the board has the responsibility to provide a return to shareholders which is better than they can receive elsewhere. The added responsibility of the board is to ensure that management is executing the strategy that was developed and implemented and producing results consistent with their responsibility to the shareholders. A financial model allows boards to understand how value is converted into cash flow and distributions to shareholders.

For employees, the firm's financial model serves an important role in their understanding of the company and its profit sources and structure. Employees need to understand how the company generates cash flow. A financial model gives employees a blueprint, or a road map, demonstrating how their work, along with other assets, generates profits. In other words, the architecture of how the company creates value to be translated into cash flow. The cash flow will be allocated to continue the cycle of value creation and cash flow allocation in which they will participate through their salaries, benefits, and bonuses. Therefore, the purpose of the company is to generate cash flow continuously for distributions to stakeholders. And it is the board's responsibility to oversee the execution of this purpose.

Customers have choices in their purchases unless a company is the only provider of a product or service. Customers prefer to deal with a firm that has a viable financial model with sustainable long-term returns. While they may seek discounts and superior services, they always prefer to deal with a company with financially sustainable operations and continuity of services.

A comprehensive financial model for any business includes revenues, profit margins, EPS, free cash flow, and tax outlays. To be meaningful, a financial model should be linked to the firm's strategy. It turns out that a strategy is followed by the need to acquire or redeploy assets necessary for the execution of the strategy and a breakdown of all components contributing to results and outcomes. Several components may grow; others may require trimming. The leadership of the organization should consider profit margins, free cash flow, and profitability in the development of a comprehensive financial model.

An effective financial model describes the outcome of a process by which the strategy is translated to an actionable plan with the deployment of assets, behind which are the necessary resources for implementation, generating profits for the bottom line, and creating value for the shareholders. To operationalize the process of translating strategy to an actionable plan, a financial model consists of three distinct components: (a) the capital allocation plan,

(b) the productivity benchmark matrix, and (c) the operating budgets of the units comprising the entire company. Each component is necessary to guide the organization toward success, and each plays a different role.

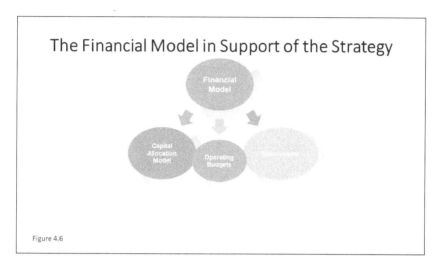

The Financial Model in Support of the Strategy

Figure 4.6

The first component of the financial model includes a supportive module that deals with the firm's capital allocation plan. (Figure 4.6) The capital allocation plan is perhaps the most important part of the overall financial model because it signals to investors and employees the specific uses of available cash flow. More specifically, it reports free cash flow and details the ways that it will be spent. In simple terms, the free cash flow is calculated based on net income adjusted for depreciation and is considered free for distribution after all investment and funding needs of the firm have been accommodated. The free cash flow is discretionary in terms of distribution because management may decide to distribute it as additional dividend payment or reinvest it in the business. More specifically, potential uses of free cash flow include capital investments, especially in plant and equipment areas; investments linked to capacity improvements; distributions to investors in terms of dividends or stock repurchases; and preemptive investments in projects that may create future strategic options to the firm. Preemptive investments may be linked to the first-mover advantage for the firm. Also, the capital allocation plan outlines the spending on strategic initiatives that may involve acquiring other companies or merging with other firms. Other areas of potential investments as part of the free cash flow include training and investments in employee benefits or incentive-compensation plans. However, a good capital allocation plan also provides the investors with a clear picture of how the free cash flow will be deployed by the management team. Another possible use is the repayment or retirement of debt. As with the horizon of a three- or four-year plan, capital allocation outlines revenue growth, projected debt repayment schedules, profit margin progression, and profitability.

From this model, investors have a clear picture of how free cash flow is allocated only when the CEO outlines a plan that shows debt repayment and debt servicing, investments in mergers, and acquisitions to buy assets necessary to execute strategy and spending on capital equipment. This way, investors have an unambiguous picture of exactly how the management team is holding itself accountable to achieve the planned or anticipated results.

Since the capital allocation plan offers a comparison relative to plans of other competitors, it serves as a target or yardstick for the achievement of results. Naturally, this plan allows the firm to benchmark its capital allocations against competitors in the industry. The percentage of free cash flow returned to investors becomes a much-watched measure for distributions returned to shareholders. If a competitor's percentage distribution is better, obviously, the firm's valuation of all other things being equal, is less attractive in relation to competitors as valuations will be out of line if the benchmarked company had a different distribution.

In these cases, there are deviations from industry norms. The CEO is required to explain where the free cash flow is used. This requires publication of the plan and its components. In the end, investors do not appreciate when management is not abundantly clear about capital allocation. As such, the capital allocation plan is an absolutely fundamental component of the financial model, and the financial model is linked to asset deployment, which is subsequently linked to the firm's strategy. To benchmark a company against competitors, the company must identify the distribution of free cash flow in the industry. In this area, the firms should strive to be in the upper quartile in the distribution of competitors.

An important but often ignored element of the financial model is the firm's tax strategy. Since tax rates drive earnings per share, and these, in turn, impact valuations, they become a priority for a global company to identify the lowest possible tax to conduct operations. Even local companies may be focusing on reducing tax rates by relocating operating facilities or operating in states with the lowest corporate tax rates. Additionally, the financial model includes projections about the average tax rate to be paid on company earnings. If the tax outlay is less than what was projected, the residual cash flows can then be reallocated to other components of the capital allocation model.

Decisions and planning both depend on the needs for building capabilities. For example, if the firm wants to buy asset capabilities, they may need to train their people more. Another option is to buy some companies. The capital allocations plan will be skewed much more in favor of the investments as opposed to the increasing of dividends or conducting a stock buyback plan. A good measure is the internal rate of return. This would entail comparing the internal rate of return of buying a company versus the internal rate of return of buying stock back.

At the end of the day, the capital allocation plan always ensures that cash is used in ways that will create benefits in excess of the company's cost of capital, and the cost of capital can vary dramatically because of interest rates. While there is not a benchmark cost of capital across companies and industries let us assume for a moment is between 8 and 10 percent. That means any company that is acquired, or any other investment that is undertaken, require a rate of return to be greater than 8 to 10 percent. Adjustments for risk may require additional compensation in returns. However, the rationale is that over the long run, if the cost to capital is not returned to the providers of capital, the business must cease to exist.

The second component of the financial model is the productivity benchmark matrix. This component is a set of measures that provides information about the productivity profile of key company resources. These measures include revenue per employee, profitability per employee, and free cash flow per employee. They provide a good measure of productivity relative to competitors. Over time, the objective is to increase those measures with the potential of having a smaller number of employees or improve measures with efficiency. This is what drives productivity and is an optimal way to be able to communicate not only to the investors but to the employees regarding the progress that is made. Investors encourage, approve of, and provide high marks for being absolutely clear on what management is holding themselves accountable for. Frequently projections do not materialize as many uncertainties may create deviations from original plans. However, a variation or deviation from the plan must be communicated effectively to the external constituency with details as to what caused that variation and deviation and subsequently, what actions would be taken to either close that gap or, in some instances, revise the financial model and revise the capital allocation model.

The third component of the financial model is the operating budget of the units or departments of the company. The budget consists of revenues, costs, and profits margin projections based on reasonable assumptions of the external environment and anticipated contributions of each unit or department to the company's overall profits. The budget becomes the primary tool in the firm's management system to monitor the financial model. As with the financial model, the budget is a balance between what can possibly be achieved and what needs to be achieved to deliver returns to shareholders. Favorable or unfavorable budget deviations impact the financial model and require detailed explanations regarding each component. These explanations lead to discussions on the appropriateness of the company's strategy. Positive budget deviations suggest perfect execution of a suitable and well-developed strategy. Negative budget deviations invite questions about the relevancy of a chosen strategy, the rightness of the asset deployment plan, and the strength of the execution plan.

The capital allocation plan, the productivity benchmark matrix, and the budgets, taken together, constitute prominent components of the firm's financial model. The absence of one of the three components leads to an ill-conceived financial model that most certainly would result in corporate failure. A financial model may fail if any of the three components is not well developed and articulated well to the constituencies.

KEY ATTRIBUTES OF THE FINANCIAL MODEL

For the financial model and its components to be suitable tools in managing the organization, communicating purposefully is necessary to provide clarity to the appropriate audience. In addition, the financial model should be realistic and based on a balance between simplicity and comprehensiveness.

Any financial model serves as a signal of information to an audience comprised of two important constituencies. First, the model is important to the internal constituency of employees and managers for their understanding of the expectation of the company's path as it advances. This understanding includes not only their roles in how they can execute strategy but also how they can begin to understand their roles in helping to execute with an established set of benchmarks. Second, the financial model is important to shareholders and investors. A financial model allows the company to develop projections for revenues each year, revenue growth, profit growth, profit margins, and cash growth over a period. Then the model should be communicated to the investors for them to gain an appreciation of and to know exactly what the company is expected to do. The model helps to develop expectations about the performance of the management team and the company's projected outcomes on a quarterly basis. Investors then measure the management team on how well they are executing against the projections that the team provided.

While the audience—that is, the shareholders and the internal constituency as recipients of the information about the financial model—evaluate the prospects of the firm, they expect the model to have three attributes. These are three important attributes that make the financial model an integral component in the firm's operations.

o   *Clarity.* The financial model must be very clear and unambiguous. While models tend to be complex and comprehensive to account for many parameters, the management should present a model in simple terms with conviction and clarity. Communications that tend to be ambiguous invite questions and doubts about potential implementation. There is always a trade-off between simplicity and comprehensiveness. While a model may encompass all parameters and factors that influence the outcome of a complex multidivisional operation, its complexity may be a deterrent in its communication to internal and external constituencies. Instead, a simple financial model may capture the most critical factors that influence outcomes, but it must be communicated effectively to the constituencies. While simplicity is desirable, the model may not be of help in projecting possible outcomes and thus may be deemed ineffective. Executives strangle with the balance between simplicity and comprehensiveness. However, to reach the balance, it is necessary to present the model with as much clarity as possible.

o *Realistic.* The financial model should be realistic, based on good information and data. The model should break down the financial structure and develop benchmarking. There is a difference between reality and aspiration. A company may aspire to be in the upper quartile of returns against competitors, but the reality may be that the firm has performance ranked in the fourth quartile. It is the job of the CEO and CFO to build a financial model that has benchmarking features that are realistic, not aspirational. If the firm has capabilities matching the fourth quartile, a financial model should capture the desire to progressively move the company to the third instead of the first quartile. It is a matter of capabilities and managing the differences and polarities between what capabilities the firm possesses today versus what capabilities it needs in the future.

o *Practical.* Third, the financial model should handle the practicality of where a company is versus where the company aspires to go. The model should solve potential friction between what can be done today versus what can be done in the future or in the long term. The financial model, with its capital allocation model and budgets, is built up with the objective of following the strategy. Once the model is set, it is broken down annually by geographic locations and divisions or units. As an example, consider a large diversified global company with many divisions. While the aspiration may be to grow the entire organization by 10 percent, practicality requires consideration of current market trends and developments. Therefore it is more pragmatic to develop a financial model that incrementally over time brings the growth of the entire firm to 10 percent. To achieve a tangible outcome with current capabilities, the firm should break down its model inputs by geography or markets and establish sensible targets. For example, one county in Australia may be targeted to grow revenues by 3 percent and improve productivity by 2 percent. In addition, due to local conditions, the cost structure required to bring the desired growth in revenue and productivity may entail an increase by 2 percent of general and administrative expenses. Taken together, this scenario of anticipated and key performance measures establishes projections for profitability from the Australian market. In other markets, revenue growth and measures of productivity and costs may fare differently, but the CEO should balance all seg-ments by geography, product line, or by industry. This allows for the development of a financial model that, in aggregate, provides a realistic and practical operating budget which is set by geography, by industry, and then by product. And then that budget, part of the management system, provides operating executives with an operat-ing budget for the year by unit or division. The model becomes a tool for evaluation and compensation. It is also customary that the operating budget be updated quarterly based on new inputs as mar-ket demand and economic conditions change over time. The budget becomes the management system by which the financial model is pulled together, business unit by business unit.

OTHER CONSIDERATIONS IN THE FINANCIAL MODEL

In addition to its components and attributes, a sound financial model should include contingencies and the ability to balance competing constituencies versus market priorities, and to use the financial model as a guide for financ-ing the business overall.

○   Contingencies are always necessary in the financial model. For ex-ample, a hurricane may take out a data center. There are no spe-cific items to account for this unanticipated event in the financial model regardless of the repairs or additional investments required for rebuilding. In many instances, insurance may cover some of the expenses, but business losses tend to exacerbate expenses not easily accounted for in the financial model. These expenses would have to be offset by other budget elements to maintain the integrity of the financial model. These are the primary roles of the CEO and management teams; they manage all those events and variations that occur every year that are beyond normal forecasting of revenues and expenses. In this setting, contingencies allow for the handling of unanticipated events and continue with adherence to the capital allocation model. Contingencies may be estimated based on prof-itability, costs, or profit margins. Contingencies play the role of a buffer between budgeted and actual revenues and expenses. The CEO is committing to the board specific targets in revenues and free cash flow based on the financial model. Indirectly, the CEO commits similar performance to shareholders and investors. However, to control outcomes and minimize unfavorable exposure, the CEO allocates budgets to various units or departments and holds a contingency in the case operating results deviate from projections.

o   Balancing competing priories for every company is an art and a science. For a firm with a certain level of profitability, trade-offs in distributions of free cash flow are apparent since there are many constraints in financing, limitations in capital investments, and expectations to meet required payments to shareholders and salaries and benefits to employees. A financial model is the most visible part of the balancing act that takes place in allocating resources to constituencies. For example, consider a company that had no credibility with the investor community as the returns to shareholders were low, and the stock price is depressed. An aggressive financial model could attract investors to provide more funds to expand the firm on the strategic path that seeks competitive advantage and value. In the short term, this may require smaller payments to other constituencies, including employees. However, in the longer term, it will provide sustainable support to all constituencies for the company.

o   Funding operations and funding investment opportunities generally come from internally generated cash flow, that is, free cash flow. The financial model provides guidance on the type of sources of funds required for asset redeployment or for major acquisitions. Primarily, debt markets and their derivative hybrid parts are used as sources for funding operations with a clear preference to using internally generated free cash flow. When debt may be a possible source for funding operations, careful analysis of the balance sheet is warranted. The financial model requires careful assessment of the impact of increased debt on the balance sheet as the total amount of debt shows the funds that have been used to acquire assets. This analysis requires an assessment of the amount of EBITDA that can support debt. Typically, the amount of debt may be a multiple of EBITDA. For example, for a billion dollars in EBITDA, the firm may be willing to have debt on the balance sheet between $2 and $3 billion. Firms use external funding. For reasonable ratios within EBITDA, the rest of the funding may come from cash flow profits.

Regarding financing investment opportunities, that is, financing acquisition of assets, executives follow a pecking order in financing assets with a preference for first using internally generated cash flows followed by fixed-loan financing and debt financing. Equity financing is only a vehicle of last resort. Equity financing leads to ownership dilution and often is associated with negative stock price reactions at the announcement of a new seasoned equity offering. Often there is a time lag between investments and expected cash flow returns. While investments are upfront, cash flow returns are uncertain and take time to materialize. The debt markets provide interim funding relief while waiting for the cash flow returns to come. Obviously, if returns fail to materialize, the firm's capital is destroyed as returns fall short of the cost of capital or the borrowing costs for the specific investment.

All these considerations go into the financial model and allow for the modeling of possible outcomes. In practice, executives look at a three-year financial model that allows for forecasting free cash flows, financing, distributions to investors, the PE multiple, and other key performance measures that assume no major exogenous events will impact the firm. Therefore, CEOs, by executing a realistic financial model in support of the strategy, can almost predict a range of stock prices. Admittedly one of the difficult parts of the execution is implementing the budget because there are always unanticipated events that create revenue shortfalls or increases, as well as other unexpected situations that emerge and require a response that is managed within that financial model.

To meet shareholders' expectations and compete with other firms for greater returns, executives often tend to be aggressive in setting budget projections for departments and units. An aggressive budget sets ambitious goals for delivering revenues and profitability, and challenges employees to exceed forecasted figures. While this approach may create tensions, it may cause innovative thinking and inspire employees to meet challenges.

Finally, the job of the CEO, among other things, is to manage expectations in terms of the company's finances for three constituent groups: the shareholders, the board, and the employees. It is typical for the CEO to use the financial model as a vehicle to make commitments to the board on the level of revenues and profitability for the upcoming fiscal year. Those commitments should be consistent with the expectations of shareholders for attractive risk-adjusted returns. After agreeing on targeted profits and revenues, the CEO breaks down the model into pieces and allocates budgets to units and departments. Typically, budgets may be aggressive to surpass targets and provide shareholders great than anticipated returns.

In recent years we observed a shift in the paradigm of the Anglo-American model of capitalism, where risk requires extra compensation. The Anglo-American model has provided to shareholders commensurable returns for risks they assumed. The shift to other alternative models, such as the corporate stakeholders' model, creates turbulence that requires a wide range of reassessment of corporate practices, including the purpose of the financial model and its usefulness. Such reassessment, however, requires leadership though which a new financial model with appropriate adjustments to stakeholders returns will be developed.

CHAPTER FIVE

Leadership

LEADERSHIP PERSPECTIVES: ACADEMICS VERSUS EXECUTIVES

A leader has power and influence in driving decision-making in a firm and directing the activities of others to obtain desirable outcomes. Much discussion in popular press and trade books has been devoted to the skills, insights, and capabilities required for a leader to be successful. Many case studies have been written about leaders who have succeeded and others who have failed. Through anecdotes, research, and observed practice, leadership is the cornerstone of success. Leaders possess knowledge and skills that allow the vision and mission of an organization to flourish. While making decisions, conventional wisdom suggests that leaders tend to satisfy rather than optimize outcomes. Armed with bounded rationality, leaders exhibit cognitive limitations that allow them to choose not necessarily the best but "good enough" options. Perhaps time is a limiting factor or satisfaction in meeting a goal is sufficient, rather than surpassing it. It is suggested that while there is a plethora of information and data, given human limitations and biases, leadership decisions often are based on rules of thumb, which reflect the wealth of information but scarcity of attention. Using the lens of practicality, leaders enact decisions that enable organization(s) to create and sustain a competitive advantage. These decisions involve executing a strategy, deploying appropriate assets in support of the strategy, and appreciating the culture within which leaders operate. These steps require finesse and a supreme understanding of the culture within which leaders operate. Understanding and navigating the culture can allow an organization immense success.

Without a doubt, academics and executives view leadership as an important construct that explains business and organizational performance. It is widely accepted that the importance of leadership persists. Research has shown across industries and individual firms that there is a positive relationship between mentions of leadership in the popular press and a firm's economic performance.

While academics and executives agree on the relationship between leadership and performance, they possess different perspectives about leadership simply because they address different questions. Academics address the broad question of, "What is leadership?" while executives focus on "how to lead." In addressing the question of what leadership is, academics have developed theories and recommendations based on data and science, rather than on wishes or beliefs. Their scientific inquiry includes analysis and data for both successful leaders as well as leaders who have failed. Successes are typically associated with a firm's economic performance, stock performance, and employee satisfaction. To arrive at their recommendations, academics examine not only cases of successful leaders but also leaders who have personally failed but also failed as a broad firm constituency, which includes their organizations, their employees, their customers, as well as their shareholders.

Executives and practitioners, when discussing matters of leadership, focus on how to lead. The conventional wisdom is to identify activities, actions, and traits that fit the facets of a leader who exceeded performance expectations and created superior profitability for the firm. There are usually uplifting stories that correlate with observed outcomes. To learn more about how to lead, one should explore the processes and contexts that produce leaders who produce excellent performances for their organizations. The processes include social psychology, which develops the actual traits and behaviors that precipitate leaders to be successful. The context also involves how to measure workplace conditions, diagnose the environment, and evaluate outcomes.

The differences in perspectives have provided several contradictions in defining leadership. Figure 5.1 provides on overview of those perspectives as we present key traits for leadership behaviors from the academic literature and from practice. While some leadership attributes and behaviors overlap, leadership in practice shapes the management team charged with the implementation of a strategy. As it will be apparent in future chapters, compensations and incentives, along with a vigilant board of directors, make leadership a precondition for business success.

Figure 5.1

ACADEMIC PERSPECTIVES

Developments in academic research have provided several insights that formed the core knowledge regarding leaders and leadership and, subsequently, answers to the question, "What is leadership?" Early academic research focused on studying the qualities of a leader as an individual who works in a large organization. More recently, more relevant research has focused attention on the context within which a leader is working and has discovered emerging leadership behaviors that involve shared, rational, strategic, and dynamic relationships of the leader, the leader's subordinates, and the environment within which the firm operates. It is not the individual's characteristics alone that make a difference. It is the environment where the behavior of the leader contributes to positive performance or outcomes. Therefore, it is the shared and dyadic relationship between the leader and the environment that produces outcomes.

Distinct Leadership Behaviors

Models of leadership include authentic leadership, transformational leadership, broaden-and-build theory, ethical leadership, and positive organizational behavior. *Authentic leadership* describes a pattern of transparent and ethical traits of a leader that encourages openness in sharing data and challenges for decision-making while being collegial and accepting of subordinates' inputs. Authentic leaders have in common the following characteristics: (a) the analytical and objective examination of data and information prior to making decisions; (b) maintenance of high moral standards; (c) willingness to share information, especially feelings as appropriate; and (d) self-awareness of strengths, weaknesses, and mindfulness of the world.

Transformational leadership depicts the behaviors of leaders who are inspirational to their followers or subordinates and demonstrate the ways in which they perform beyond expectations. These include performance results in response to radical changes in the organization that indicate the abilities of the leader to motivate and influence subordinates to take a course of action that benefits the organization. A transformational leader places the good of the organization ahead of self-interest and individual gains.

In the *broaden-and-build theory*, individuals with positive psychological behaviors—such as positive feelings, optimism, and confidence—make great leaders because they have the propensities to broaden their own behaviors and build additional capabilities around themselves in the organizations. By enlarging or expanding one's behavior as a leader, the results can include novel ideas and the development of actions that result in superior organizational performance.

Ethical leadership describes the style of leadership that is indicative of conduct that exudes personal actions and interpersonal relationships that are characterized by high moral standards, principled behavior, and transparent decision-making. In this setting, an ethical leader advocates and promotes such conduct to subordinates within the firm as well as exhibiting these behaviors by example.

Finally, the *positive organizational behavior model* suggests that certain concepts create a positive climate within a firm and thereby enhance the firm's performance. A leader who advances hope, resiliency, efficacy, optimism, happiness, and well-being creates an environment where decisions lead to superior performance.

While distinct leadership behaviors provide a broad view as to what is leadership, they mostly emphasize the behavior of a leader who advances a leader–follower (subordinate) relationship. It is presumed that each leadership behavior aligns the actions of the leader with those of the subordinates to produce outstanding firm performance. Setting goals, providing direction and support, and reinforcing or emulating behaviors like those of the leader foster an environment where subordinates are motived to follow the leader's decisions and produce exceptional performances. The traditional academic models interpret leadership as an exchange or a transaction between a leader and subordinates or followers. The transactional exchange aligns leadership behavior (transformational, emotional, among others) with the interests of the followers. Therefore, in an organization, a leader does not need to exhibit all the behaviors of the traditional model but a specific behavior of the model.

Most recent academic research has advanced the notion that the transactional exchange between the leader and the followers/subordinates could be further augmented when the leader provides visionary and inspirational messages, expresses emotional feelings, stresses ideological and moral values, and provides an environment with intellectual stimulation to subordinates.[30] It is certain that a transformative leader raises subordinates' aspirations and activates their higher-order values in a way that allows followers to identify with the vision of the leader, feel better about their contributions at work and then perform far beyond simple motivation and expectations. It has been established, based on research,[31] that transformational leadership is associated with effectiveness and other performance outcomes, including productivity and low turnover across many types of firms, levels of analysis, and cultures. What is more definite is the process through which a transformative leader influences followers' attitudes, behaviors, and performance.[32] Key factors that contribute to this positive outcome include

---

[30] A. Bryman. *Charisma and Leadership in Organizations* (London/Newbury Park, CA: Sage, 1992).

[31] B. J. Avolio, B. M. Bass, F. O. Walumbwa, and W. Zhu. *Multifactor Leadership Questionnaire: Manual and Sampler Test*. (Redwood City, CA: Mind Garden, 2004a).

[32] H. Liao, A. C. Chuang. "Transforming Service Employees and Climate: A Multilevel, Multisource Examination of Transformational Leadership in Building Long-Term Service

establishing a sense of commitment to subordinates' satisfaction, perceived fairness, autonomy and feedback at work, responsibility, and how followers come to feel about themselves and their teams in terms of efficacy, potency, and cohesion.[33], [34]

Additional research has identified the parameters that mediate or moderate the relationship of the transformative leader with that of followers' levels of motivation and performance at the individual or team level as well as organizational level.[35]

Research regarding the correlation of the charisma of the CEO and the performance of the organization remains inconclusive. Some research studies show that CEO charisma is not related to organizational performance as measured by net profit margins and shareholder returns. Other research points out the opposite result.

Research on leadership has primarily focused on hierarchical organizations with traditional leadership models. Traditional leadership models follow the notion that the organization is structured with command-and-control features in a hierarchical model. In recent years, however, new innovative structured approaches appeared in the marketplace that do not resemble the traditional production-oriented firm. Leadership research has addressed leadership dynamics for organizations operating in today's knowledge-based economy.[36] Organizations in this regard are considered complex, and researchers apply the complexity theory to study leadership. In this context, leadership is examined as an interactive system of dynamic interactions

---

Relationships," *Journal of Applied Psychology*, 92, 2007, pp. 1006–1019.

[33] F. O. Walumbwa, B. J. Avolio, W. L. Gardner, T. S. Wernsing, and S. J. Peterson. "Authentic Leadership: Development and Validation of a Theory-Based Measure," *Journal of Management*, 34, 2008, pp. 89–126.

[34] J. Schaubroeck, S. S. K. Lam, and S. E. Cha. "Embracing Transformational Leadership: Team Values and the Impact of Leader Behavior on Team Performance," *Journal of Applied Psychology*, 92, 2007, pp. 1020–1030.

[35] R. T. Keller. "Transformational Leadership, Initiating Structure, and Substitutes for Leadership: A Longitudinal Study of Research and Development Project Team Performance," *Journal of Applied Psychology*, 91, 2006, pp. 202–2010.

[36] B. B. Lichtenstein, M. Uhl-Bien, R. Marion, A. Seers, J. D. Orton, and C. Schreiber. "Complexity Leadership Theory: An Interactive Perspective on Leading in Complex Adaptive Systems." In *Complex Systems Leadership Theory: New Perspectives from Complexity Science on Social and Organizational Effectiveness*, ed. J. K. Hazy, J. A. B. B. Goldstein, and B. B. Lichtenstein (Mansfield, MA: ISCE Publ, 2007), pp. 129–141.

between employees who interact with each other in unpredictable ways with complex feedback loops. Those interactions yield performance that is adaptive and continuously evolving. The results include innovation, knowledge, and further adaptation to change. In this format, leadership starts from any point within the organization and evolves through any interaction between employees or partners. In this framework, leadership is not centralized; rather, it emerges within complex firms.[37]

Academic research also points to several trends: (a) Leadership is a holistic exercise. Leadership is not only about the leader; it also involves the subordinates, the senior leadership team, the context and all levels of the organization, and their dynamic interactions. (b) Leadership involves a process of exchange between the leader and the subordinate. The process involves behavioral and strategic elements as well as the sharing of information. As the leader and subordinate process information, their interactions and the ways that the exchange affects the other, the group, and the organization is important. (c) From the content perspective, leadership may be authentic, transformational, or visionary. From the process perspective, leadership may be shared, complex, or strategic. (d) More leadership is being distributed and shared in organizations.

Shared leadership is based on patterns of reciprocal influence, which further develop relationships between members of the organization.[38] Additionally, shared leadership reflects a dynamic, interactive influence process among individuals with the objective of leading each other to achieve team or organizational goals.[39]

---

[37] J. K. Hazy, J. A. Goldstein, and B. B. Lichtenstein. "Complex Systems Leadership Theory: An Introduction." In *Complex Systems Leadership Theory: New Perspectives from Complexity Science on Social and Organizational Effectiveness*, ed. J. K. Hazy, J. A. Goldstein, and B. B. Lichtenstein (Mansfield, MA: ISCE Publ., 2007), pp. 1–13. Similar research appears in M. Uhl-Bien, R. Marion, and B. McKelvey. "Complexity Leadership Theory: Shifting Leadership from the Industrial Age to the Knowledge Era," *Leadership Quarterly*, 18, 2007, pp. 298–318.

[38] D. V. Day, P. Gronn, and E. Salas. "Leadership Capacity in Teams," *Leadership Quarterly*, 15, 2004, pp. 857–880.

[39] C. L. Pearce, and H. P. Sims. "The Relative Influence of Vertical vs. Shared Leadership on the Longitudinal Effectiveness of Change Management Teams," *Group Dynamics: Theory, Research, and Practice*, 6, 2002, 172–197.

Leader and Leadership Development

There is a difference between the development of leaders and leadership development. Leader development focuses on the ways that individual leaders develop, while leadership development involves a focus on the process of developing several individuals in the organization, including executives and subordinates. Leadership development provides ways for individuals to develop and hone skills to further advance in their roles.

Leadership and Change

Change management is devoted to the linking of leaders' actions with organizational change and subsequent outcomes. In fact, leadership is implicitly associated with a process of change. The appointment of a new leader in any organization signals upcoming changes.

THE EXECUTIVE'S PERSPECTIVE

The role of a leader is to ensure that a company has a strategy in place that is well aligned with the marketplace. Once this strategy is in place, then the leader must guarantee that the firm possesses the assets, the people, the skills, and the capabilities to execute that strategy. A financial model, by which performance will be measured, allows for the communication of whether a strategy is working or not working. The job of the leader is to bring together all the elements necessary to execute the strategy and achieve the desired outcomes, along with enhancing competitive advantage. Also, the leader is tasked with the responsibility of creating the environment of the firm to carry out the desired strategy. This direction can be one where people either believe in performance and accountability, hard work, discipline, and curiosity and fulfill these roles, or a culture emerges that is centered around dissembling and passive-aggressive behaviors. The latter is a culture that will create difficulty in realizing the desired goals of the strategy. Additionally, these are all characteristics of organizations that have not really subscribed to the leadership that needs to be positively projected on in a relentless, disciplined way.

VIEW FROM THE TOP

Leadership is the single biggest challenge for organizational success. Poor leadership will still lead the organization. A firm's strategy is important, as are the types and qualities of assets it deploys. A good financial model is critical, but at the end of the day, the single biggest determinant of success is leadership. While not precisely defined, leadership is the art of influencing people. It is not a management system that establishes rules of command and control, but leadership sets the influence of others. It is about taking people to a place where they would otherwise not go or not be able to get there without the influence of a good leader.

In practical terms, leadership is a balance between being realistic and being honest and factual, while at the same time, creating hope, a plan, and a pathway to lead people to a destination that they absolutely could not get to by themselves. Shareholders pay executives well to achieve an outcome that is different from what would happen under normal operations or normal circumstances. Leaders drive their teams, and a CEO drives the whole organization, to achieve beyond what the employees of an organization think they could do themselves. Leaders work, and they work best in partnership with other leaders. In other words, leadership is not a solo mission. It is about interacting, communicating, partnering, and bringing out the best in other leaders and employees in the organization.

Leaders lead from many power bases. The two most important power bases of leaders are those that stem from an intellectual power base and the emotional base. These two bases represent the two extremes of the spectrum of alternatives. These two bases often represent polarities. Leaders are smart enough and have the intellectual depth that allow them to develop strategies. Additionally, the leaders can build a financial model as well as build and redeploy assets. All these activities demonstrate that leaders can lead from a purely intellectual perspective. However, on the other side of the spectrum, the other side of the polarity spectrum, is the emotional aspect. Good leaders not only lead from the brain, but they also lead from the heart. The most effective leaders can lead from both dimensions. They bring together the intellectual and emotional elements and bring together the brain and the heart. When those parts merge and complement each other, this intersection creates passion. The result is the emergence of the outcomes that are superior to those of leaders who only lead from one of those two dimensions or bases. Part of the emotional leadership base is the ability to be empathetic. Empathy, which means to understand people and understand what they are going through as they go down this leadership path, allows leaders to relate to the people employed in the organization and enables those employees to feel valued and understood.

When examining leaders and observing what they do, certain traits and characteristics stand out. Leaders are not necessarily popular. They often make mistakes, but they are good listeners and can reverse course when necessary. Leadership is a choice, not an obligation, and it requires courage, focus, and decisiveness. The leader's curiosity and interest in search and discovery helps to generate future opportunities for the organization and explore new markets and products. Interacting with others in the organization requires fairness, thoughtfulness, authenticity, and integrity. Finally, charisma and self-confidence help solidify performance. In the next section, we present more details about those characteristics of a successful leader.

Popularity

Leaders are not necessarily popular. Good leaders are not reliant on constant adulation, praise, and positive feedback from the individuals with whom they work. Leadership is not about popularity, but it is about influencing, and it is about convincing people to believe that the leader and the strategy can produce success and advance the organization. People like to follow leaders who are successful. Success has a multidimensional aspect: success with shareholders, success with customers, success with partners, and success with employees. In fact, as analogous to soldiers and majors in the army, you would not want to work for a general who loses every battle. The general may be the nicest general in the world and could have the best strategy in the world, but at the end of the day, if he loses the battle, no one wants to be in that army under his leadership. Therefore, it is incumbent on the leader to create an environment that is conducive to and supportive of people and their beliefs that if they work hard, and if they execute the plan, they will be successful.

Leaders as Good Listeners

When a leader implements a strategy, deploys the right assets, and develops a financial plan, rarely do the resulting operations follow those plans to the letter. There is almost immediately obstacles or changes that occur in the implementation process. A good leader can see which components of the plans are working, which are not working, and then make appropriate adjustments to correct the course. Much of the input that the leader provides is not only from observations but also stems from listening and leading from the front and actively participating in the completion of the strategy, not leading from the rear.

Leadership Mistakes

Leaders often make mistakes. They make mistakes all the time and under unexpected circumstances. It is not poor judgment but often misreading facts, misinterpreting information, assessing risk differently, and making decisions that lead to suboptimal outcomes or even results that are not value-enhancing. Often decisions involve forthcoming options based on assumptions about the resolution of future uncertainties. When uncertainty, however, is resolved, options that a leader thought will be value-enhancing may turn out to destroy value, and the leader should admit mistakes and missteps. Being unpretentious and humble while responsible about the outcomes establishes positive viewpoints about the soft qualities of the leader. Several times these mistakes are reversed when updated information is provided. These revisions demonstrate that good leadership is all about listening, not just listening from the organization, but listening from all dimensions and then making adjustments. Napoleon was a master at this. The general always sat up on a hill and looked at the battle so he could make adjustments during the fighting. Napoleon's approach shows the tremendous importance of seeing the entire scope of an organization's operations, so that (a) a leader has a macro-view of the operations, and (b) the leader can fine-tune or tweak elements to bring them more into sync with the entire operating structure.

Leadership Is a Choice

Given an opportunity for a leadership role, some people show that they are good leaders, while others demonstrate that being a good leader is not their strong suits. And at some point, mid-level managers should make a choice as to whether they want to be leaders since leadership is hard work and does involve discipline and persistence. Many people think that as they progress in an organization, as they get further up the organizational hierarchy, they do not have to work as hard. Instead, they think that they can preside and take input from all the people who work for them. The truth is that you must work even harder as you take on leadership roles as you must have a plan and carry out the plan that creates the structure and timelines for departments and employees to execute. You must have the self-confidence to drive and lead the organization to an outcome individuals under your leadership did not think they could get to by themselves.

In addition to these qualities, there are several other characteristics that make the prospects for success positive.[40] The following are these qualities with descriptions of each one.

Courage

Courage involves optimism and self-confidence. When everyone doubts what you are doing, courage allows you to move forward, especially when you have a vision that is different from the general thinking of an organization. Additionally, it takes courage to stand up to people. It takes courage to take on the accountability and responsibility to be out in front of those under your employ and say, "I believe in this; this is the direction we are going. I believe in the abilities of all of you and know that together we can achieve the amazing results that this plan will allow us to realize."

---

[40] Many of these characteristics appear in Robert Iger, *The Ride of a Lifetime* (New York: Penguin Random House, 2019).

Focus and Decisiveness

Focus is a critical part of good leadership, as is decisiveness. Many leaders rely on a task force format to make decisions. In these scenarios, the task force reports back the results of their work and often does not make a decision. They report the results of their meetings to enable a decision. Alternatively, a leader makes a decision based on facts. It is unlikely that the leader will get 100 percent perfect of the facts, so a leader may make decisions based on about 70 percent or 80 percent of the information available to make a decision. If you wait for all the information needed, a leader will never make a decision. By the time you would finally make a decision, it would be too late because the environment or the market would have already changed. If you make a decision at that point, it would be the wrong decision. If you have self-confidence, you are willing to admit, "Hey, this hasn't worked. This was a bad decision." And then you reverse course. There is nothing wrong with changing direction based on new information. In an analogy to being a captain of a ship, changing direction due to adverse weather conditions would allow you to keep the ship in the direction that it has set to reach and do so without risking adverse conditions to both the ship itself and those onboard.

Curiosity and Discovery

Leaders must be curious and interested in discovering new things and new ways of doing business. A leader cannot just accept what's right in front of him or her. A leader must be able to look around corners, or at least have some people who are close to him or her and can look around those corners to investigate, among other things, alternate operational strategies, new techniques, and ways to innovate. To look around those corners requires curiosity. Why is something the way it is? Why do we accept certain things for the way they are? That is curiosity. It is challenging the status quo and ensuring that the operational and human capital sides of the organization are doing the best that they can and advancing to the best of their abilities.

Fairness

Particularly fairness with people. People always make mistakes, as many as a CEO or perhaps more. Often people are not employed in the proper positions, which can lead to missteps. The leader is very hardnosed about performance, but at the same time must be fair. And being fair usually involves honesty and empathetic communication with the employees as to what they are doing well, what they are not doing well, and what you as the leader expect of them.

Thoughtfulness

Not only thoughtfulness as it relates to thinking through strategy, thinking through tactics, thinking through execution, it is also being thoughtful about people in day-to-day operations and as situations arise. What is going on with their families? What is going on in their lives? Spending time trying to understand the psychology of people who work for the leader always creates a positive outcome. Understanding their needs and wants and how they could be satisfied may provide ways of improving performance as this understanding allows employees to feel that they are respected and understood holistically, not just for the work that they do.

Authenticity

People know immediately when you are authentic and when you are not. When leaders stand up in front of an audience, judging from statements people can figure out in roughly ten minutes whether a leader is authentic. Organizations have an uncanny ability to quickly decide whether someone is authentic. If you are authentic, that helps with the mission of influencing employees and leading them to a place they could not reach on their own. If employees view you as inauthentic, they tend to tune you out. When they tune you out, there is no way that the organization can accomplish its mission and its objectives. You must be relentless—relentlessness in execution and relentlessness in ensuring that the details are understood. Relentless in driving people to a different outcome. This tenacity drives the organization forward and prevents detracting behaviors from being obstacles to the achievement of the strategy and resulting outcomes.

Integrity

Integrity is doing what you say. This does not mean that you do not change or alter the way you do things because you often have to change. For example, you may have to change your opinion about a leader. Integrity comes from being honest about why you initiated the change. This entails communicating and being authentic in describing the change and the reasons you made it.

Self-Confidence

Leaders must project self-confidence, not arrogance, but self-assurance. Employees only want to work for leaders they think are confident; that is, leaders who believe in themselves. They believe in what they are doing. People do not want to work for or follow someone who is filled with self-doubt and epitomizes insecurity. Now, we all have self-doubts, but the art of leadership is to let people know you have doubts through your ability to relate to them empathetically but still create a sense of confidence in what the organization is doing and in moving the organization in the right direction.

Charisma

Charisma is another positive dimension that can add even more to the characteristics of the leader. Charisma is important, but charisma is different from self-confidence as it is a style that creates attraction, among other things. Charisma can help the short term to engage members of the constituency and develop a strong support base. Fundamentally, leadership is mostly about hard work, and it is about self-discipline. It is not about delegation. Delegation is just a tool that the leader uses to advance the direction and attainment of the strategy and goals of the organization. The leader cannot delegate the accountability and the responsibility for the organization. The leader accepts that accountability. Accepting that accountability and responsibility requires hard work and discipline in order to achieve the desired results. At the end of the day, performance outweighs charisma.

LEADERSHIP AND ORGANIZATIONAL STRUCTURE

Leaders influence the direction of the organization and the way the firm is organized. One consideration that influences the organizational structure of a large company is leadership. A good leader can understand where the organization is; for example, if the organization is running very well. With good financial systems, you have good capabilities and very capable managers. This structure typically would call for more of a decentralized management system. Capable leaders will be closest to the market, closest to customers, closest to the people, therefore being able to make the necessary decisions. Those leaders work independently, but in a good way, support the overall strategy more effectively in a decentralized mode of an organizational structure.

On the other hand, if the organization lacks good processes, the leader cannot create a disciplined organization. The type of structure may have deficits for good managers and talent. This type of structure for control purposes requires centralization. Centralizing allows for reengineering and redoing processes to get control of the organization. Then over time—and this is a key part of the leader's competency skills—identifying the right people to be appointed in the right positions. As a result, the leader with a new team in place can delegate decision making. Having the wrong people creates chaos and a loss of energy, discipline, and focus. This approach is more appropriate in a centralized organizational structure.

ACQUIRING HUMAN CAPITAL AND LEADERSHIP

Regardless of the organizational arrangement, one of the key responsibilities of leaders is to ensure that they have people surrounding them who believe in the mission, the strategy, the direction in which the organization is moving, and have the character values that support the leader. It is the CEO's responsibility to get people who have different and diverse backgrounds but share many of the same common values. Integrity and authenticity, empathy, willingness to accept accountability and responsibility, excellent communication skills, ability to accept mistakes and/or missteps, and self-confidence are some of the value traits a leader should look for when building his or her team. These traits allow for the creation of a positive work environment that is collaborative and ethical in its execution.

However, when selecting people surrounding the CEO, skills tend to be important. For example, a CFO needs to be disciplined and good with numbers and financial models. The CFO does not need to be a salesperson. The VP of sales, on the other hand, needs to be extremely empathetic and have great communication skills. The leader should be surrounded by people who share the same values and the same or similar trait characteristics of the CEO but also have the right skills and occupy the right positions. Additionally, a leader can assess his or her own strengths and weaknesses and hire executives who provide strengths where his or her weaknesses reside.

Football provides a great analogy to the acquisition of human capital. In football, the coach is very instructive. You can have a great left tackle, but if you have that left tackle playing quarterback, the team will not work well. You can have a great receiver, someone who is fast and has good hands. If the coach positions him to play the offensive line, the player will be completely miscast. Therefore, the role of the coach is to ensure you have the right skills in the right positions. This means you need to understand what skills you need in an organization to execute the strategy. This is where the skills of the CEO are very necessary. As the positions are determined, human characteristics and values need to be considered as they are relatively fixed. If you have a team of leaders that share values and characteristics, well over time, those values and characteristics get transmitted down through the organization and begin to create culture.

ARE LEADERSHIP SKILLS TRANSFERABLE?

The skill component of leadership skills is highly transferable. If you have a great financial executive, can you take that skill set and go to another organization? Absolutely. What are not as transferable are the human traits, the values and characteristics. You can take someone with high integrity, great self-discipline, and great self-confidence and put the person in a terrible environment. In that environment, all those values will not dissipate, but they will erode. Values become an important part of the culture. Generally, skills are transferable; values and traits are less transferable because they are individualistic, but they are also collective. If an individual gets transplanted into an organization that does not share those values or those traits, it becomes very difficult for that person then to be able to perform at a level consistent with his or her own value structure and consistent with the performance the individual wants to derive.

THE ROLE OF TRUST IN LEADERSHIP

Many believe that trust is an important characteristic of a leader. Trust is something that is *earned*. It is not a unique trait for an executive and is earned with integrity, honesty, and empathy. While someone may have a choice to be a leader, that choice also includes decisions. The decisions a leader must make involve doing what he or she says, carrying out actions that are ethical, and following through with deliverables. If someone does what he or she says, those actions are carried out with integrity. Additionally, being fair creates trust as well. While trust is important, it cannot exist without the underlying values and characteristics of a leader.

LEADERSHIP AND INSPIRATION

To be successful, a leader must have a vision. If the leader does not have a vision, it is very difficult to lead. A leader must have a vision of what he or she is trying to create; everything flows from that. This includes departmental visions and action items, budgets, communications, and marketing strategies. If the leader has no idea what he or she would like to accomplish, there will be no vision and no goals. Leaders must have visions of what they want to create. And from those visions, strategies emerge, which then flow to the assets, which then flow to the financial models, and subsequently to the organization through communication, integrity, trust, discipline, and relentless execution. Therefore, the starting point is that leaders must know what they want to accomplish. If they do not know, it is doubtful they will reach their goals.

STRENGTH-BASED LEADERSHIP

Leading the organization includes identifying the strengths of the entire team, including the executive staff. Heidrick and Struggles developed a leadership model based on five or six characteristics that describe the value and benefit of this type of understanding. The Hendricks & Struggles model encompasses characteristics that include business acumen, empathy, intellect, and other strengths. All these traits are valuable, but it is *how* those strengths are put together and executed experientially through the day-to-day business operations as well as running an organization. The following football analogy demonstrates this point.

When the Philadelphia Eagles draft players, the scouts and managers go through an enormous evaluation of the strengths of potential team additions. Some of the questions that aid in the evaluation process include: How long are the player's arms? How big are their hands? What is his football IQ? Additional questions address the determination of the additional metrics of strength and levels of strengths of each player. The answers to these questions provide a plethora of information, but the information does not amount to much value until team management can get the potential team members on the field to observe how they execute, how they assimilate, how they integrate those strengths, and how they adapt those strengths to the unique circumstances of the business environment.

The strengths-based leadership approach is a great tool, but it is not providing a complete picture. It is the CEO who assimilates the results of the strengths-based approach with the practical nature of his or her team. A good CEO or leader is constantly assessing the strengths of the organizational team, determining what the organization is doing well overall, what they are not doing well, and how to develop areas of weakness. The latter includes encouraging members of the organization to capitalize on the strengths of every individual and the team as a whole and try to minimize some of the weaknesses. If weaknesses are glaring, some of those weaknesses may be difficult to overcome. In these cases, the CEO must find individuals who have some of those skills or strengths in order to offset weaknesses in others. For example, a CFO may have great facilities with numbers and excellent communication skills but may not be a great leader for his or her team. The CFO may communicate well but may not be transparent and open. In some instances, there may be positives and negatives regarding certain qualities. Sometimes people have real Achilles heels that must be addressed if they are going to be able to execute the job they have undertaken and drive the performance that is required.

POWER AND LEADERSHIP

Someone in a leadership role usually has authority and power. This authority and power come from two different power bases, the intellectual and emotional. Within those power bases, there are many gradations. For example, people have a power base based on those they know in the organization, which includes familiarization and affiliation with other people in the organization. Some people lead because they are competent and intelligent, qualities that people will respond to in leaders. Other people respond to more of an emotional leadership style. There are six styles of emotional leadership, which include authoritative, coaching, affiliative, democratic, coercive, and pacesetting. Leading with emotional intelligence will help create a balance between achieving the company's goals and creating solid work relationships.

Finally, one of the power bases is the positing a leaders is placed in the hierarchy of a firm. In a command-and-control world, people in higher positions in the hierarchy tend to have more power than people who are in lower positions in the hierarchy.

Leaders must adjust their leadership style to the environment that pervades the company. Let us say the company is in crisis mode. What we have just gone through with COVID-19 is a good example of a crisis mode. Crisis modes are not times for endless task forces but rather quick and diligent action. These are instances that require leaders to step forward, get facts, get information, make decisions regarding the ways that the company will operate in the time of crisis, as well as address impacted business that is directed to and from them.

Within those power bases, there are different leadership styles. There are democratic leadership styles, autocratic leadership styles, and consensual leadership styles[41]. Those leadership styles must be adapted to each situation, and there are times when the best leadership style is democratic. Alternatively, there are times when decisiveness is required, and an autocratic leadership style is appropriate to take the organization out of a crisis. At other times, you must step back and take a more affiliated, more consensual approach to decision-making. What is important to the leader and to the decisions that need to be made is that they are consensual and democratic, and that the leader displays an open and transparent approach. In other words, everyone has an opportunity to participate and influence what it is the organization is trying to handle. However, when it comes to execution, there is no room for democracy or affiliation or task forces. It is all about the relentless pursuit of excellence in implementation. Therefore, the power bases and the types of leadership styles are supremely important because those leadership styles need to be adapted to the environment.

In a very high-performing organization that is producing great results, an autocratic-style leader as the CEO will be most likely fail. On the other hand, an organization that has direction, a culture that is totally undisciplined, and has no accountability, no responsibility, and is performing very poorly requires a strong leadership style, perhaps an autocratic leader to get the team moving or involve a new team so the organization can move in a better direction.

Leaders can always abuse power. There are all kinds of abuse of power, but it stems from a lack of key personal characteristics, traits, and values, not the other way around. In other words, a person who has high levels of integrity, is honest, open, and transparent, and will rarely abuse his or her power in an organization. A person who is dishonest, dissembling, not confident, and a poor communicator has a higher propensity to abuse his or her power in a hierarchy. Therefore, abuse of power stems from leadership values, not power and leadership styles need to be commensurate with what the organization needs. With the power bases, people lead with their different strengths with the goal of moving the organization forward.

---

[41] A broad term of all these alternatives refers to affiliation leadership styles

ADAPTABILITY

Leadership is contextual. It is dependent upon the environment, the context, and the leadership style of the person exhibiting it. Leadership is adjusted to the context. It is natural or situational. One critical question is the adaptability of the leader in different settings; that is, how a leader can apply his or her leadership skills in various organizational contexts. Let us assume a leader has become accustomed to an environment that is based on continuity and perpetual growth. Can the same leader operate with success in an environment that is very disruptive with complexity and in crisis mode?

In our view, it is harder for the leader to adapt to a different scenario because people have primary leadership styles. These leadership styles are not so completely fixed that a leader cannot adjust. A good leader is willing to take feedback, is willing to acknowledge mistakes or missteps, and is willing to make adjustments. By definition, a good leader who has characteristics like curiosity, self-confidence, and open-mindedness is usually better prepared to make adjustments in his or her leadership style or elsewhere that adjustments need to be made. However, people have a primary leadership style, and it can be very difficult to change that leadership style completely.

This is where the role of the board becomes important as it provides an understanding of where the company is and what the company needs, and then match those conditions with a leader with the right leadership capabilities and style. But these are situations in which boards sometime make misjudgments. In some cases, they do not know where the organization is and, therefore, appoint the wrong leader. In other cases, the board does not know what the organization needs and is unable to find the right leader. Or they just make mistakes because sometimes leaders do not show their true colors until they are in a position of leadership.

However, people can adapt. There are great examples of people adapting, but at the end, in our view people have primary leadership characteristics and traits and styles. And these characteristics, traits, and styles need to be matched with the right environment for the leader to be able to execute and perform at a high level. In the five components framework— which involves strategy, assets, the implementation of a financial model, leadership, and culture—a leader is provided with an opportunity to make adjustments within the context of the framework. Those adjustments then become less individual, less personality-based, and more systematic within that framework.

WHAT IS MORE IMPORTANT FOR A LEADER, EMOTIONAL IQ OR INTELLECTUAL IQ?

Ideally you have both an emotional IQ and an intellectual IQ. The best leaders have both. There are good strategists and executors who can engage people emotionally as well as intellectually. The emotional IQ—the ability to relate to people, motivate people, and inspire people to an outcome that they could not reach themselves—is more important than the pure intellectual framework. The characteristics of emotional IQ are more important than intellectual IQ. In other words, a leader can always hire a consultant to help figure out an intellectual problem that requires a solution. However, a consultant can never help a leader relate to the organization that she or he is leading. Those characteristics are much more on the emotional IQ spectrum than on the intellectual IQ spectrum.

NEGOTIATIONS FOR A LEADER

While many believe that the ability to negotiate is one of the traits of a leader, it is truly a skill. A leader may learn additional negotiation skills or hire others to handle negotiations on his or her behalf. Negotiations are specialized skills, like legal skills or technical skills. However, the art of negotiation requires a high emotional IQ to understand how to negotiate. It is much more an emotional transaction than it is a logical transaction, particularly when the leader is buying companies. In these situations, you're dealing with the emotions of CEOs, management teams, boards, and shareholders. That is usually much more important than just intellectual rigor. Therefore, negotiation skills are a skill set, but certain elements of negotiations require emotional intelligence, which becomes a good trait for a leader.

THE LEADERSHIP TEAM

In our decision-making framework we believe a leader with the right traits and characteristics can lead an organization to successful outcomes. However, this cannot be accomplished without building the right team to provide engaging input, involve in execution and provide support. Building the right team is an art and a science. Potential individual members should be assessed and evaluated for fit through a holistic process that involves assessment and judgments about (a) experience and expertise, that is, technical knowledge, skills and abilities that someone possesses (i.e., industry, technical exposure, education, depth of knowledge) (b) Capabilities that are associated with competences critical to deliver outcomes (i.e., shape strategy, inspire and influence people, disrupt and challenge, initiate innovation (c) Potential which underscores and enables delivery of favorable outcomes (i.e., agility, learning, adaptability and resilience) and (d) culture fit and impact which allows for alignment of values with the organization (i.e., collaborative style, seriousness of purpose, sense of direction). The leader's success depends on his or her ability to build talent and teams that will drive the strategy for results while continuously improve current practices.

CHAPTER SIX

The Role of Organizational Culture

INTRODUCTION

Corporate culture as a concept originated in the disciplines of anthropology, political science, psychology, and sociology. While the notion of culture in organizations is not new, it gained prominence in the 1980s with the publication of several books, including *In Search of Excellence*,[42] *Corporate Cultures: The Rise and Rituals of Corporate Life*,[43] and *Theory Z*.[44] Academics and executives agree that organizational culture is an important consideration in business leadership, and a strong culture produces superior performance compared to firms with weak cultures. In particular, a recent survey confirms that 91 percent of top executives consider that culture is "very important" or "important" for their firms, with 54 percent of executives believing that culture is one of the top three value drivers for their organizations.[45] Academics and executives agree that understanding culture helps decision-makers assess and evaluate the challenges faced by an organization

---

[42] Tom Peters and Robert Waterman. *In Search of Excellence* (Grand Central, NY 1988).

[43] Terrence Deal and Allen Kennedy. *Corporate Cultures* (Addison–Wesley, Boston 1982).

[44] William Ouchi. *Theory Z* (Addison–Wesley, Boston 1981).

[45] J. Graham, J. Grennan, C. Harvey, and S. Rajgopal. "Corporate Culture: Evidence from the Field," *NBER Paper*, 2019.

in confronting changes in the competitive environment. Moreover, under-standing culture helps executive leaders develop a strategy that requires the deployment of assets with a suitable financial model that, when executed with good leadership, yields superior performance.

Managing culture, while complex and multifaceted, nevertheless is a powerful tool in bringing together diverse people with a variety of skills to produce consistent and purposeful outcomes. Academics have produced a volume of research findings about culture helpful in decision-making by focusing primarily on three key aspects of culture: (a) What is culture? (b) How does culture evolve in an organization from the time a founder starts a company into the future when a company experiences a crisis or continues successes? and (c) Can culture be managed to improve a firm's performance?

While the first two aspects of the work of academics offer an appre-ciation of the phenomenon of culture and its progression in the life of an organization, they are not of great interest to practicing executives. It is only the third part of the work of academics that coincides with the interest of executives. Executives believe that by managing culture, they can improve outcomes to stakeholders. Understanding the dynamics of organizational culture and how they impact performance is one of the top items on the agendas of every corporate executive. In fact, in a 2018 survey that covered responses from 1,348 executives, the overwhelming majority (92 percent) believe that the firm's value improves when corporate culture improves. Also, 84 percent of executive responders in the survey identified the need for improving culture as a priority, while only 16 percent of executives believe that their own firm's cultures require no change.[46] All this evidence suggests that executives place emphasis on managing the culture of the organizations they lead as they implicitly believe that the "right" culture impacts value. Academics and practitioners may have different views as to what culture is and how it evolves, but both evidence and practice suggest that managing culture pays dividends to stakeholders.

To present the diversity of views about culture, we followed figure 6.1. We report findings from academic research about core values and norms, performance, and competitiveness. We also write about the software and firmware components of organizational culture terms attributed to

---

[46] Graham et al., "Corporate Culture."

practicing executives when they discuss culture. In addition, we report the link between culture and strategy.

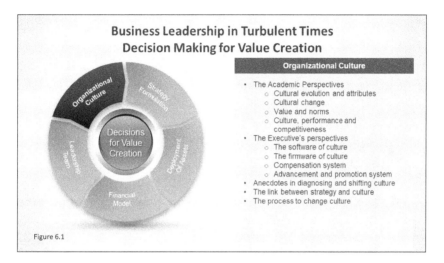

Figure 6.1

THE ACADEMIC PERSPECTIVE

Academic scholars treat organizational culture as a nexus of unique characteristics that involve the firm's internal climate that synthesizes the DNA of the organization. While distinct for each firm, culture is partially articulated or formalized via statements or messages but evolves over time. Its foundation is based on common and shared learning experiences of the people working in a firm. It influences, affects, and regulates the decision-making process. As competitive market forces change, culture may be an asset or an impediment for the firm in its efforts to adjust to new market conditions. Academic work has advanced via theories and empirical studies, including two separate but complementary definitions of culture. One considers culture as "a pattern of assumptions that a given group has invented, discovered, or developed in learning to cope with its problems of external adaptation and internal integration. These assumptions have worked well enough to be considered valid, and therefore, to be taught to new members as the correct way to perceive, think and fell in relation to these problems."[47] The other defini-

---

[47] Edgar Schein. *Organizational Culture and Leadership* (Jossey-Bass, 1988).

tion maintains that culture is a "system of shared values and norms." Values define what is important to the organization, and norms define appropriate attitudes and behaviors for the members of the firm. Both definitions are complementary in that assumptions about values and norms determine the workings of the organization. These assumptions were originally developed by the founder of the firm and taught to new employees. Employees lacking these values and norms, or are unwilling to accept these shared values and norms, will not be members of the culture. The spreading of culture to employees resembles the biological phenomenon of spreading an epidemic through the population. Culture propagates through a transmission mechanism that involves three elements:

1. *Leadership and the leader.* For culture to expand, it requires a leader, analogous to the primary source of an infection. A leader believes in the assumptions of shared values and norms and can influence other followers.

2. *Teams.* It requires a group of people working together with the makeup of the group analogous to the population at risk. The group of people eventually is instilled by the leader with the shared assumptions of values and norms that reflect the culture of the organization.

3. *The environment of the group.* An encouraging environment creates a positive response for the spreading of the culture, while an unfriendly environment with barriers of communication and constraints in the behavior of people, leads to suppression of culture.

The spread of culture to the firm's employees is not based on the traditional economic model, which advocates the idea that people respond to incentives of monetary rewards and penalties to maximize their self-interest behaviors. Instead, the spread of culture resembles a biological phenomenon, and the emergence and dissemination of culture are influenced by the founder's value or leadership qualities in general, the composition of the team within the firm, and the environment. Authority via leadership directs the firm's employees to accept voluntarily a culture that is based on shared values and norms. The question of practical importance is once rooted in culture, how do these shared values change? Cultural change is what executives are always after.

Shared values and norms may be spread via two avenues. First, the transmission may take place from the top down with authority and leadership. Charismatic leaders, usually founders of successful organizations through the force of personality, create shared values to be adopted by the members of the organization. Leaders harness the behavior of the firm's employees to promote financial goals such as profits and investment return, but also goals on decisions that involve ethical standards, morals, and integrity. In corporate culture, the leader is perceived as the orchestrator of the company's activities who defines the moral and ethical boundaries of the organization and the processes via which the work is done. An organization often has no capacity or ability to assimilate an outside opinion, and naturally, the leader's moral compass by default is the primary source of values and norms. For leaders with an excellent track record, the culture remains strong, even if the environment changes and leads to deteriorating performance for the firm. With a strong culture, the transition to a new leader does not guarantee a change in culture.

The second avenue for spreading shared values and norms in the firm is through a bottom-up process. A culture may be developed from the behavior of people within it, not necessarily from the top. This occurs over time, when the organization hires new talent based on criteria that are different compared with those at its founding. During the hiring selection process, the firm naturally prefers employees with traits that fit the culture, expecting that they will adapt to the environment faster. This "fit-the-culture" mentality helps in improving performance and profits under normal economic conditions. However, in many instances, the firm wants to hire employees to benefit a diversity of views, innovative thinking, and other considerations that will help the performance of the organization while shifting the economic environment. This requires hiring talent that may not fit the culture but is needed to reduce risks of performance under changing economic conditions. Essentially, the hiring selection resembles the challenge of diversification for a portfolio manager who should identify winners, select sectors to deploy funds, and manage risk to increase the value of the overall portfolio. Those hired who do not fit the culture initially but contribute to the firm's success will become agents for transmitting changing values and norms within the firm.

It is well known that providing solutions to challenging problems requires common ground and assumptions on behalf of all participants in the decision-making process. These assumptions shared by participants deal with values and norms acceptable to all members of the organization where these values have validity as they have been repeatedly tested and passed the test of validity based on solutions to past challenges. Shared values reflect what is considered crucial to group members with respect to several distinct dimensions, including morality, ethics, integrity, importance, and significance.

Norms are appropriate attitudes and behaviors in day-to-day work and interactions. Norms may include reporting unethical behavior, developing new ideas, and working in teams under tight deadlines. There is a difference between shared values and norms, but both are connected. While shared values reflect the ideals that the employees strive to fulfill, norms indicate the extent to which employees walk the talk or follow day-to-day practices that attempt to live out these values, thus contributing to the organization's success.

Values and norms are represented with formal policies or informal practices in the organization and can be observed by all employees. For example, the HR policies for hiring, promoting, and terminating employees and the governance of the firm are considered parts of the formal policies and informal practices often referred to as formal institutions. When there is alignment between culture, consisting of shared values and norms and formal institutions, a company has an effective culture that yields positive outcomes. Outcomes, formal institutions, and norms are all observable. What is not observable, however, is the shared values that are well-rooted assumptions and beliefs that allow the firm to operationalize its decisions. These assumptions are deep into the beliefs of employees as being valid based on past experiences, word of mouth, and repeated practices that produced positive performance or outcomes.

The culture of an organization is expressed through a series of artifacts, which include elements describing key symbols of the culture. Artifacts are surface-level representations of culture. While they are easily observed, artifacts are difficult to interpret by new members of the organization. Artifacts often include:

- Ceremonies, tributes, and rituals practiced by employees that may involve retirement dinners, new product introduction ceremonies, meetings announcing new priorities, and events celebrating company milestones and anniversaries.

+ Physical space, architectural, and work arrangements such as layout, furniture, lighting, and working from home.
+ Stories about the way decisions are made or how people interact that are told about the firm by its employees.
+ Symbols such as a dress code at work and formalities in interactions with employees, clients, or the public.

Formal policies represent practices for an organization and may include:

+ Policies and procedures
+ Hiring guidelines
+ Organizational charts
+ Promotion, appraisal, and reward systems
+ Termination procedures or no-layoff commitments
+ Perks for employees, including company cars, parking spaces, and access to a cafeteria.

All these artifacts synthesize the climate at the firm and represent part of the culture.

The relationships between value, norms, and artifacts appear in figure 6.2.

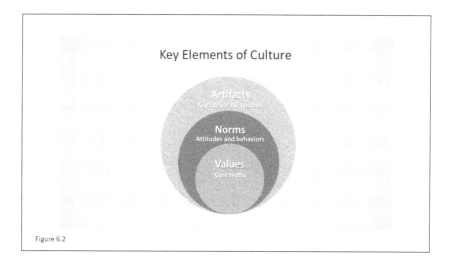

Key Elements of Culture

Artifacts
Key corporate symbols

Norms
Attitudes and behaviors

Values
Core truths

Figure 6.2

A metaphor of a tree is a useful representation of the essence of a deep-rooted organizational culture. Above the ground, the branches and leaves are all observable elements of the firm's culture. These are artifacts and provide a visible description of the culture of the organization. The ground surface supports the trunk of the tree (culture) with the right mix of fertilizer and soil. The mix consists of formal policies for various business operations and processes, informal norms, and explicit statements of values for the organization. However, the essence of culture is in the roots of the tree, which is below the surface, where values are used in practice to make decisions, and several assumptions about the way processes work are taken-for-granted. A well-rooted tree is not susceptible to powerful winds as it remains strong under adverse weather conditions. Similarly, an organization performs well and has longevity despite changes in the business and economic climate only when its core elements of culture are well rooted, the ground surface is well kept with formal policies and explicit statement of values, and several artifacts are observed and maintained. The culture makes the organization strong enough to sustain changes in the competitive environment.

CULTURAL EVOLUTION AND ATTRIBUTES

Organizational culture primarily evolves over time. It starts with the founder's lasting impact—the attitude, the aspirations, and the long-term intentions of the founder. The founder becomes the initiator of the foundation for the culture, and for a long-serving successful founder, the values and artifacts are reflected in the firm's values and aspirations. As the firm continues its evolution, succeeding leaders establish norms consistent with the values originally developed by the founder. Values and norms adjust slowly over time based on and reinforced and augmented with a reward system.

A well-articulated culture eventually is developed when a firm follows with continuity and consistency a reward system based on a set of values and norms. However, group thinking and absence of challenge for the leader(s) may create a culture full of contradictions, questionable behaviors, and ambiguity. All these characteristics reflect emerging organizational rigidities that, if not corrected, continue in perpetuity. For example, founders who had impacts on culture include Steve Jobs (Apple), Walt Disney (Disney),

Michael Dell (Dell), Sergey Brin and Larry Page (Google), Oprah Winfrey (Harpo Productions and *OWN*, the Oprah Winfrey Network), Bill Gates (Microsoft), Larry Ellison (Oracle), Ralph Lauren (Polo Ralph Lauren), and Herb Kelleher (Southwest Airlines). Jack Bogle, founder of Vanguard, personified the investment manager's cost-leadership strategy. Sam Walton's lifestyle matched its low-cost strategy at Walmart.[48]

Early academic research viewed corporate culture as a by-product of values held by the society at large. That is, it was perceived that corporate culture is a set of values, beliefs, and behaviors usually consistent with those held by a society. Organizations are part of a culture comprised of inherited artifacts, processes, habits, and values. Many viewed the informal, nonmaterial, interpersonal, and moral bases of cooperation and commitment as more important than the structured controls stressed by the rational system. Later research, however, shifted to focus on measuring aspects of culture, especially employees' attitudes and perceptions in the context of delegation and coordination in decision-making within the firm.[49] This emphasis brought into attention the examination of culture relative to the firm's financial performance. Peters and Waterman, in their work *In Search of Excellence*, provide key observations about how culture may contribute to success in an organization. They identified eight attributes that make an organization successful and innovative.[50]

1. Employees experience a bias for action in which they are encouraged to act and undertake initiatives while the culture recognizes which failures are acceptable and which are not acceptable as they lead to disasters.
2. A culture that evolves around the needs of the customer will lead to successes, especially when consumer needs change over time.
3. A culture that provides employees with autonomy and incentives for entrepreneurship will be successful.
4. Productivity can be achieved when employees are treated with appreciation and incentives.

---

[48] At one time, he drove a beat-up Ford pickup, got $5 haircuts, went camping for vacations, and lived in a modest ranch home in Bentonville, Arkansas.

[49] Daniel Denison. *Corporate Culture and Organizational Effectiveness* (New York: John Wiley & Sons, 1990).

[50] Tom Peters and Robert Waterman. *In Search of Excellence* (Grand Central, NY 1988).

5. Developing a culture with meaningful values that make people proud will yield positive outcomes for the organization.

6. Expanding business through mergers is only desirable if the culture of both firms is aligned.

7. An organizational structure that is characterized by simplicity and lean staff, where the focus of culture is on results and operations, is much more preferred compared to a complex arrangement that involves career staff employees.

8. Regardless of a centralized or decentralized operational structure, a successful company carefully manages the core value of its culture along with a few top strategic priorities.

Collectively, all these attributes from *In Search of Excellence* highlight the importance of cultural attributes that lead organizations to success but cannot be misconstrued as principles. What is clear, however, is that these eight well-articulated attributes provide the following key recommendations to executives.

+ First, a culture that is based on measuring success in numbers only will lead to failure of any organization since people and firms are not rational in the ways finance, accounting, and other disciplines are typically taught.

+ Second, the human capital of any firm is considered an asset, but the complexity of human beings should prevent managers from treating them as factors of production. Rather, managers should treat them as sources of intellectual capital capable and motivated for innovating.

+ Third, a firm's culture should tolerate ambiguity to allow for experimentation and innovation with a clear understanding of the boundaries for failure and disappointment.

In Search of Excellence lacks scientific rigor as it is based on anecdotal evidence of few large corporations, and many academics have criticized the methodology and results obtained.

CULTURAL CHANGE

A corporation resembles micro-societies and experiences a constant challenge to foster cooperation among employees with the objective of advancing the firm's goals and performance. Culture change in a corporation is considered a manageable process. Through hiring and terminations, corporations can adhere to or change certain values by selecting employees who are aligned with values and norms. By avoiding the more difficult approach of changing employees' minds, firms can also create incentives through an employee compensation system to provide appropriate motivation for adapting to culture change.[51] Yet it is important to identify the causes of culture change and the mechanisms that allow new values and norms to replace older ones. Studies have shown what triggers culture change in an organization include the following:

- *Dramatic changes in the firm's external environment.* Emerging rigidities due to change are eliminated when the firm's competitive strength is challenged, and adaptability and survival override any resistance to change. As a result, the firm readjusts its values and norms.
- *New strategy and structure.* Change in leadership accelerates the implementation of a strategy and structure with consequences on the change in culture.
- *Reversal of fortunes.* When original competences turn into liabilities and require changes in values and changes in linking values to incentives and compensation, priorities can change. For example, GM's bureaucratic culture, combined with its innovative M-form structure, was once considered the key contributor to superior performance. However, that culture became a liability when the external environment changed following the oil-price shocks in the 1970s and the entry of Japanese carmakers into the United States. Therefore, GM's strong culture led to organizational inertia. This resulted in a failure to adapt to changing customer preferences for more fuel-efficient cars, and it prevented higher quality and more

[51] L. Guiso, P. Sapienza, and L. Zingales. "Corporate Culture, Societal Culture, and Institutions," *American Economic Review,* 105, 2015, pp. 336–339.

innovative designs. GM lost customers to foreign competitors that offered these features.

Executives have recognized that culture is one of the top value drivers for a firm. In survey research, 84 percent of executives indicated that they are not satisfied with the cultures of their own firms and believe it requires change.[52] Therefore, it is not surprising that culture change preoccupies the attention of top executives, especially of newly appointed CEOs who want to develop and implement a new strategy and changes in their firms' organizational structures. In this respect, the culture should be aligned with the new strategy.

COMPONENTS OF CULTURE: VALUES AND NORMS

Describing the culture requires the identification of values and norms. Academics have proposed seven proxies for values that describe the firm's culture.[53] These include:

1. *Adaptability.* This refers to the ability of the firm to take initiatives, taking advantage of opportunities. The firm has a fast-track decision-making process, and it is willing without penalty to experiment.
2. *Collaboration.* This refers to interactions among employees and management and shows to the extent to which they are team-oriented, collaborative without serious conflicts, and supportive.
3. *Community.* This refers to the firm's attitude toward diversity, inclusion, the environment, and being open to the community.
4. *Customer-centered approach.* This refers to the firm's priorities to learn, listen from, and attend to the needs of customers, lead the market with products and services, and be proud of its service orientation.

---

[52] Graham et al., "Corporate Culture."
[53] J. A. Chatman, D. F. Caldwell, C. A. O'Reilly, and B. Doerr. "Parsing Organizational Culture: How the Norm for Adaptability Influences the Relationship between Culture Consensus and Financial Performance in High Technology Firms," *Journal of Organizational Behavior*, 35, 2014, pp. 785–808.

5. *Integrity.* This refers to high ethical standards, honesty, and transparency that characterize employees and management.
6. *Detail orientation.* This refers to paying attention to details, using analytical methods, and focusing on quality.
7. *Results oriented.* This refers to performance results and focuses on achievements, being competitive, and attaining milestones.

A complete characterization of culture also requires proxies for norms. While norms may encompass many items, the most widely accepted include the following:[54]

- Agreement between goals and values
- Consistency and predictability of actions
- Coordination among employees
- Trust among employees
- New ideas developed within the firm
- Urgency with which employees work
- Employees comfort in suggesting critiques
- Long-term orientation in decision-making

The above proxies of values and norms offer a good picture of a corporate culture based on which surveys and additional research has been performed to focus on aspects of culture and outcomes.

THE LINKS BETWEEN CULTURE, PERFORMANCE, AND COMPETITIVENESS

The firm's performance measured by operating profits and other financial variables is typically explained by a host of factors, including asset structure, leverage, type of strategy followed, and costs. If values and norms that contribute to culture are important, as executives contend, they should be linked to performance.

---

[54] The categorization of values and norms is based on the study by Graham et al., "Corporate Culture."

Despite several methodological issues, researchers document the relationship between culture and performance in several studies. Performance is measured by the return on investment (ROI) and operating cash flows, but it is adjusted to account for firms with different levels of operating, financial leverage, and market capitalization. The link between culture and performance is through the extent to which there are strong values and norms. Firms with strong culture benefit from having: (a) employees dedicated to achieving organizational goals, (b) enhanced coordination and control within the firm, and (c) improved goal alignment between the firms and its employees. Naturally, firms with strong cultures outperform firms with weak cultures. In addition, for incremental changes in the competitive environment, firms with strong cultures can easily adjust internal processes as confronting change is incremental. However, when changes in the competitive environment become dramatic, an organization with a strong culture will encounter difficulties in adjusting, and therefore, performance will be reduced. Consequently, when the business environment changes often, and competitive forces shift erratically, the firm's strong culture becomes a liability in adopting changes.[55] Several multiple-perspective studies and studies across different countries validate this link between culture and performance. Additionally, firms with strong cultures tend to report strong short-term operating performance, and indirectly, the strength of a culture becomes a reliable predictor of short-term firm's performance.[56] Finally, many firms in their annual reports and various communications tout their corporate values. These so-called transparent, or advertised, cultural values include statements about ethics, integrity, transparency, innovation, and teamwork. While these advertised cultural values appear to be important, they do not seem to be correlated with measures of short-term and long-term performance of the firm. Instead, when the values are based on employee perceptions, research shows that performance and culture are correlated. This leads to the conclusion that it is not what is advertised but what employees perceive to be the norms and values of the organization that are linked to performance.

---

[55] J. B. Sorensen. "The Strength of Corporate Culture and the Reliability of Firm Performance," *Administrative Science Quarterly*, 47, 2002, 70–91.

[56] G. Gordon and N. DiTomaso. "Predicting Corporate Performance from Organizational Culture," *Journal of Management Studies*, 29, 1992, 783–798.

Additional research from survey work offers evidence of a relationship between corporate culture and measures of financial performance and competitiveness. Survey responses from executives about culture are linked to financial data publicly available to determine whether the subjective views of executives about the importance of values and norms are correlated with observed measures of a firm's performance and competitiveness.[57] The proxy for culture is based on crowd-sourced employee reviews that often rate a firm as, "One of the best places to work," or information that appeared in *Glassdoor* ratings. Employees satisfied with their work environments, where norms and values motivate them to perform their tasks, will rate their environments favorably. The proxy for competitiveness is Tobin's Q, a measure of market value of the firm relative to its book value. A higher Tobin's Q ratio indicates a more competitive firm as reflected in its market value.

The link between culture and competitive advantage is direct. There are at least three mechanisms that make culture improve a firm's competitiveness. First, if the culture yields consistent profits and improvements in market value, the firm's competitiveness is improved. Second, the firm achieves competitive advantage if the culture, with its values and reward systems, is organized in a way to capture value by producing services or products that are rare, difficult to imitate, and valuable to the consumers. And third, if culture adapts, the values and reward system changes as the business evolves. For example, it is best to develop a strong and strategically relevant culture in the first few years of a firm's existence. Strategy scholars have documented that the initial structure, culture, and control mechanisms established in a new firm can be a significant predictor of later success.

In summary results of academic studies offer the following insights:

1. Executives believe that corporate culture is characterized by the values of adaptability, community, results orientation, and collaboration, and it encompasses norms that include trust, long-term decision-making orientation, agreement about goals and values, and coordination among employees.

---

[57] Graham et al., "Corporate Culture."

2. Leadership plays a prominent role in determining the effectiveness of culture. Nearly 67 percent of executives indicated that leadership reinforces an effective culture.

3. The culture of the organization matters so much that 54 percent of the executives would not consider a merger with another firm if cultures are incompatible.

4. Almost 70 percent of executives indicate that culture plays a significant role in reporting quality financial statements. A strong culture leads to effective compliance and accurate reporting, thus the high quality of publicly available financial information.

5. Almost 85 percent of the S&P 500 companies surveyed described a section on their reports or on Web communications about their firms' cultural values. Most frequently cited values are integrity and respect (70 percent) and innovation (80 percent).[58] However, these advertised values are not correlated with the publicly traded firm's performance and/or measures of profitability.

6. When culture is measured based on how values are perceived directly by employees, rather than what the firm advertises, a culture of integrity is positively associated with a firm's performance and profitability. The evidence suggests that it is not what the firm *calls* its culture that matters the most, but it is what the employees *perceive* to be the culture that creates a better-performing organization.

7. A firm's competitiveness is explained by cultural values and cultural norms. Values and norms are defined in the previous section. Higher cultural values and norms are associated with improved competitiveness; this result holds regardless of the firm's size, industry, capital intensity (investment-to-capital ratio), number of employees, and other firm parameters.

Overall, academic studies have presented evidence that culture matters, and despite methodological issues, cultural values are correlated with performance and competitiveness.

---

[58] L. Guiso, P. Sapienza, and L. Zingales. "The Value of Corporate Culture," *Journal of Financial Economics*, 117, 2015, pp. 60–76.

THE EXECUTIVE'S PERSPECTIVE

Many executives believe that culture is the foundation of all firms and can make or break the success of any company. It is so important that many executives feel culture can influence the firm's ability to find solutions to unknown problems.

It is not by coincidence that many executives believe culture is something that you respect but change. However, changing the culture is playing with fire, as the old saying, "Culture eats strategy for lunch," highlights the significance of culture to the continuity of an organization. And if you do not develop the right culture over time, the chances of being able to get anything other than sort of mediocre results over the long term are greatly impaired. Culture really matters. For executives, culture is a lot of things and includes organizational structures, decision-making, delegation, management systems, and reporting.

Executives believe that there are two sides to the culture in an organization. The *software side* of the culture deals with behavior, organizational values, and executive leadership. The *firmware side* of the culture involves hard-coded elements that deal with the architecture of the management system that consists of tools and a framework of decision-making. Tools involve measurement systems, compensation systems, and promotion systems. The framework for decision-making reflects a traffic light network that handles the decision-making process within the firm in a centralized or decentralized fashion. Both sides are important and collectively influence the success of the strategy, the quality of an asset deployment plan, and team leadership.

THE SOFTWARE OF CULTURE

The software side of the culture is about values and how the people think about what the organization is. What they think the organization is then directs their behaviors. In many ways, culture is what people do when no one is watching. A firm may build management systems to watch, monitor activities, and develop reports, but the software of culture is really what people feel, what they think, and how they act when they are outside that formal sort of management and reporting system. As an example, do people think the company is customer-oriented? If they think that the firm is customer oriented, their behaviors will be modified to reflect that orientation on the customer. If they think that the culture is all about achieving quantitative measures of performance and all about results, their behaviors will begin to mirror that. If they feel that the culture is an "old boys' network"—in other words, the only way to advance professionally is by, "Who you know, not what you know"—their behaviors will reflect that. Soon you can observe behavioral patterns and informal structures developed in the company that are outside the formal structures. Values are cherished, things like customer orientation, commitment to excellence, or commitment to aspiring to more than what you can be, the values around results, and the values around integrity. If those behaviors and values are not constantly reinforced, there the culture around those values will fade away and eventually will disappear.

The leadership of the firm reinforces the culture and acts in a manner consistent with the values and norms of the organization. For example, a leader cannot talk about integrity and then take the team out to dinner and cheat on the expenses. Similarly, a CEO cannot have a policy around not staying at high-end hotels, and then, when the senior executive team show up locally, they stay at the best hotels. You cannot talk about people all being in this together, and when you show up at the headquarters, there are parking spaces reserved for the senior management team. You cannot announce cost-cutting measures and then have the CEO show up in a private jet or being picked up by a limousine. Those are all examples of behaviors that are modeled by the senior leadership and certainly the CEO. The behavior of the senior team must be in alignment with what they purport they want the organization to be from a cultural standpoint. For a specific culture, a misalignment of behaviors between employees and leaders creates chaos and most certainly influences outcomes and performance.

Transparency and integrity are two important values that leaders often advocate. Executives set an ethics hotline in place and other measures to implement a culture of transparency. If the ethics hotline never responds to employee concerns, or worse, if there is some retaliation involved, the culture is destroyed. There is no way you can then ever create a culture of high integrity and transparency if leadership fails to be modeling and living that behavior day in and day out. Values become a critical component of the soft side of culture in an organization. We call that the North Star rules for getting along with people. Most companies try to have a culture of collaboration, but if the senior team, for example, is constantly fighting and bickering, there is no way you can build a team or a collaborative culture deeper in the organization. Culture and leadership become especially critical for the success of a merger between companies. Executives should understand what the original DNA of the company was and how well that will fit with the new culture. A very strong centralized command and control system may be in place, and a leader is considering acquiring a company that has a very decentralized, very laissez-faire type of culture. The chances of those two cultures meshing well are very low, and it can undermine the value that is attempted to be created through mergers or acquisitions. Some of these cultures go way, way back.

To demonstrate how two cultures may improve or collapse a company we offer two examples. One was at EDS, which had a very strong authoritative culture. It was built on a military-style DNA, and it was all about the top people, who all did very well. Everyone else had to work very hard to try to get to the top of the organization. That environment created a very much of a doggy-dog kind of culture, and that is hard to scale and develop a company with multiple divisions and a similar culture.

The second example is Computer Science Corporation (CSC). CSC had a culture of loyalty. If you were loyal to the company and you stayed around, you sort of ascended through the hierarchy. However, ascending through the hierarchy was not aligned with the idea of people assuming more responsibilities. As leadership is a privilege, not a right, CEOs and executive leaders assume more responsibilities. So that created behaviors throughout the organization in which the top team was not being engaged in modeling the types of behaviors and values that are necessary to create a high-performing culture. These are the soft attributes of culture that are critical to understanding and especially important during M&A transactions. When HP was bought by CSC, the good news was that both cultures of the company were very much customer-oriented, they were very services-oriented with focus on providing value to clients. However, one culture had a very rigorous management system and the other a relaxed management system. The company that did not have the rigorous management system was an old boys' network, and women did not feel that they could progress and included in the culture. Whereas the other culture was based more on, "You will be promoted, and you will be compensated based on your performance." In 2008 EDS Hewlett Packard acquired EDS to create HP Enterprise Services with focus on transforming enterprises and achieving measurable business outcomes. In April 2017 CSC and the Enterprise Services Division of Hewlett Packard merged to form a new entity a fortune 500 firm, DXC. Not surprisingly, when those two management teams came together, they did not mesh very well, and culture change was required.

THE FIRMWARE OF THE CULTURE

In addition to the software part of the culture, the firmware of the culture includes harder, more rigid components of culture. These involve the architecture of the firm's management system and the tools required for decision-making. The architecture includes formal management systems in terms of decisions, measurement systems, compensation systems, and promotion systems.

Management systems facilitate decision-making in a diverse organization. In terms of decision-making, there are two choices: Decisions can be either centralized or decentralized. The selection is partially based on the maturity of the company. In other words, with the right leadership capability at the lower levels of the company, it is effective to delegate authority and decisions at the lower levels of the company. It is well known that a decentralized organization is typically better because it can move faster, is more creative, is more innovative, and responds better to local business conditions and local customer or client requirements. It is also easily scalable. However, in a turnaround situation or in instances where cost reductions are expected, all levels of the organization should be marching in the same direction. If you do not have information systems that allow you to monitor very closely what is happening in a decentralized world, then a centralized model is usually more appropriate. Therefore, if you have good, robust processes that are aligned to the strategy that you have in place, then a decentralized model can work. If you have processes that must be completely reengineered to run the business consistent with the strategy that you put in place, centralizing those processes will provide better outcomes. Those processes must be reengineered, and they have to operate and be architected. Only after you are comfortable that those processes or producing the results that you are looking for, can you begin to delegate the operation of those processes out closer in a more decentralized model.

In designing a management system in a centralized versus a decentralized organization, it is critical to determine early on what kind of decisions need to be made and where in the company these decisions need to be made. For example, where do you want merger and acquisition decisions made? At the level of the CEO, or at the level of the division of the firm? Where do you want pricing decisions made? Where do you want HR decisions made? Promotions, demotions, how do you want performance management to be done, and what criteria should be used? Do you want that to be done consistently through the company, or do you want it done differently in a decentralized model? Answers to these questions become critical components of the architecture of the management system.

METRICS

Measurement systems involve metrics that allow for measurement of performance and outcomes. First, a hard part of assessing culture is deciding what to measure. There may be many items to be measured. Firms focus more attention on a handful of well-articulated metrics of performance. Typically, organizations get what they measure. The CEO can talk about customer satisfaction in great detail, but it is not helpful if it is not measured. A leader can talk about profits, but if profits cannot be measured in the organization, people's behaviors and cultures will never appreciate the significance of profits. Likewise, the CEO can talk about growth but if investments are not made either in developing skills for employees or making tangible purchases in assets, most likely the organization will not experience growth. The measurement system then becomes a reflection of the culture and strategy that you are trying to put in place.

Jim Collins[59] often talks about the flywheel for firms that make a difference and become influential. Understanding the components that drive the flywheel and then measuring and reporting on key elements that make a difference are essential to the success of great companies. Many management teams make the mistake of trying to measure dozens of things, sometimes

---

[59] Jim Collins. *Good to Great: Why Some Companies Make the Leap and Others Don't* (Harper Collins, 2001).

with overlapping concepts. That really does not work because people cannot focus on many things. That puts the onus on the leadership team to be very clear as to what you are going to measure. Then that creates another major component of the sort of the firmware of culture.

Another component of the firmware of the culture is compensation. Does the CEO get paid the same way as the senior leadership team? If the focus is on revenue growth or profits, is the CEO's compensation aligned with for the company's revenue growth or profits? The reward system, particularly the compensation system, must be aligned with what is measured, and what is measured must be aligned with the strategy that has been in place along with the objectives required to achieve the strategy. Therefore, compensation is an important part of the hard side of the culture.

An additional component of the firmware of a culture is the advancement of employees. In many organizations, the ability to get promoted and advance is as powerful as the compensation system. Therefore, for a given culture the question is what type of people the CEO would like to promote? Will the CEO promote people who are not only good performers but also exhibit behaviors consistent with the values and the culture that he or she is trying to create? Or people are promoted only on performance outcomes? How does senior management handle this bifurcation?

Executives are often evaluated based on (a) the results and outcomes that they achieve, and (b) how they achieve these results based on the current culture in place. In other words, executives in culture-driven organizations are not only accountable for outcomes but also are expected to achieve results in a way consistent with the culture of the organization and answer the question, Do you exhibit the culture and behavior that the firm is looking for? A simple assessment tool based on a quadrant analysis is helpful. We can envision the horizontal axis of the quadrant to show gradations for results (outstanding/average/below average), and the vertical axis shows gradations of culture support (outstanding/average/below average).

According to this stratification, there are several people within the organization that may fit in different quadrants. For example, a senior manager could obtain very good results, but the people reporting to him could not stand the manager because he or she was not a team player and had alienated wide swaths in the organization. That person was probably the most difficult person to manage in a company and continues to reinforce the behavioral and cultural action aspects that you are looking for. On the other hand, the person who gets great results and exhibits the values, the sky is the limit. The person who exhibits great behavior but does not get the results, is usually given a second, third, or sometimes a fourth chance, or is assigned to another area in the organization to be more successful. Then there are employees who do not get results and do not share the cultural values and behaviors. The typical outcome is that eventually exit the business. However, the hardest person to assess and evaluate is the employee who gets results but does not share the company's values. Many people call that passive aggressive. While there are all kinds of terms for it, fundamentally, these are employees who get results and are unable to exhibit and model the behaviors which are consistent with the culture that the CEO is trying to create. The stratification presented in this quadrant analysis provides invaluable input and informs decisions about promotions, advancement, and compensation.

Therefore, in summary, firmware consists of tools that include measurement systems, management systems, compensation systems, and promotion systems. All these tools are part of the firm's culture and provide formal mechanisms to accentuate and drive culture. On the software side, values, behaviors, and leadership all contribute to the organizational culture.

ANECDOTES IN DIAGNOSING AND SHIFTING CULTURE

To demonstrate how culture is related to leadership and strategy, we present various anecdotes. Most of them are based on real work and actual circumstances. They provide signals that show shifts in intended employee behaviors and, consequently, to the culture of the organization.

The Parking "Signal"

The new CEO of a multinational NYSE-listed firm decided to demonstrate that his leadership team is not different from the firm's other teams. On his first week on the job, he eliminated the reserved parking spaces for senior executives and replaced them with spaces for individuals with handicaps and pregnant women. When senior executives arrived, they realized they had to park on the higher floors and walk down the stairs to come to the office. Some of them changed the time they arrived at the office and arrived earlier to secure a parking space closer to the office building. Anecdotes like this show the symbolism and the intent of the CEO to value all employee equally in an organization and provide strong signals for expected behaviors. Those little things send strong signals, especially when this change comes from the new CEO of a company.

Downsizing the Corporate Floor

Another anecdote involved the executive floor of a corporate office for a major firm. A newly appointed CEO moved the executive floor to a new floor and completely renovated fifteen offices of senior executives by downgrading the furniture. In addition, these offices were converted to an open floor plan, and sixty-two new employees arrived. The executive offices moved from the top floor to a lower level, and many offices were without windows. These actions represent expected shifts in behavior and offer strong signals of what is valued to all company employees. Several employees as a result of these action start thinking that "Gee, the values that we thought we had are no longer as important. Here are the new values."

The 90 Percent Rule

A new CEO should always look at how things really work and begin to understand what symbols or rituals may be required to change the culture. The new CEO should try to understand what can be dealt with in the short term and what can be dealt in the longer term. For example, many executives believe, "Ninety percent of what makes a difference requires no talent." The 90 percent rule involves activities and efforts that are mostly common sense, such as showing up on time and being prepared for meetings. It is surprising how often the expectation of being punctual for meetings is not followed by senior managers, thus demonstrating that they are not disciplined enough to participate in a meeting. At a minimum, the expectation is that senior executives should show up on time, be prepared, be engaged, communicate, and operate within the management system. In addition, being prepared for a meeting is an absolute requirement. It is not productive when several team members are not well prepared, and the executive spends time getting everybody in the meeting on the same page just because several members neglected to do their homework to understand the issues involved. The 90 percent rule demonstrates the belief that minimum expectations for rituals and effort are required in a culture that expects participation in decision-making.

Direct Reports and Subordinates

Another anecdote involves the interaction of senior leaders with the CEO. Several times senior managers present challenges about their business to an executive and bring with them their entire team. After they make an artificial introduction, they turn the presentation over to their subordinates. This approach suggests that the senior manager may not be knowledgeable or feel confident enough to articulate issues and challenges of his own business unit.

The PowerPoint Rule

Many senior leaders prefer PowerPoint presentations but are unable to articulate the strategy without visual aids. As senior leaders are expected to discuss strategy with a wide audience, from subordinates to clients and others, it is expected that they do so without PowerPoint presentations. Therefore, it is more essential to understand and articulate strategies and challenges without visual presentations. Many times, executives limit such presentation to four or five slides and request any reports not to exceed three pages. Those guidelines send signals to the rest of the organization about what is acceptable behavior and what is not acceptable behavior. If executives tolerate unacceptable behavior, the rest of the organization will yield mediocre results.

It Takes Time to Change Culture

Culture is not something that changes in ninety days. Based on the above anecdotes, the CEO may change guidelines, symbols or artifacts within ninety days on arriving at the firm, but the change in culture takes much longer, perhaps a year or two. Culture is measured in years, and it is the consistent modeling of behavior that is aligns the culture with the firm's strategy. CEOs are expected to develop measurement, reporting, decision-making, and compensation systems which become supportive diagnostic tools for strategy execution.

Buying into the Strategy

Many times senior managers participate in meetings and seem to agree with the CEO on strategy and key operating decisions. They often do not buy in to the strategy, and so no evidence of commitment. What is surprising is that while those cases are rare, senior managers avoid presenting views about improving strategy or moving forward the dialogue. Under these circumstances, for them to stay on the team becomes a difficult proposition.

In other instances, in discussions about strategy, senior managers openly support views presented by colleagues, but after the meeting, they present their reservations to the CEO. These cases reflect a culture of a lack of courage and confidence on ideas and suggestions that may improve the dialogue. The yes-executives are not tolerated in a culture that requires constant, transparent dialogue and discussions with the senior team.

Divisions without Shareholders

Operating executives of well-performing divisions tend to have expectations for improved compensation and increased investments. However, compensation should be a function of how the firm performed and how the division performed. A division without shareholders should expect to compensate unit executives only after the company made profits and after the shareholders have been satisfied with the price appreciation and dividends. Only when a division becomes independent typically through a spinoff transaction, the executive's expectations for improved compensation and investments can be fully met.

'Rough Justice'

The cultural differences between two organizations may be so wide that when they merge, the combined management team does not have good synergy. One example is when a new company is acquired by a bidder and the past CEO of the target firm confesses to the new CEO, that "The way we do things around here, Mike, if people really work hard but they had some bad breaks, then we give them a break. We have this concept called 'rough justice,'" to which the new CEO, Mike, replied, "Okay, but let me tell you. If you do not achieve what we need to achieve here, my idea of rough justice is that you're gone."

Apparently, the biding firm's culture is based on rewarding results, while the target firm's culture is based on rewarding efforts and hoping for results. "Rough justice," that is not something someone will ever see on a chart, not something that a management team would ever review in a document, but that was the behavior that the rank-and-file believed in when the executive team was not around, a classic example of values in a culture. Obviously, Mike had to change the values in the culture immediately to assert his expectations about what counts more. The symbols in a culture often indicate what the real DNA of the organization is.

Symbolism

There is no more powerful way to project the expectations of a culture than presenting simple acronyms that amplify the DNA of the culture. A symbolic acronym may summarize the focus and culture of the organization. Symbolisms encompass all aspects of the organization, including leadership, customer focus, aspirations shared, and execution excellence.

Change is Constant, Culture Change is Inevitable

Large and small companies are exposed to disruptive innovations as change in the business environment is relentless. Firms with the ability to change their culture fast they adopt their products and services to a changing market. This is especially true in technology firms where constant innovations create disruptions and the need for survival requires adaptability. In this environment, the ultimate competitive advantage is a fast-adopting culture to changing business conditions. Research from the consulting field shows that almost 70 percent of corporate transformations fail, and 70 percent of those failures are attributed to cultural rigidities.[60]

THE LINK BETWEEN STRATEGY AND CULTURE

It should be stressed that the firm may have completed the best strategy formulation plan supported by the best financial model with an asset deployment program that will help maximize company returns and value. But if that culture is not properly aligned with the strategy, the execution of the strategy is doubtful unless lightning strikes take place, and counting on lightning strikes is not a good strategy!

There is no clarity, however, if culture follows strategy or strategy follows culture. If you are creating a culture around adaptability, around serving customers, about being externally focused, not internally, then when you adapt and change a culture, it is expected because you are adapting to the changes in your market and within the customer set that you are serving. So change in strategy is a reinforcement that you have a dynamic, open, transparent, customer-oriented, externally facing culture.

Admittedly, culture change is one of most difficult things to accomplish, even by successful CEOs. This is especially true when a company requires a turnaround due to a failed product or service, competitive market pressures, or a wrong strategy. A new CEO may be treated by employees with a hope for success or doubts about future successes. Typically, one third of the people in an organization accept the new CEO with great enthusiasm, one third are negative and do not buy in to the new strategy or new way of doing business, and the rest are "watching," meaning that they are on the sidelines. The key to cultural change is to know who the people are in each of these categories and to make sure you are applauding and encouraging people, particularly those who are enthusiastic for change. Employees who are against changes will be difficult to turn around and most likely will transition to new roles or to opportunities outside the organization.

---

[60] Carolyn Dewar and Reed Doucette "Culture: 4 Keys to Why it Matters." McKinsey Organization Blog March 27, 2018.

Probably the single most important part that will facilitate a change in culture is the right leadership team. Without an effective and committed leadership team, culture change becomes difficult, and without culture, it is much more challenging to achieve anything other than the norm. What helps change the culture is evidence of results and good performance. In an organization where people are willing to and accepting of change, improved performance creates more followers who believe in the course of action designed by a new CEO. More and better results create momentum, and this produces more followers and more engagement and buying in. However, the precondition for this momentum is to produce results and add credibility to the strategy that is followed.

Culture is related to the other components of our decision-making framework. Indeed, culture is the most important. A good culture can usually execute a mediocre strategy well; a lousy culture can absolutely torpedo an outstanding strategy. These are what many refer to polarities or extremes.

WHAT IS THE PROCESS TO CHANGE THE CULTURE OF THE ORGANIZATION?

A new CEO, typically with the support of an external third party, a consulting firm, performs a cultural assessment. A survey is designed, and all employees are asked to fill it out. A statistical analysis of data responses provides a good picture of the current culture of the organization and includes information about perceived values and norms that have been developed. It is not unusual to observe that the culture among the workers is pretty much aligned, but there may be broad dispersion with the management team. In other words, the way employees manage themselves as a group in several instances may be different from the way senior management operates.

One approach that has been developed for assessing organizational culture is the "CLEAR paradigm," which stands for:

C: *Client-focused culture.* A deep understanding of the needs of clients and customers provides success to the firm that is committed to delivering exceptional service and value to all its customers. Customer-centricity, innovation, and relationship management are key drivers for a client-focused culture.

L: *Leadership.* Top company leaders display integrity and shared values and use factual evidence to support their decision-making and gain trust through the organization, and inspire and influence employees. An environment based on collaboration between top leaders and employees provides a positive change in performance. Drivers for leadership include integrity, influence, employee development, diversity, equity, and inclusion.

E: *Execution excellence.* When decisions are made, the implementation of those decisions requires commitment to excellence and flawless execution. Execution excellence allows organizations to be recognized as leaders in their industries. Drivers for execution excellence include best practice orientation, achieving and exceeding milestones, lead change, and persisting to achieve results.

A: *Aspiration.* The entire organization aspires collectively to be better tomorrow than what it is today. Individually and collectively, all employees are committed to continuous improvements and aspirations for a better future organization. Drivers for aspirations include focus on growth and quality, surpassing milestones, establishing best practices, and leading change.

R: *Results.* Emphasis is based on results. While efforts are recognized, employees and executives assume individual responsibility and are accountable for tangible results that improve performance and profitability. Key drivers for results include accountability, resilience, and motivation.

While different approaches may be suitable in specific organizational and industry settings, CLEAR provides a strong diagnostic tool in identifying the drives and shared values that impact culture. It also offers a framework within which senior leaders can assess the teamwork performed within the firm, the type of collaborative style, and the sense of purpose and direction of the organization as it is perceived by employees and senior management.

The results of an analysis with a diagnostic tool like CLEAR provide the foundation to the CEO for where the current culture and its key value drivers are. With appropriate personnel changes, the next step is to align a new set of values with a management system that aligns performance with culture. The alignment is not instantaneous as it takes time to implement changes and requires commitment on behalf of the CEO as it is an art and a science.

FINAL THOUGHTS

Culture matters; it is respected. But evidence shows most of CEOs, especially newly appointed ones, are not satisfied with the current culture of the organization and strive to change it. However, if there is no alignment between values and collective habits, a culture change may not yield desirable performance results. Academic work has provided insights as to what culture is, the process of developing shared values, and attributes of collective habits. It has also documented that only employee-perceived values of integrity and ethics, not advertised values from company communications, influence a firm's performance and competitiveness.

A well-developed strategy supported by an asset deployment plan and strong leadership may fail in execution if culture is not aligned with values and collective habits that make things work. Leadership is necessary to develop a culture to align the values and collective habits of employees with performances. Without strong leadership, there is not a strong culture. And without culture, the firm cannot achieve anything more than nominal performance, if at all. Finally, while necessary, it is not sufficient for the leadership team to develop a well-developed competitive strategy without alignment of cultural values of the firm and its leadership. In this respect, the saying, "Culture eats strategy for lunch," is valid.

CHAPTER SEVEN

Corporate Governance and the Role of the Boards of Directors

DECISION-MAKING AND AGENCY COSTS

Our decision-making framework assumes that executives' and shareholders' interests are aligned. A strategy developed by executives, with an appropriate asset redeployment plan which is supported by a viable financial model and consistent with the culture of the organization, will have great probability of success as measured by key performance indicators. In the context of this framework, the CEO's leadership will yield results benefiting the interests of shareholders and success. This success is thus translated to value added for shareholders. However, despite good intentions, not all executives undertake decisions that compensate shareholders for the risk of investing in the firm. Popular and business press outlets have pointed out detailed accounts of corporate fraud, accounting irregularities, and several corporate failures[61] that document the occasional behavior of CEOs to operate in their own self-interests.

---

[61] There are many examples of shocking and outrageous stories that point out the self-interest behavior of managers. Richard Scrushy, CEO of HealthSouth, was accused of overstating earnings by $1.4 billion between 1999 and 2002 to enrich himself with additional

In fact, many researchers have provided evidence of self-interest among CEOs. These occasions include examples of class action lawsuits, financial restatements, and bankruptcies. For example, between 2004 and 2018, more than two hundred class action lawsuits were filed annually. These lawsuits resulted in declines of $120 billion in company market capitalization during the same period.[62] Between 2005 and 2017, almost 12,700 financial restatements were made by CEOs of publicly traded firms.[63] Several bankruptcies were the results of fraud committed by insiders and CEOs as more than 2,200 publicly traded firms filed for Chapter 11 during 2000–2018.[64]

The source of self-interest behavior stems from the separation between ownership and management. Due to specialization and division of labor, CEOs with specialized expertise serve as agents for shareholders. But simultaneously, they control key decisions that occasionally provide executives with opportunities to take actions to enrich themselves at the expense of shareholders. This scenario is referred to as the "agency problem," and the resulting costs are described as "agency costs."[65] Agency costs include perquisites for CEOs, financing and investment decisions that do not match the shareholders' risk expectations, and differences in goals and aspirations between well-informed executives in charge of the resources of the firm and less well-informed shareholders. Researchers estimate that there is a 10 percent

---

bonuses and compensation. Dennis Kowlowski, CEO of Tyco, funded a $2.1 million birthday party for his wife using company funds. Most recently, Adam Neumann, the CEO of WeWork, was forced to depart the company in 2019 when it was revealed that a high number of senior positions were held by his family and friends, and that the company granted a $740 million personal loan to him and purchased for $6 million the trademark "We" from him. Several corporations have experienced declines in stock values as a result of CEO behaviors, including companies AIG, Countrywide Financial, Enron, Theranos, and WorldCom.

[62] Cornerstone Research, Stanford Law School, "Security Class Action Fillings: 2018 Year."

[63] Center of Audit Quality, "Financial Restatement Trends in the US 2017" (www.thecaq.org/financial-restatement-trends-united-states-2003-2012).

[64] Delloitte "Ten Things about Bankruptcy and Fraud: A Review of Bankruptcy Filings" (2008). Appeared in https://bankruptcyfraud.typepad.com/Deloitte_Report.pdf.

[65] Principal-agency problems are a central topic for research in academics, and it is traced to the original work of Berle and Means, *The Modern Corporation and Private Property* (New York: Harcourt, Brace and World, 1932). However, Jensen and Meckling had highlighted details of the problem as it applies to financing and investment decisions in their article "Theory of the Firm: Managerial Behavior, Agency Costs and Ownership Structure," *Journal of Financial Economics,* 3 (4), October 1976.

probability that an average exchange-listed firm is engaged in fraud in a given year. They also find that if the fraud is uncovered, the costs to shareholders is between 25 percent and 37 percent of the company's equity value.[66]

While the agency relationship between CEOs and executives provides alarming concerns about the self-interest behaviors of CEOs, it should be noted that despite the potential of agency costs in any organization, CEOs are not uniformly and completely self-interested. Executives demonstrate moral salience, a knowledge that certain actions are inherently wrong even if they are undetected and left unpunished. It is not accidental that academic studies find that CEOs who strongly identify with the company are less likely to accept perquisites or make decisions that are contrary to the interests of shareholders.[67]

THE BOARD OF DIRECTORS

To discourage and alleviate potential self-interested behavior on behalf of CEOs, a set of mechanisms has been developed that provide a monitoring system to align the interests of CEOs and shareholders. Known as corporate governance, the system involves constituencies, internal or external, to the company and provide direct or indirect CEO oversight with checks and balances. External monitors include the capital markets, regulatory enforcement agencies, media and analysts, and the legal environment that offers guidance on the rule of law. Internal monitors include the board of directors, the auditors of the company, and its creditors, suppliers, customers, and the union(s).

How the monitoring system is arranged depends on two considerations. The first consideration is economics. To be economically feasible, the cost of maintaining a complex mechanism of monitors should be less than the cost of implementing these mechanisms. Certain mechanisms may not be

---

[66] I. J. Alexander Dyck, Adair Morse, and Luigi Zingales. "How Pervasive Is Corporate Fraud?" Working paper, University of California, Berkeley, November 2019, pp. 1–47. (Retrieved January 2020.)

[67] Steven Boivie, Donald Lange, Michael L. McDonald, and James D. Westphal. "Me or We: The Effects of CEO Organizational Identification of Agency Costs," *Academy of Management Proceedings*, 2009, pp. 1–6.

important if their costs are enormous relative to corresponding benefits for shareholders. Second, the monitoring system depends on the orientation of the firm. If the primary obligation of the company is to maximize shareholder value, as the Anglo-American model has advocated in the last two centuries, corporate governance focuses on those mechanisms that increase the value of the company's equity. If, however, the firm has a societal obligation beyond increasing shareholder value, the corporate governance supports actions that produce stable employment, reduce risks to debt holders, and primarily improves the community and environment.

Unfortunately, there are no universally accepted corporate governance standards. Legislation has provided regulatory guidelines to address shortcomings of monitoring mechanisms. Sarbanes-Oxley of 2002 (SOX) mandated a series of requirements to improve auditing processes and transparency of reported information and made CEO's and CFO's misrepresentation of financial statements subject to criminal charges. The Dodd-Frank Reform and Consumer Protection Act in 2010 mandates shareholders' rights to have an advisory vote on executive compensation (say on pay) and the right of institutional investors to nominate board candidates directly on the company proxy (proxy access). In addition to those legislative rules, third-party organizations such as the Institutional Shareholder Services (ISS) and MSCI ESG ratings publish governance ratings on companies in an attempt to protect shareholders' interests. Finally, the increased prominence of activist investors, the advocacy for environmental, social, and governance (ESG) sustainability and the new model for governance in private equity firms all play indirect roles in improving governance practices. Most recently, The Business Roundtable has provided guiding principles for corporate governance.[68]

While new trends and improved practices in corporate governance have helped reduce possible conflicts of interest between CEOs and shareholders, one mechanism that monitors closely the self-interest behavior of CEOs is the board of directors. Mandated by regulations for exchange-traded public companies, the role and functioning of boards of directors has received considerable attention by researchers and policy makers.

A recent study by NACD in 2019 surveyed 1,400 companies listed on a stock exchange and provides interesting statistics about directors and boards.

---

[68] *Roundtable Principles of Corporate Governance*, 2016.

The median director's age is sixty-four, and the board consists of nine directors with median retirement age of seventy-three. The board meets seven times per year and the tenure on the board is 7.4 years. The total number of board seats between 2009 and 2013 were 5,254. During the period between 2014 and 2018, the total number of board seats was 4,767, which shows a trend that boards have shrunk.

WHAT DO DIRECTORS DO?

Good corporate governance helps firms prevent corporate fraud, scandals, and acts of potential criminal and civil liability of the firm. It is also good business. In this respect, boards are critical and have some important responsibilities by fulfilling a dual mandate. First and foremost, boards are the agents of the shareholders and provide an oversight function by acting diligently in the interests of shareholders. In essence, they work for the shareholders, and the shareholders transfer power to the board of directors to manage their investments. The board's fiduciary responsibility is to create returns for the investors and indirectly manage corporate risks. Hiring and firing of the CEO, measuring corporate performance, evaluating performance, and awarding compensation are parts of the board's oversight capacity. Boards must step back and understand where the company is, the "personality" of the company, and the company's stage of evolution. To fulfill their fiduciary responsibilities, which include the hiring of a CEO or attracting other board members, a board must understand what the company needs. And the company's needs are often different depending on its life cycle stage, its evolution, its current and anticipated performance, and where it is juxtaposed in conjunction with the industry and competitors.

The second part of the dual board mandate is the provision of advice and constructive input to the CEO and senior leadership of the firm. In this advisory capacity, the board provides insights to management regarding the strategic and operational direction of the company with particular attention to the company's risk exposures, investment, product market, and financing plans. The engagement of the board with daily operations is limited. Board members are selected based on their skill and expertise, including previous experience in a relevant industry or function.

A board ideally works as a team to advance the interests of shareholders while working collegially with senior management. Depending on the stage of development and track record, boards may be classified as developed, advanced, or world-class. A developed board satisfies core governance and compliance requirements and demonstrates focus with regard to future strategy and execution. In addition, the board is proactive in anticipating board-membership skill gaps while demonstrating forward-looking focus on executive talent and CEO succession. A key feature of a developed board is its forward-looking orientation. An advanced board exhibits the characteristics of a developed board and demonstrates a track record of overseeing profitable company growth and balances time spent in committees versus full board engagement in debates and reach decisions on the most critical issues. An advanced board is not only forward looking, but its overall performance contributes to the company's profitability. Finally, a world-class board exhibits the characteristics of an advanced board, but in addition, board leadership is fully engaged in company leadership, demonstrates the capacity to adapt to changing market directions with required strategic, financial, and human capital changes, and reflects and reinforces the positive culture and values of the firm. In essence, a world-class board is not only forward looking and high performing but also serves a strategic purpose for the company.

THE STRUCTURE OF THE BOARD OF DIRECTORS

The dual responsibilities of the board bring attention to the qualifications of directors elected by shareholders, the frequency of the elections, and the size of the board. All these considerations provide a glimpse of how directors perform the fiduciary role of protecting the interests of shareholders and indirectly managing the risks of the enterprise.

Directors are classified as internal if they are selected or influenced by the CEO. Outside directors tend to be independent, but their independence may be questionable. For example, lawyers or investment bankers who are directors of a firm while simultaneously they or their businesses do business with the firm. These directors are considered not completely independent and are classified as "affiliated" directors. Academic studies find that prior to 1995, a typical US publicly traded company's board was comprised of 55

percent outside directors, 30 percent inside directors, and 15 percent affiliated directors.[69] More recent studies document that company boards have
become more outside dominated, and insider director representation has
dropped in recent years to about 13 percent. In addition, the total number of
directors is eleven, a drop from fifteen in the 1960s.[70] With the most recent
regulatory developments of Sarbanes-Oxley, boards have become larger,
more independent, form more committees, meet more often, and tend to
be more accountable.[71] Given these circumstances, the demand of directors
post-SOX has increased substantially, but the willingness of directors to
serve has been moderated by the potential litigation from bad actions. As a
result, director pay has increased, and directors' liability insurance premiums
have increased as well.

Many times the firm organizes its governance using staggered or a classified board. This practice allows directors to be elected to a three-year
term rather than one-year terms, with one-third of the board standing for
election each year. Staggered boards prevent the reelection of the majority of
the board in a single year and are considered a formidable protection against
takeover bids. Over the last twenty years the popularity of staggered boards
has declined significantly,[72] and research has provided mixed results on the
impact of these forms of governance on shareholder wealth. Early findings
suggest that staggered boards prevent attractive merger offers and insulate
CEOs from bad decisions.[73] Most recent research shows that long-term operating performances of firms have improved with staggered boards.[74] The
reason is that staggered boards protect long-term business commitments

---

[69] Eliezer M. Fich and Anil Shivdasani "Are Busy Boards Effective Monitors?" *Journal of
Finance*, 61(2), 2006, pp. 689–724.

[70] Lehn, Kenneth, Sukesh Patro, and Mengxin Zhao. "Determinants of the Size and
Composition of U.S. Corporate Boards: 1935–2000." *Financial Management*, 38(4), 2009,
pp. 747–780.

[71] James S. Linck, Jeffry M. Netter, and Tina Yang. "The Determinants of Board Structure,"
Journal of Financial Economics, 87(2), 2008, pp. 308–328.

[72] Only 32 percent of firms had adopted staggered boards in 2014, down from 57 percent
in 2005, with the trend declining even further in recent years.

[73] Gregg A. Jarrell and Annette B. Poulsen. "Shark Repellents and Stock Prices: The Effects
of Antitakeover Amendments since 1980." *Journal of Financial Economics*, 19(1), 1987, pp.
127–168.

[74] William C. Johnson, Jonathan M. Karpoff, and Sangho Yi. "The Bonding Hypothesis
of Takeover Defenses: Evidence from IPO Firms," *Journal of Financial Economics*, 2015.

that would have been disrupted by a hostile takeover or commit CEOs to long-term investment horizons, thus allowing firms to be innovative and develop proprietary technologies or improved services.

There is ample evidence that boards do their jobs by dismissing poorly performing CEOs. Performance typically is measured based on risk-adjusted stock returns or the company's accounting profits. Poor company performance serves as a leading indicator of CEO turnover as the board takes action,[75] albeit often reluctantly, to terminate the CEO.[76] Also, the size of the board matters. Firms with smaller boards tend to turn over CEOs faster compared to firms with larger boards. This suggests that smaller boards tend to be more hands-on and watchful of CEO actions. Also, board size and firm competitiveness tend to be negatively correlated.[77] When boards are dominated by outside directors, CEO turnover is highly likely when the firm's competitiveness declines as it is in firms with insider-dominated boards.[78]

Board members are experienced professionals with subject matter expertise and often have multiple board appointments. One would have thought that busy directors might not devote enough time and expend sufficient effort in the affairs of the company. Analysis of many firms shows that busy outside directors serve on boards whose corporate performance is weak. In fact, when the majority of outside directors serve on three or more boards, firms exhibit lower levels of competitiveness and weak profitability. Shareholders respond positively to announcements of departure of busy directors. When directors of a company become busy, mostly from multiple board appointments, shareholders of firms where they serve often react negatively to the announcement.[79] Also, more than 20 percent of directors in the S&P 500 companies hold multiple boards seats. Nearly 85 percent of S&Ps 1500 firms share at least one director with other S&P 1500 firms.

---

[75] Jerold B. Warner, Ross L. Watts, and Karen H. Wruck. "Stock Prices and Top Management Changes," *Journal of Financial Economics*, 20(1–2), 1988, pp. 461–492.

[76] The CEO turnover is often explained as the wish of the CEO to spend time with family, a face-saving explanation, rather than on the admission of having the CEO forced out.

[77] David Yermack. "Higher Market Valuation of Companies with a Small Board of Directors," *Journal of Financial Economics*, 40(2), 1996, pp. 185–211.

[78] Michael S. Weisbach. "Outside Directors and CEO Turnover." *Journal of Financial Economics*, 20(1–2), 1998, pp. 431–460.

[79] Eliezer M. Fich and Anil Shivdasani. "Are Busy Boards Effective Monitors?" *Journal of Finance*, 61(2), 2006, pp. 689–724.

Directors who serve on multiple boards may reduce their workloads if one of the firms on which they serve is acquired by another company that eventually terminates the board. Thus directors on multiple boards are affected. Evidence suggests that following the termination, the performance of the other firms that continue to employ the affected directors are considerably improved. Reductions of board appointments are associated with higher profitability and market valuation. This suggests that when directors are terminated from board appointments of firms where directors work less elsewhere, their companies benefit.[80]

BOARD COMMITTEES

Typical operational functions of the board include (a) adding value on key business issues and aligning CEO strategies with shareholders' returns; (b) developing succession plans for the CEO and each director on the board; (c) peer benchmarking to self-assess and evaluate each board member's contribution and the board's contributions overall; (d) overseeing processes and practices to ensure effective risk management and compliance with regulatory and other requirements; and (e) adding to the debate for the direction and strategy of the company by leveraging board members skills, capabilities, and diversity. All these board functions are operationalized by committees charged with specific tasks.

There are three committees that are critical for the smooth functioning of a corporate board. The first is the nomination and governance committee. Its responsibility is to ensure the board is active and engaged in the affairs of the corporation with skills and ability to execute its responsibilities. The committee is involved in searching for new talent for directors and overseeing CEO turnover. The second is the audit committee. Its job is to ensure the integrity of the financial structures, systems, and reports of the company. It ensures that outside audit firms have no inherent conflicts with the company being audited while placing more accountability for performance and transparency on the CEO and the CFO. In addition, the audit committee is concerned with potential operating risk exposures and the management of

[80] Roie Hauser. "Busy Directors and Firm Performance: Evidence from Mergers," *Journal of Financial Economics*, 128(1), April 2018, pp. 16–37.

the financial risks of the firm. That is a huge responsibility just as important as ever to ensure the integrity of the financial systems and results of the company. Audit committees also focus on whistleblowers to make sure that there is an open line of communication into the audit committee for people who see any wrongdoing.

In most cases, ethics groups report directly to the board's audit committee. This committee is responsible for maintaining a very open, transparent, and nonretaliatory approach to employee concerns in day-to-day operations. This indicates that the audit committee has a major role in enterprise risk management in addition to the responsibility of the integrity of the financials and ensuring that employees have a pathway to report any wrongdoing that they see. However, there should be a balance. Audit committees ought not to be creating issues where issues do not exist. They need to make sure that their systems, programs, and policies encourage the culture in line with the strategic goals and directions of the companies, but they need to be very careful not to overstep their bounds.

A third important committee is the compensation committee. Its role is to ensure that the management team and the CEO are held accountable for the firm's performance while being compensated appropriately. The link of CEO and performance should be direct. By tying compensation to performance, the board effectively aligns the interest of shareholders with executive management and provides incentives to management to act as owners of the firm.

Sometimes during the course of business, the board may determine the need for forming special committees. For example, the firm may need a special committee to look at a transaction that involves a merger or an acquisition, or there is some other pressing issue, such as a crisis that requires special attention. Typically, those special committees come together around a particular issue and then they disband when that issue has been resolved. Sometimes boards will put technology committees together because of the importance of technology, cybersecurity, and the need to manage potential risk exposures. Other times, boards will form a finance committee to ensure that the right capital structure is in place, or the right controls are put in place in an effort to preempt possible unfavorable financial outcomes.

In practice, many CEOs are not strong believers in having many committees as they think this practice creates a bureaucratic atmosphere with possible overlapping roles and mandates. Many CEOs favor small boards of ten, maybe as many as thirteen members so that they can appropriately staff the committee that will be more actively engaged and ensure that the work can get done. The larger the board, the more difficult it is to keep it together as a collaborative, focused, united team.

Over time, academics have provided insightful observations about the functioning of boards and how committees may influence the selection of board members as well as how CEOs interact with committee board members. Using large data of publicly traded companies, it is now understood that when the CEO serves on the nominating committee, fewer independent directors are appointed. Additionally, announcements of independent director appointments are treated with lack of enthusiasm by shareholders.[81] When inside directors, not independent directors, dominate the finance and investment committee of the board, research has found that the firm's performance improves. [82] As a company expands and grows, the work of the board and its committees tends to augment the professionalization of the firm. The committees of large firms tend to have more tasks assigned to the committees, while smaller firms with higher CEO ownership have fewer tasks. As the firm becomes more mature and the ownership more diverse, the board and its committees tend to play larger roles in corporate governance. Boards of diversified firms devote more time to monitor the activities of the CEO. In contrast, boards of growing firms devote more time to discuss and approve strategic competitive moves.[83] Finally, the quality of accounting reports and the firm's quality of earnings are improved when the makeup of the audit committee membership consists of independent directors. This suggests that board structure tends to be more independent of the CEO and more effective in monitoring the corporate financial accounting processes.[84]

---

[81] Anil Shivdasani and David Yermack. "CEO Involvement in the Selection of New Board Members: An Empirical Analysis," *Journal of Finance*, 54(5), 1999, pp. 1829–1853.

[82] April Klein. "Firm Performance and Board Committee Structure," *Journal of Law and Economics*, 41(1), 1998, pp. 275–303.

[83] Rachel M. Hayes, Hamid Mehran, and Scott Schaefer. "Board Committee Structures, Ownership, and Firm Performance," 2004, unpublished working paper

[84] April Klein. "Audit Committee, Board of Director Characteristics, and Earnings Management," *Journal of Accounting and Economics*, 33(3), 2002, pp. 375–400.

Board self-evaluation and assessment

The board also must frequently evaluate itself. There are plenty of mechanisms to carry out evaluation, but often they are more of an exercise than a vehicle to drive change. For example, based on the industry does the board has the expertise to understand the industry? It is surprising how many boards do not have a good working knowledge of the industry that the company is in.

A recent survey conducted by PwC in 2019 provides insightful details about the views of over seven hundred directors of public companies. The survey reports the results of directors' assessments and trends in corporate governance of major public companies. In particular, results show that 61 percent of directors report that their boards conduct assessments, while 72 percent say that their boards have made changes in response to their assessment processes, up from 49 percent in 2016. As a result of the director assessments, according to the survey, 42 percent of boards are adding expertise, 27 percent of boards diversify the board, 26 percent of boards changed the composition of committees, and 15 percent of boards indicated that they ousted a director.[85] One startling finding in the survey was that 61 percent of directors on boards with CEO chairs say that at least one fellow director should be replaced. In contrast, on boards with an independent chair or a lead independent director, only 47 percent of directors felt that at least one fellow director should be replaced. What is very surprising is that 83 percent of directors, including more than 50 percent of female directors, report that they do not support laws mandating gender board diversity. In addition, fewer directors say board diversity is very important; only 38 percent report that gender diversity is important. Additionally, they report only 26 percent think racial and ethnic diversity is important, down from 46 percent and 34 percent, respectively, from a year ago. While directors believe that gender, racial and ethnic background, age, years of experience, and socioeconomic background are important determinants of diversity, they believe board diversity is fading over time as a key issue in assessing boards across this dimension. Directors, including a majority of women, reject diversity mandates advocating that boards will become more diverse

---

[85] PwC's 2019. "Annual Corporate Directors Survey. The Collegiality Conundrum."

over time and that the process will happen naturally, without external or regulatory requirements.

CEO COMPENSATION AND THE ROLE OF THE BOARD OF DIRECTORS

Popular press is full of anecdotes of outsized payments to corporate CEOs granted by boards. Many critics of high executive pay urge boards to curb top-level pay to make CEOs accountable when performance is weak. Other critics argue that executive compensation should be reduced in the interest of social equity. While some of the arguments may be justified in a few cases, overall excessive compensation is not the biggest issue confronted by a board compensation committee. When the relentless focus on how much CEOs are paid attracts public attention, it takes away from the key issue boards are asked to address, *how* CEOs are paid. Academic studies have provided evidence of the alignment of executive pay and performance.[86] During the 1990s, most public companies adopted compensation policies that gave executives bonuses for stock price appreciation, cash flow, and earnings growth. For a large sample of companies, approximately 20 percent of the total CEO compensation is now based on salary, and the rest is contingent through direct stock awards, stock options, and/or deferred compensation. The percentage of compensation in salaries has steadily declined in the last decade, suggesting that boards reward CEOs based on performance incentives. For a typical public firm in 2004, the average CEO total compensation was $3 million, but only $1 million was salary, which is 33 percent of the total compensation. In 2014, the typical compensation was $4.5 million, but the salary was approximately $0.85 million (almost 18 percent of the total), while the rest was stock, options, and deferred compensation.[87]

Other academic studies have examined how executive compensation changes when stock price performance is improved. In other words, how sensitive is the CEO pay to stock price performance of the firm. Studies

---

[86] M. Jensen and K. Murphy. "Performance Pay and Top-Management Incentives," *Journal of Political Economy* 98(2), 1990, pp. 225–264.

[87] Historical data from Execucomp in Berck and DeMarzo, *Corporate Finance* (Pearson, 2017), pp. 998–999.

found that for every $1,000 increase in a firm's value, CEO pay changed on average by $3.25, reflecting primarily an increase in stock ownership, $2, and $1.25 in salary.[88]

MISGUIDED EXPECTATIONS ABOUT BOARDS AND DIRECTORS

All these practices contribute to board effectiveness and support the smooth functioning of the board as a mechanism for overseeing and advising senior management. However, there are several misconceptions about what the board should not do. These misguided ideas are not supported by research and constitute myths in practice.[89] Some of these erroneous assertions include:

1. A CEO should never serve as chairman of the board.

In 2005, almost 71 percent of companies in the S&P 500 Index had a dual chairman/CEO, while only 53 percent of the firms in 2014 followed this practice. Similarly, during the same period, the percentage of firms where an independent director served as chairman increased from 9 percent to 28 percent. During this period, boards were inundated with shareholder proxy requests that the roles of CEO and chairman of the board be separated. The rationale for these actions was based on the notion that the role of the chairman of the board and the CEO present conflicts of interest. An independent chair, alternatively, offers rigorous and watchful oversight of the organization and management, helping shareholders achieve their objectives. However, empirical academic works does not support this assertion. [90] Results from

---

[88] Michael Jensen and Kevin Murphy. "CEO Incentives—It Is Not How Much You Pay But How," *Harvard Business Review*, May/June 1990.

[89] David Larcker and Brian Tayan. "Seven Myths of Board of Directors" (Stanford, CA: Stanford University Rock Center for Corporate Governance), September 30, 2015.

[90] Brian K. Boyd. "CEO Duality and Firm Performance: A Contingency Model," *Strategic Management Journal*, 1995. More recent studies provide further evidence on the topic. See, for example, Aiyesha Dey, Ellen Engel, and Xiaohui Liu. "CEO and Board Chair Roles: To Split or Not to Split?" *Journal of Corporate Finance*, 2011.

studies shows that there is no statistical correlation between board independence and firm's operating performance. In fact, some studies find that a forced separation between the two roles creates unfavorable stock price returns at the time of the announced decision and that subsequent operating performance is lower. In summary, the evidence suggests that combining the roles of CEO and the chairman of the board, a business model of organizing public companies in the United States, does outweigh the benefits and costs of an independent board chairman.

2. Interlocked directorships are detrimental to shareholder interests.

An interlocking directorship is a practice where a member of one company's board of directors also serves on another company's board. Critics argue that interconnected boards compromise independence and create an implicit psychological reciprocity not serving in the best interests of shareholders of both firms. Supporters place a premium on improved information flow among directors and shared ideas about operations and strategies that lead to better outcomes for firms observing interlocking directorships. Best practices are then transferred across firms efficiently through the broader network of directors. Empirical research supports the proposition that interlocked directorships are in the best interests of shareholders.[91]

3. Directors serving on boards face unlimited risks.

The popular press projects the notion that directors face unlimited liability risks perhaps because of the high-profile cases of Enron, WorldCom, and Tyco, where directors were forced to pay out-of-pocket expenses to settle class action litigation. When asked in a survey conducted by PwC, more that 75 percent of board directors believe that the liability risk of serving on

---

[91] Cesare Fracassi and Geoffrey A. Tate. "External Networking and Internal Firm Governance," *Journal of Finance*, 2012. For additional evidence in M&A transactions, please see Ye Cai and Merih Sevilir. "Board Connections and M&A Transactions," *Journal of Financial Economics*, 2012.

boards has increased, but only a small fraction of directors think of resigning due to increased personal liability.[92] Studies from the legal profession report that the actual risk for directors paying out-of-pocket is very small. In addition, there are directors enjoying considerable protections against personal financial losses with liability insurance (D&O insurance) and various indemnification agreements that allow the company to pay costs associated with class action lawsuits. Overall, directors enjoy considerable protections against exposure to their personal wealth. The real concerns of directors who perform poorly are associated with their reputations, time, and efforts associated with a lawsuit.[93]

4. When a company fails, the board has failed to fulfill its responsibilities.

This misconception does not consider the nature of possible failures. Corporate decisions require some risks, and if the board has not exercised good diligence, it has failed its role in exercising its fiduciary role. These instances are not typically observed. Instead, there are instances where failures reflect the competitive nature of market forces, unexpected shifts in consumer preferences, and other unique circumstances that have not been well anticipated. And occasionally there are not red flags presented to the board. Absence of preconditions for a potential future problem and detection of a failure is impossible. Academic research shows that regardless of the reason for any failure, directors are punished as they are ousted from board seats or become targets of activities, all suggesting that they lose their reputations.[94]

---

[92] Corporate Board Member and PricewaterhouseCoopers LLP, "What Directors Think, 2009: Annual Board of Directors Survey. A Corporate Board Member/ PricewaterhouseCoopers LLP Research Study. Special Supplement," *Corporate Board Member*, 2009.

[93] Bernard S. Black, Brian R. Cheffens, and Michael Klausner. "Outside Director Liability," *Stanford Law Review*, 2006.

[94] Suraj Srinivasan. "Consequences of Financial Reporting Failure for Outside Directors: Evidence from Accounting Restatements and Audit Committee Members," *Journal of Accounting Research*, 2005.

These misconceptions, while shedding light on the debate of the role of the board, add scrutiny to the work of directors. As is common in many labor market segments, several practitioners believe the labor market for directors consists of good and bad directors. The National Association of Corporate Directors (NACD)[95] has sketched the profile and reported the following defining characteristics of "bad directors": (a) lack of attention to details and failure to analyze complexity while focusing only on big picture items; (b) a narrow field of focus by developing an agenda that differs from both the board's and the management's perspective; (c) a sense of entitlement by recognizing authority and positions of power while ignoring corporate social responsibility; (d) an absence of cooperation and a deficit in financial and legal literacy. Directors fitting this profile may be recognized as technocrats with a narrow-band expertise; a representative of just one point of view or just one group of shareholders; a financial stumbler, who possesses too limited financial knowledge to participate in complex discussions; a partisan, who interprets corporate decisions from a certain political view; the unprepared, who spends limited time in preparing for the board meetings while showing interest in discussing broad issues; the storyteller, who tells unrelated war stories with distracting views; and marquee directors, who command name recognition but differ on issues requiring discussion. While the overwhelming majority of directors fulfills the expectations for their fiduciary duties and possess requires skills, recognizing isolated cases of bad directors helps the board contribute in advancing the interests of shareholders. This indirectly helps management as the role of a director is not to provide for management. Instead, "it is to assure that management is provided."[96]

PRACTICAL CONSIDERATIONS

The dual mandate provides guidance for boards to do the following:

1. The board needs to make sure that the company has a strategy in place, and that the strategy is in tune with the marketplace that

---

[95] Michael Pocalyko. "A Field Guide to Bad Directors." *NACD Directorship*, July/August 2018, pp. 22–28.

[96] Norman Augustine, former Chair and CEO of Lockheed Martin Corporation.

the firm competes in and ensures that the chosen strategy makes sense and will allow the company to grow and prosper. The board also needs to make sure that there are appropriate assets in place to execute that strategy. In other words, boards must be very mindful to not agree to strategies that cannot possibly be executed because the company does not have the capability of doing so.

2. Boards need to know when to be hands off. In other words, there are times when a board just does not want to be a nuisance or do any harm. An example of that would be the 2020 COVID-19 pandemic. CEOs and management teams have had to put plans together to determine how to manage amid the pandemic. In a situation like that, boards do not want to give CEOs and management teams more to do. They need to step back and let the management team execute their responsibilities. There are also times when the board needs to monitor very closely the activities of management. For example, maybe the company is not performing as well as it should, or it is not meeting its expectations, or there is some other crisis that the company is forced to deal with. That is a time for the board to monitor what is going on very carefully.

   And then there are times when the board must take over, and that is when perhaps the CEO or the management team is unable to execute their responsibilities. Then the board needs to step in and take control. However, there are isolated cases where boards intervene in times when they should not be intervening, and when they should be exerting their control, they are unable to decide and wait too long.

3. Boards must approve appropriate objectives. Boards need to understand how a company should be performing and how to monitor progress. They can then set the appropriate objectives for the CEO and the management team for compensation purposes. And of course, boards have the big responsibility to manage the compensation of the CEO and other named executive officers of the company. Bards also have responsibility for risk management. Understanding corporate risk exposure is a topic that is gaining more and more importance as we go forward. Normally, risks are calibrated in two dimensions: the likelihood that an unfavorable event will happen,

and the impact of this event to the company. Those risks that have a higher probability of happening and a huge impact on the company need to be monitored and dealt with at the board level. For example, a major cyberattack. The likelihood of a cyberattack is much higher than it was ten years ago, and the impact on the company could be extreme. We have countless examples, like Equifax and others, in which a cyberattack led to a significant revenue loss of the company and this required to change the executive team. Enterprise risk management is an absolutely critical board responsibility. And then perhaps, the most important responsibility of all, is selecting a CEO and ensuring that there is a viable, robust succession plan in place for the CEO.

4. Countless examples provide evidence that boards have good succession plans in place. For example, Disney had a pretty good succession plan in place. GE had one as well when Jack Welch left. Lou Gerstner at IBM had a very good succession plan in place. Apple did as well when Steve Jobs was ill. But there are several cases where a good succession plan has not been put in place. The board and the company was then put at risk. Selecting a CEO requires a lot of diligence on the part of the board. Again, the board needs to understand where the company is and how the company is positioned to determine the skills needed by the CEO. The Board should determine priorities in terms of the sill set of a CEO. Does the company need technology skills or general management skill? What experiences from past appointments are deemed necessary to lead the organization? In the spectrum of high EQ and IQ which behaviors are more desirable to match the firm's needs for future success? Is a task master more desirable than someone who can delegate and allow senior executives to develop?

All these issues should be assessed by the board within the context of what the company requires for the next phase of its growth and development. And by definition, for the board to understand what the company requires, directors actually have to understand the company. So, the board's ultimate responsibility is to make sure it is informed at a level commensurate with its responsibilities. For example, board directors should know the top CEO succession candidates. They should know many of the senior members of the management team. They should be able to articulate what the strategy is, and they ought to be able to understand how the company is performing in absolute terms and relative to its competitors. In fact, boards have a responsibility not just to show up at meetings five or six times a year but also to understand the business. This allows them to discharge their agency responsibilities to the shareholders.

BOARD CHALLENGES IN THE TWENTY-FIRST CENTURY

Reputation for Directors

Directors are motivated to represent the interests of shareholders and often are provided compensation that includes stipends and bonuses. However, reputation may be a salient feature that makes them work to improve shareholder wealth as they strive to be perceived as "good and sensible" business leaders. Perhaps reputation is more important than compensation. With good directors being in high demand, this creates opportunities for retaining current seats or even getting multiple board seats. This is more pronounced when a CEO serves as a member of the board of directors of another company when compensation is hardly a motivating factor in supporting the interests of shareholders. Studies show that CEOs who are not performing well in their companies are less likely to gain board seats, and well-performing CEOs tend to gain board seats. These findings point out that reputation is a strong factor in board seat assignments.

Growth and Inequality

An issue confronting boards today is the extreme wealth inequality that globalization has produced over the last twenty-five years. It is perceived to be unsustainable for a CEO to be paid 700 to 800 times more than the average company employee. On one hand, one can argue that we have a lot of people in India with an annual salary of $15,000, and therefore the comparison in salaries of a CEO of multinational firm relative to the firm's employees is not appropriate. On the other hand, there is evidence of a gap between the compensation of a CEOs and the compensation of middle management or the median salary in a company. This wealth gap may create an issue around how capitalism is practiced in the United States and elsewhere in the Western world.

In fact, the Anglo-American model of capitalism has developed in parallel with the positive externalities of globalization. If someone looks at the 1980s, globalization started after the demise of the Soviet Union, ushered in by Prime Minister Margaret Thatcher and President Ronald Reagan, which left just the United States at the pinnacle of the pyramid. And then the introduction of technologies like the internet created a globalization model. The globalization model has done enormous good. It has accelerated more people out of poverty than ever in the history of the world. It has solved huge problems, but it also created unintended consequences, including wealth inequality and environmental damage just to mention a couple.

While the primary responsibility of any board in the United States is shareholder returns, large asymmetries in salaries within any public company has created a debate about a renewed board mandate that perhaps should include returns to stakeholders and employees. Multiple shocks in the economic system, such as the dotcom and financial crises of 2008–2009, and most recently the COVID-19 pandemic. These have renewed the debate in much broader terms of having board members consider stakeholder returns in their decisions Ultimately, it may be necessary for the board to begin talking about societal issues as successive crises have pointed out to inequalities across the population.

Activism

Often motivated by institutional investors that challenge corporate decisions and demand change in strategy, activism presents challenges to Boards. There is no need for activism. Boards often react very negatively to activism. However, activism does the job of ineffective boards, not the other way around. And because some Boards are not doing their jobs very effectively, directors feel threatened by activism. So it is important that boards stay together, work together, hammer out possible differences on strategy matters and risk management, and are responsive and transparent to the shareholder base, particularly in times of a transition.

When Boards are doing their job, making sure that companies are performing well with good strategies in place that return value to shareholders, activism disappears. For boards to perform this way it means directors know the company well and understand its challenges. Activism may arise because Boards do not perform their duties of overseeing strategy or disagreements begin to emerge among directors with respect to the direction of the company. When fractions materialize, that is very deleterious to the company, to the management team, and ultimately to the shareholders and employees. Often, fractions in Boards provide an opening for activism. Several executives believe that activism is required when boards are not doing their jobs. The CEO also has a major responsibility in shareholders activism. In some instances, activism is welcomed by CEOs who are exposed to split Boards. Good performing Board not only ensure CEOs perform at levels above expectations but work very hard to stay together and to stay on the same page.

Board's Active Participation in Strategy Formulation

The active participation of the board requires engagement in the formulation of the strategy. Directors do not develop the strategy, but they approve the strategy. Directors need to understand the strategy, so engagement really starts with the strategy. It is customary for a multidivisional company to have a board meeting at different sites. Boards should not sit in the big mahogany boardroom but be involved in understanding key operating issues, visit facilities and discuss the challenges of regional offices. Having the opportunity to meet and mingle with other people provides an invaluable perspective about the workings of the firm.

Board members could ask questions, listen to the others, and get a feel for what is going on. For example, the CEO can also bring in customers to share with the board how the company is meeting their needs or explore areas for improvement. Another example is to bring investors or analysts in a Board meeting to solicit their perspective on the company's future course. Business partners can also be invited in. These are all vehicles that the board can use either formally on an agenda or informally. Visits to various parts of the company allow for a better handle on what the company is up to, what the culture is, and how freely people speak. During informal gatherings, board members can also get a very good handle on how other employees and senior executives understand the strategy of the company. There is nothing more disheartening for a board that has approved and supported a strategy than to be in meetings with employees where they cannot articulate the strategy.

The Role of Institutional Investors

In several Fortune 500 companies, institutional investors represent a predominant shareholder base. Companies have a balance of active investors who trade frequently the firm's stock and passive investors who maintain stock exposure for longer term. Passive investors represent investment asset managers like Fidelity Investments, Vanguard, and Wells Fargo. There has been a trend over the last five or six years toward more passive investing. There is considerable growth in index funds, and management of funds has been more efficient and cost-effective. The reason for these trends is that many active managers' investment strategies have not created much alpha; that is, substantial risk-adjusted returns relative to passive, index-based approaches to investing. Most of it has been beta. And if you conclude that most of it is beta, then you are probably better off in an index passive fund than you are in an active fund. Typically, big asset managers are not actively involved. It is almost impossible to be actively working with management even if active managers hold a portfolio of forty or fifty companies. Instead, they meet with management once or twice a year to better understand the firm. The lack of active and more frequent involvement of asset managers as shareholders potentially makes the model of corporate governance less responsive than it could be. Similarly, pension funds with large holdings in many companies perform like typical asset managers, with a few exceptions of activism.

However, the pendulum swings back and forth. In the 1990s and early 2000s, there was a rise of activist investors, and there is still a lot of activist investors today. But underneath, we have seen a huge flow of money from active managers to passive index funds. ETFs is another example of more of a passive investment as opposed to buying the stock and the company. When institutional investors become shareholders, it is worthwhile for them to understand the company, to be involved in the company, and to understand the fundamental strategy of the company going forward.

Board Diversity

One of the key issues that has brought public attention during the 2020 COVID-19 pandemic is diversity in corporate boards. Until the early 1990s, boards were dominated by white male directors. In the new business environment challenged by the pandemic and economic inequality, the composition of the board of director in terms of race, gender, and ethnicity has become a much-discussed issue in governance. Imbalances in the composition of corporate boards primarily as it relates to gender is not new. For example, it has been documented that in 2014, women's share of board seats in the United States was 19 percent, while in Japan, it was 3 percent and in France 30 percent.[97] Although there is evidence of benefits in terms of firm's performance from boards with gender diversity, only recently has there been momentum toward increasing the number of women on boards.[98] Nominations for female directors are often initiated from shareholder resolutions introduced by institutional investors or peer pressure from progressive business groups on CEOs. Institutional investors have expressed strong support in increasing board diversity,[99] and investment banks have encouraged board diversity for IPO firms. In 2020, Nasdaq proposed a new rule requiring that for a company to be listed on the exchange it must have (a) at least one director who self-identifies as a female, and (b) at least one director who self-identifies as black or African American, Hispanic or Latinx, Asian, Native American or Alaska Native, Native Hawaiian or Pacific Islander; two or more races or ethnicities. Furthermore, the company should explain why it does not have at least two directors on its board who self-identify in the those categories.[100]

[97] *Catalyst Census: Women Board Directors.* (New York: Catalyst, 2014).

[98] Renee B, Adams and Daniel Ferreira. "Women in the Boardroom and Their Impact on Governance and Performance," *Journal of Financial Economics,* 94 (2), 2009, pp. 291–309.

[99] J. S. Lublin and S. Krouse. "State Street to Start Voting Against Companies That Don't Have Women Directors." *Wall Street Journal,* April 23, 2017.

[100] "Nasdaq to Advance Diversity through New Proposed Listing Requirements," Nasdaq Press Release, December 1, 2020. https://www.nasdaq.com/press-release/

If diversity is a topic of interest to shareholders, we would anticipate that their voting behaviors will reflect strong support of candidates based on race and gender diversity. Indeed, a detailed research study shows that shareholders place a voting premium on diversity, and diverse candidates experience support during elections at the annual shareholder meetings.[101] Based on a comprehensive database of directors' race and gender from 2003 to 2018, diverse candidates experienced shareholder support during director elections. Between 2003 and 2018, the number of directors elected to companies' boards increased by 140 percent, from 3,973 to 9,546. During the same period, the number of female directors increased by 310 percent, from 468 to 1,917 in 2018, while the number of male directors increased by 118 percent, from 3,505 to 7,629. Also, the number of black directors increased 149 percent, from 249 to 619. The study results demonstrate an overwhelming support in elections for women candidates and for candidates with African American or black ethnicities, both resulting in more diverse directors' boards. Gender diversity is more pronounced than race diversity, but both have been dominant trends in defining board composition. The trend for more diverse boards is expected to accelerate in the coming decade as many institutional investors adhere to ESG principles.

GLOBAL ISSUES IN GOVERNANCE

The practice of corporate governance is not uniform across the world although firms complete globally. Let us take Europe for example. They do not practice Anglo-American capitalism. Their model is more balanced with shareholders, employees, unions, and other stakeholders all represented on board. That changes the entire governance model. When employees or heads of unions are members of the corporate board, that changes completely how the CEO manages a company. For example, the separation of the CEO from the chairman of the board is critical. In US over half the Fortune 500 companies combine the roles of the chairman and the CEO. In European companies, oversight is much different. In addition, there are two boards,

nasdaq-to-advance-diversity-through-new-proposed-listing-requirements-2020-12-01.

[101] I. Gow, D. Larcker, and E. Watts. "Board Diversity and Shareholder Voting," *ECGIA Working Paper Series in Finance*, December 2020.

the supervisory board and the operational board. The supervisory board oversees strategy and risk management, while the operational board works on tactics and oversees and advises management on daily functional, human resources management and operational matters.

Countries with capital markets exercise regulatory oversight for public companies. Securities commissions, typically in the similar structure to SEC, oversee disclosures and information and enforce rules and regulations to avoid fraud. But regulations are not the same across countries. The US SEC has been more active in enforcing regulations during the Sarbanes-Oxley era. Japan is a totally different model as it not transparent. It is much more of an old boys' network because it grew out of the Kyoritsu, post–World War II management and governance model. There have been some cracks in those foundations, but the transparency level in Japan is still not nearly as geared to shareholders as the American, or for that matter even the UK model.

In absence of convergence of regulatory frameworks across the globe, the challenge for global public companies is how to address the multiple regulatory environments in which the firms operate. This challenge persists, and corporate boards often spend time addressing global regulatory constraints.

ASSET DEPLOYMENT AND THE BOARD

The board should be knowledgeable on matters related to asset deployment. Several boards include members with previous M&A experience. Other board members may have subject matter expertise on key product lines, technology or retail investing. One or two members may have come out of the private equity world and understand that turnarounds, growth and exit strategies.

Fundamentally, the board should feel comfortable with the strategy that the CEO has proposed. Then they monitor the execution and the performance against that strategy. If the board is completely unhappy with the strategy, directors must ask a fundamental question: "Is this because the CEO and the management team don't understand the industry, or is it because they don't have the skills to put a strategy together?" The former question deals with strategy formulation while the latter deals with strategy execution. If a board does not think the CEO and the management team have come up with a viable strategy, this may dictate a change in leadership. If the Board thinks that the management team lacks credibility in executing strategy the CEO will be required to take a corrective action by bringing a new team and/or this may necessitate leadership change. Regardless of the course of action it is important for the board must have the skills to determine adequately whether the company has the right strategy in place and the right team to execute the chosen strategy.

But if the board is incapable of determining whether the right strategy is in place, then by definition, it is probably not capable of determining if they have the right CEO. Then the secondary measurement is the performance. So if you think you have the wrong strategy and you got lousy performance, that usually indicates it's time for a change.

A good CEO linked to a good board go hand in glove. It is very productive the board and the CEO work very collaboratively and that they are in agreement. It is important that the board is transparent with the CEO, sharing with the CEO what directors think. After a board meeting, the chairman of the board should always give the CEO valuable feedback. And it is important that the chairman try to keep the board together so that there's not factions. The chairman should encourage the board members to speak their minds and advocate that they ought to have the courage of their convictions and tell the CEO in board meetings what they think. There is nothing wrong with that transparency. Transparency and openness in communications build trust. There are times when board members do not always agree, but exchange and transparency create trust. And the CEO has to trust the board, and conversely the board has to trust the CEO. If that trust is broken for whatever reason, then the outcome is damaging to all parties involved. And it becomes more destructive when the Board is divided into factions, for example when four members support the CEO, and another four members think the CEO's not doing the right job. Obviously, a dysfunction at the board level and dysfunction between the board and the CEO, it is problematic for the firm. Often shareholders will generally pay for the dysfunctional environment eventually with declines in market value of their ownership.

THE ROLE OF BOARDS IN THE FUTURE

It is difficult to predict the future of boards. Going forward, boards will be confronted with some issues that they have not had to deal with as much up to this point in time. For example, it has been postulated that ESG criteria are better determinants for sound investment decisions and are used as factors in measuring the sustainability and societal impact of an investment in a business or in a company. Select topics dealing with the environment include climate change, energy management, water usage and sourcing, natural resources, emissions, and biodiscovery. Social topics that the firm's board should consider also include health and safety of employees, human rights, employee rights, and data privacy. With respect to governance, the board should consider topics such as business ethics, compliance, board composition, shareholders' rights, bribery, anticorruption, and fraud.

Unlike the governance topics, where many directors understand broad issues, social and environmental topics tend to be industry-specific and require extensive education and adaptation to the norms and industry conventions for directors to drive meaningful oversight of risks, impact bottom-line results, and address value-chain consequences. When all these preconditions have been met from the board's perspective, the question that requires thought analysis is: what programs and what culture and what processes are required to be put in place to comply with ESG methodology? Answers to this question are becoming a growing concern for investors and the role the company has in adhering, and in some cases leading on issues like this. The Business Roundtable has advocated for several years now the need for Boards of directors to take a more balanced approach between shareholders and stakeholders.[102] The Roundtable has introduced eight standards as guiding principles for good corporate governance. Two key principles advocate that the board and management should consider stakeholders' interests in creating value. In particular, the Roundtable provides guidance on the following:

- The board and management should engage with long-term shareholders on issues and concerns that are of widespread interest to them and that affect the company's long-term value creation.

---

[102] *Principles of Corporate Governance*, Business Roundtable, 2016.

- In making decisions, the board may consider the interests of all the company's constituencies, including stakeholders such as employees, customers, suppliers, and the community in which the company does business when doing so contributes in a direct and meaningful way to building long-term value creation.

The principles advocating a balanced approach in considering the competing demands of all stakeholders have received notoriety and were published by the *Wall Street Journal* and other media outlets. When organizations like the Business Roundtable start to take up issues like this, it is very important that boards are paying attention to it as well.

We can draw two conclusions regarding the boards of public companies based on practice and academic research.

First, there is overwhelming evidence that good corporate governance with a well-functioning board produces economic and financial benefits to the firm. In responses to a survey study by McKinsey and Co., institutional investors attach a premium for a well-governed company. The premium varies from 11 percent for companies operating in North America to 40 percent for companies operating in emerging country environments.[103]

Second, the board has the responsibility to oversee strategy, review the asset deployment program, approve the financial model, determine the best leadership team for the organization, and indirectly influence the firm's culture. More specifically, the board has the responsibility to make sure there is a workable strategy in place. As a direct linkage, the board approves the strategy. The board has the responsibility to make sure that the company deploys the right mix of assets to execute the strategy. This may include mergers, acquisitions, or divestitures. In addition, the board has a direct responsibility for the financial model because the board authorizes the budget and ratifies the capital allocation model of the company. Moreover, the board approves distributions to shareholders by determining the amount of dividend payments or the size of stock buybacks to be implemented. As a result, the board has a direct linkage to the financial model. In addition, the board has the ultimate responsibility to identify, hire, and guide the leadership of

---

[103] Paul Coombes and Mark Watson. "Global Investor Opinion Survey 2002: Key Findings" (McKinsey & Co., 2002). Accessed April 2, 2015. See www.eiod.org/uploads/Publications/Pdf/II-Rp-4-1.pdf.

the company. By appointing a CEO, the board ensures that there is an incentive compensation plan, measurement systems in place, and that the right objectives and goals are well understood by all levels of employees. Indirectly, the board's decisions influence organizational culture.

Within this setting the board has the responsibility to create an environment where the firm's employees play a role that involves ethical standards, openness, transparency, and accountability. In essence, the board carries the responsibility to review, ratify, and supervise the execution of the five-elements framework we have advocated throughout our chapters.

CHAPTER EIGHT

Execution and Strategy Implementation

THE BLUEPRINT FOR SUCCESSFUL BUSINESS OUTCOMES

Our framework for decision-making offers a blueprint for successful outcomes. Having a strategy in place with appropriate deployment of assets, supported by a viable financial model and strong leadership, along with a culture passionate about the mission of the company offers a strong foundation on which success is highly probable. As a metaphor, building a successful business is like building a house. A blueprint is based on the vision of how the house will look like on completion. The strategy outlines the plans or steps that will be required to build the house, and a good architect—the leader and orchestrator of all activities—with the support of a culture of energized and skilled professionals, will complete the construction of the house. Our decision-making framework represents the strong foundation on which a functional and operational organization can be built. While abstractly our framework with five key elements (strategy, asset deployment, a financial model, leadership, and culture) provides a good starting point, it is far from offering guarantees for success.

In practice, the way our decision-making framework is executed or operationalized really matters.[104] Without all the elements linked cohesively, the framework lacks purpose and direction. A strategy without the assets, assets without a strategy, a strategy and assets without a financial model, the financial model without a management team that is passionately engaged both intellectually and emotionally contribute to outcomes that are attributed to pure lack. All elements should be aligned with a focus on the formulation of a strategy. The strategy must reflect a careful and realistic assessment of the firm's aspirational goals and be consistent with the company's real capabilities. Even with the implementation of a good strategy, which is the first significant part in the building of a strong foundation, there are, unfortunately, no guarantees for successful outcomes.

A MISSING LINK: THE ROLE OF EXECUTION

In the strategy formulation process, the firm and its leadership gather appropriate information and data, analyze alternatives, identify opportunities, and consider the firm's internal strengths and weaknesses. An aspirational plan is developed based on the strategy that involves the deployment of assets as well as a financial model that supports the strategy with the intellectual and emotional engagement of the leadership and the employees of the organization. This blueprint is nothing more than a set of plans based on assumptions and conjectures, albeit realistic and sensible. Elements of the blueprint are linked and are consistent with organizational resources. However, the firm's leadership cannot use the blueprint as plug and play and expect to obtain results. This is where execution or implementation comes into the picture. Often the missing link to any strategy formulation is execution as it is somehow assumed it is a mechanical process.

Execution involves the conversion of the blueprint into a set of concrete action steps that will create desirable outcomes. It is conjectured those desirable outcomes are the ones predicted when developing the strategy and the supporting five elements of the decision-making framework. Until the

---

[104] Often in business, execution and implementation are synonymous. In our decision-making framework, however, execution is more action oriented and requires alignment between planned activities and desirable outcomes.

execution is complete, the strategy is still aspirational and involves hypotheses and assumptions. It is only when the leadership of an organization acts to execute the strategy that the process of testing the hypotheses and key assumptions originally used in formulating the strategy begins. To validate the hypotheses and consequently confront the realities of the competitive marketplace, coordinated work is required on behalf of employees within the organization. The work involves making decisions with the emotional and intellectual engagement of all people across the firm while deploying assets based on the financial model and following the strategy.

The execution of the strategy, however, is not a straightforward proposition. It is not a mechanical, linear process as many believe, where plans and actions create predetermined outcomes. Broad external trends, such as rapid technological changes, unanticipated economic volatility, and global uncertainties especially in turbulent times, all provide an environment within which plans, if not adjusted appropriately, will result in a failed strategy. Additionally, as people within the company execute plans, part of the strategy formulation, the internal hierarchy, the organizational structure, and the firm's culture may strengthen or weaken desirable outcomes. At this time it is important to understand why a well-conceived strategy may fail. The simple answer is there are many obstacles to the execution of the strategy.

Many believe that execution is more important than strategy. There are two perspectives on why there is this belief. The first perspective focuses on the significant process of finding opportunities during the execution of the strategy that lead to innovation, not failure. It is believed that during execution of the strategy, management could adjust plans while at the same time explore opportunities that create innovations and a path toward securing a competitive advantage. The second perspective contends that the success in strategy execution hinges on whether the strategy formulation process empowers managers and employees. Lack of involvement of key employees early in the process of strategy formulation results in a lack of commitment and a sense of limited accountability on behalf of the employees to see the firm do well. These two perspectives, one that advances innovation during the execution of a strategy and the other that highlights possible failures if people do not "own" the strategy formulation, represent two points of view. Both viewpoints underscore the importance of strategy execution and highlight its possible successes or failures.

OBSTACLES IN STRATEGY EXECUTION

A possible failure in strategy should be viewed in the contexts of understanding the (a) difference between strategy formulation and strategy execution and (b) the decisions and trade-offs required when a strategy based on aspirations and hypotheses turns into an executable plan. Understanding the difference between strategy formulation and strategy execution provides key insights into the ways that planning and execution diverge. Knowing the process of executing a plan and the processes and decisions that comprise it are vital in understanding when one has to make compromises or divert slightly.

First, strategy formulation primarily focuses on *effectiveness*, the big-picture view of the world within which the firm competes. In contrast, the execution focuses on the *efficiency* of converting action plans and resources into outcomes with the lowest possible costs and highest degrees of productivity.

While there is disagreement as to what is more consequential, effectiveness or efficiency, both are important for business success. Effectiveness is associated more with the notion of doing the right things, which means having an excellent game plan or a strategic plan. Efficiency means finding the best ways to accomplish outcomes. Because strategy execution tends to be more difficult to accomplish than formulation, many contend that efficiency is more important. In contrast, others feel that effectiveness is more important than efficiency because it is essential to be on the right track or digging in the right spot. Otherwise, even the hardest-working employees would be unsuccessful in focusing their best efforts on doing the things that add value to the firm. In essence, decisions about formulation (effectiveness) of a strategy tend to be very important to the success of the firm.

Regardless of the point of view, strategy formulation and strategy execution require different skill sets. The strategy formulation is primarily an intellectual process, while the execution phase is an operational process based on time and resource constraints. The strategy formulation requires analytical and intuitive skills, along with coordination among the leadership of the organization, which has a scientific flavor with tools and techniques. The execution of the strategy requires leadership skills and motivational techniques to be coordinated among many employees of the company. It is considered an art, not a science, as it relies on skills in motivating, buying-in to the strategy, and engaging the passion of employees. While the strategy formulation lies in the hands of senior executives and is mostly process-driven, the execution, alternatively, is mostly employee-driven and the responsibility of middle- and lower-level management.

To execute the strategy, management reviews the firm's capabilities and organizational structure to determine the best actions to implement the plan and how these actions can be conceived and organized. There is not an optimal path, rather, several trade-offs emerge during the execution phase. For example, the leadership can determine to develop and retain current talent or recruit externally to carry out the plans. To do so, the provision of a variety of incentives to align the interests of employees with desirable outcomes can be developed. Additionally, developing performance standards based on which employees are promoted or terminated would be part of this process.

The root causes of deviations from a well-conceived strategic plan are obstacles that occur in the context of strategy execution. Obstacles clarify what needs to be done for executives to achieve desirable outcomes from a well-developed strategy. In addition, obstacles are attributed to leadership deficits, organizational rigidities, cultural inertia, and misaligned processes and control mechanisms. To overcome obstacles, management is required to make adjustments in plans to resume the direction of implementing the strategy and achieving desirable outputs. Getting back on track may require trade-offs in decisions.

Obstacles Related to Leadership Deficits

It is universally accepted that a reasonably good strategy with thoughtful execution provides results. In contrast, a perfect strategy when not followed by an excellent execution may produce lousy results. Execution is critical and may explain why CEOs and companies fail. Failure in execution is associated with not being able to follow through. It is about not being disciplined. It is about not sticking to the strategy or the game plan that involves the key components of the decision-making framework, that is, strategy, asset deployment, the financial model, leadership, and cultural.

Having a reasonable strategy in place that is consistent with the industry is a common assumption regarding a firm. The firm possesses the assets and the capabilities to execute the strategy. Executives have developed a financial model, there is a team in place, a measurement system, a compensation system, and the software and the firmware of culture reasonably well aligned. The only thing that can really get in the way is execution. And execution is about discipline, it is about follow-up, it is about the willingness to get into and understand the details, and the stick-to-itiveness over a period time, not giving up. Execution is not about stopping the actions for the implementation of a strategy when you meet an obstacle or even if management runs into some headwinds that may steer the organization in a different direction.

The misconceptions made by many CEOs include assumptions that once they take on the role of CEO, they do not need to be involved with details. They often believe that they can delegate and have teams conduct the follow-through. The misconception is that the CEO role is a presiding one as opposed to an active, involved, hands-on approach. The CEO is responsible for the entire organizational operation. This understanding is particularly important in companies that are not doing well and need to be turned around. Having a new strategy in place with new assets and a new financial model requires traditional hands-on leadership by the CEO.

On one of end of the spectrum are CEOs who understand the market, capabilities, where the growth will occur, where profit pools are, and are outstanding at formulating a strategy. The following questions emerge: (1) Could they then develop a financial model? (2) Could they attract a team to execute? (3) Could they devise a management and measurement system that aligns compensation with performance measures? (4) Are they willing to establish and implement an operational management system, roll up their sleeves, and get into the details in order to ensure success?

At the other end of the spectrum, are executives who are outstanding with regards to execution. These executives have instituted a well-developed management system with appropriate performance metrics. They have the necessary processes in place and the pertinent data so that they can manage using data and facts in integrated and beneficial ways. The problem lies with the strategy that they have in place; it is the wrong strategy for the company in the industry it is in. This is what is known as trying to get blood out of a rock. Without the right strategy, the greatest execution in the world does not produce results.

In practice, under realistic conditions, a CEO could formulate a compelling strategy with the ability to execute the strategy. Sometimes a good chief operating officer (COO) may assist in the process, but execution is often more important than strategy formulation.

Obstacles Related to Organizational Rigidities

An organizational structure depicts the hierarchy and decision-making authority within the firm. It reflects how authority is distributed within subunits of the organization and how control of decisions is delegated from the CEO to divisional operating executives. Through trials and errors, organizations gravitate toward a structure that is both effective in formulating a sound corporate strategy and efficient in executing the strategy at the divisional level.

It is true that organizational structure changes as a firm grows and adapts to a changing environment. Small firms can accommodate a simple structure, but large firms require a multidivisional or matrix structure to address increases in size and complexity. A functional structure works when a firm has a narrow focus and small geographic footprint. A differentiation strategy fosters innovation and creativity only when decision-making is decentralized.

The relationship between strategy formulation and organizational structure is interdependent and dynamic, never static. The structure of the organization must be adjusted to the firm's stages of development or it will become a liability for the execution of the strategy. Therefore, an obstacle to the execution of a strategy is often the resistance to change within the firm's structure to accommodate a strategy that reflects the evolution of the organization in a competitive environment. Often this misalignment between strategy, structure, and execution reflects a CEO's oversights related to the context of decisions.

Obstacles Related to Cultural Inertia

Shared values and common traditions permeate the culture of a firm, especially one that has confronted challenges and threats in the past. The firm's culture, however, is difficult to change when external conditions change drastically. Accelerations or slowdowns in growth, changes in the business model, exits from current markets, or entries into new markets all create pressures on the firm's culture to deliver performance and desirable outcomes. While these new problems require a different approach in order to handle solutions, it is probable that the corporate culture may have inertia from past problems. These past problems may have been confronted successfully, but the culture cannot change fast enough to accommodate new challenges. Cultural inertia then becomes an obstacle in executing a new strategy to reorient the firm toward new performance goals and/or to change its overall course of action to be more effective in the competitive market. When the environment changes, the firm must refine, hone, and upgrade to ensure that core rigidities do not emerge. When original core competencies turn into liabilities, the current culture requires drastic change. Only with cultural change can the firm adapt as the business evolves. The execution of a strategy becomes smooth when these cultural rigidities disappear.

Obstacles Related to Misaligned Management Processes and Controls

Management processes and control systems are helpful in measuring efficiencies within the firm. Those processes allow senior executives to allocate resources and improve outcomes. Over time, processes and control mechanisms have been slowly adopted to accommodate incentives, culture, and people. Feedback mechanisms allow the firm to compare desirable output with actual output and take corrective action if necessary.[105] The single-loop mechanism simply compares actual outcomes with planned/desirable outcomes. Goals and objectives are appropriate when the environment is relatively simple, and goals and objectives may be measured with high degrees of certainty. Operating budgets, sales measures, and production targets are simple mechanisms to ensure adjustments in any deviations from expectations for the organization when the structure is stable. Over time, this structure becomes rigid and uncompromising

---

[105] Chris Argyris. *Organizational Learning: Theory, Method and Practice* (Reading, MA: Addison-Wesley, 1996).

to changes. When the environment becomes unpredictable due to fast changes, as in turbulent times, the structure becomes an obstacle for the execution of a new strategy designed to confront the realities of a new, changing environment. With simplicity in measures of outcomes, the system becomes a liability in executing a new strategy determined by competitive market shifts.

EXECUTION AND GAPS

It is not realistic to expect desirable or expected outcomes to be identical to the actual outcomes. A strategy formulation process is an aspirational plan based on many simplified assumptions that only by pure luck could be validated. Eventually there will be deviations (see Figure 8.1). Departures from expected outcomes may be positive or negative in relation to projected performance. At the same time, the execution of the strategy and the adherence to our 5-elements framework offers a unique opportunity to discover new investment prospects, new markets, and new products and services that, when considered, may create future growth opportunities for the organization.

As the CEO executes the plan, a constant evaluation of results or outcomes should be taking place. In a case where the results are consistent with expectations, there is no need for corrective action. If, however, results are not consistent, the root cause of the deviations from expectations should be identified, and corrective action should be undertaken. Unfortunately, in many cases when corrective action is required, people do not make decisions based on facts. They tend to make decisions on emotions or anecdotal evidence. It is critically important that when managers get a lot of data and evaluate input from a fact-based platform, changes that are made are well rooted in the reality of the strategy and the execution. Management systems and processes serve as integrating and alignment-creating mechanisms to bring required changes for the execution. Additionally, leadership should allocate time to separate the deviations from expectations.

In practice, the CEO identifies a limited number of priorities and develops a plan with his or her team to execute against. Following the agreement with the team, the CEO follows up on the key success parts that are required for the execution of the plan. After a critical success path is identified from a steady focus on the part of the CEO, there can be the assurance of a delivery of results. It is not uncommon for the CEO to be absorbed with daily distractions that will not allow his or her full attention to the adherence to this critical path. Also, it is essential for the CEO, while the execution is taking place, to engage customers, investors, and employees in an effort to obtain invaluable feedback and anecdotal data to be used to compare against results or outcomes.

As the execution of the strategy is unfolding, there will be an occasional performance gap, a difference between what was projected or expected and what is currently achieved. Performance gaps are not extraordinary. What is important is to uncover the root causes and explore ways of taking corrective action. The gap is often attributed to a process that is not working, a problem with human capital, a technology problem, or a shift in the marketplace. Indeed, it is necessary to understand what the root cause is so that corrective actions can take place. Handling and responding to symptoms is not an approach helpful in keeping the management system and processes directed in the path of success and exploration of future opportunities.

Performance gaps often may carry negative connotations in terms of a divergence between a plan of activities and outcomes. However, on a positive side, they may offer opportunities for reevaluation of the strategy. As part of this reevaluation, there may be an emergence of expanding of firm boundaries. These may include pursuing new products with new investment projects, new services, differentiated customer segments, and even cost savings.

In summary, deviations between projected/desirable outcomes and actual outcomes are explained by the obstacles presented previously and the opportunities that have not realized at the time the strategy was formulated. These deviations are manifested through two avenues:

+ *Performance gaps:* These gaps are deviations between actual performance or outcomes/results with projected or desired results.

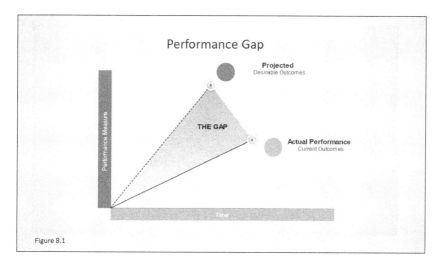

Figure 8.1

A performance gap may inform the strategy, and through a series of feedback loops, allows for changes of the strategy based on what is discovered in the execution. Revisions may take place on an annual or quarterly basis and be monitored through measurable objectives. Also, a performance gap could very well be because that market's attitudes or preferences have changed, and the company's strategy is incongruent with market needs. If in following that the strategy requires revision based on those new facts, parts of the 5-elements decision-making framework, such as asset deployment and the financial model, are not cast in stone. They must be adaptable, flexible, agile, and adjusted to changes in circumstances. An example may be the airline industry during the 2020 COVID-19. Airline strategies evolved over time and eventually focused on maximizing plane seat capacity through a network of connections, ensuring that there were as many point-to-point routes as possible for convenience. The financial model to support the strategy was based on maximizing the revenue per passenger or the revenue per plane. During the pandemic, the almost 90 percent drop in passenger traffic created a new market reality, forcing executives to rethink that entire strategy. Extreme market conditions, like the ones we observed during COVID-19, created a large performance gap, necessitating changes in strategy. Similarly, technological and societal changes reflect the evolution of an industry creating performance gaps that require reexamination of the strategy.

+ *Opportunity gaps:* These gaps are deviations between actual performance results and results that would have been obtained had the firm pursued new opportunities in new product markets, new services, and/or financial or business methods.

An opportunity gap is the performance lost due to a missed attractive business opportunity discovered during the implementation phase of the strategy. As new information is revealed about the business environment during the strategy execution phase, the firm's capabilities may offer a suitable match with evolving market conditions worth pursuing for value creation and profits. The newly discovered alignment generates future strategic options and requires development of a supplementary operating plan. At that time the senior management has the option to (a) either activate a separate operating plan to pursue it independent of the unfolding operating plan, or (b) revisit the initial implementation plan and make necessary changes to incorporate the new strategic option. In some instances, the revised plan is so different that the original operating plan has been discarded. Regardless of the decision, an opportunity gap generates valuable strategic options, not obligations for the firm to pursue them immediately. The CEO should consider the trade-offs between staying on course and focused on the implementation of the original execution plan and the pursuit of newly discovered options. Figure 8.2 shows the impact on performance when both opportunities are not pursued and when there are deviations between actual and desirable outcomes.

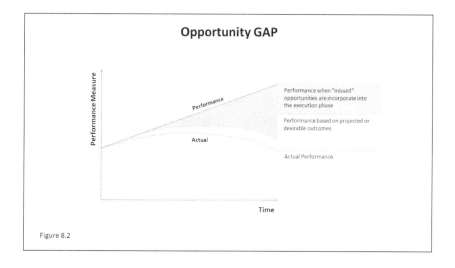

Figure 8.2

However, a caveat is in place when an opportunity gap presents new avenues for expansion of a product or service portfolio of the firm. It is not advisable to be far afield from the strategy because the firm could wind up taking on things inconsistent with the strategy and the vision. Instead, by adding new pieces, assets, or activities, alignment becomes more challenging. Without proper alignment, unrelated albeit valuable pieces end up being a major distraction to the overall execution and accomplishment of the strategies and goals that the organization has in place.

AMBIDEXTERITY

Identifying performance and opportunity gaps during the execution of a strategy offers executives an opportunity to adopt to new facts and conditions. Adaptiveness requires organization to utilize two contradictory and seemingly opposite capabilities. [106] On one hand, when adaptive, the firm has the ability to exploit existing capabilities, resources, and information to improve and streamline performance results further. On the other hand, when the firm is adaptive, it affords the opportunity to explore new avenues for innovation or growth by rethinking existing resources and developing

---

[106] Michael Porter. *HBR's 10 Must Reads on Strategy* (Boston: Harvard Business Review Press, 2011).

new capabilities. The simultaneous balancing act of exploring and exploiting while executing a strategy is what it is called *ambidexterity*.[107]

Ambidexterity becomes a critical element in improving both effectiveness and efficiency of any organization. While exploiting current capabilities by narrowing a possible performance gap, efficiency is improved as outcomes are enhanced and resources become more productive. Effectiveness is also increased as opportunities from the exploration of new areas raises competitive advantage or improves synergistic capabilities with the current assets.

Both exploitation and exploration are required during the execution of a strategy. A company that only exploits existing resources and capabilities may improve its performance but will eventually attract competitors. More competition changes in market dynamics may erode the company's strategic posture. Exploiting existing resources signals that the company is profitable and competitive by relying on current assets, existing capabilities, and practices of the past. Conversely, a company that constantly explores new opportunities by reconfiguring resources to develop new capabilities will eventually shrink its current competitive advantage and weaken its presence in the marketplace at the expense of an uncertain future.

The best example of a firm that created a great future in uncertain times is IBM.[108] A large established company, IBM in the 1980s encounter difficulties when faced with the need to radically change its business model and build capabilities for sustained innovation. While the world was changing, new competitors eroded IBM's market share and profits and the firm undertook a dramatic turnaround to respond to disruptors and reestablish market leadership. The execution of a new strategy allowed IBM through exploitation and exploration to change gradually by taking advantage of its strength and stability while innovating and developing emerging initiatives helpful in the long-term success. Capabilities were adopted, integrated, and reconfigured, which allowed for the adaptation

---

[107] Charles O'Reiley, Bruce Harreld, and Michael Tushman. "Organizational Ambidexterity: IBM and Emerging Business Opportunities," *California Management Review* 51, 4, Summer 2009, pp. 48–80.

[108] Details about the challenges of IBM in the 1980s appear in two Harvard Business School Case studies "IBM's Decade of transformation: Turnaround to Growth (Case 805-130) and Uniting Vision and Values (case 807-030)."

to a changing external environment. Evolving technologies and new markets offered new innovative capabilities while existing markets solidified strengths and offered stability. The ability to exploit and explore during the execution phase of the strategy informed and helped IBM to gather intelligence and advance supply chain knowledge, and provided unique insights about current and future customer needs.

Leaders believing in ambidexterity take a holistic view of the firm as they execute strategies. They pay attention to (a) management processes of executing a strategy, and (b) the culture of the organization. The management processes involve actions and tasks to be completed to create results, usually profits and shareholders' value. In addition, management processes include a reward and performance measurement system to evaluate productivity and offer rewards for efforts in meeting expectations or for exemplary efforts. The culture of the organization, which consists of shared values and collective habits when leveraged, could produce creative solutions or innovations during the execution phase.

In an environment where ambidexterity is practiced, an alignment between management processes and culture results in a successful exploration of new opportunities and exploitation of current strengths and capabilities, all yielding a high-performance organization. Implicit in this alignment is the need to undertake corrective actions to narrow possible gaps. This implies change, and in this vein, strategy execution has a heavy dose of organizational change and change management as deviations from expected outcomes necessitate corrective action and adjustments. Corrective actions may lead to human capital changes, changes in processes, changes in management systems, and possibly changes in performance/rewards metrics. In addition, alignment implies that it is reasonable for management to expect performance or opportunity gaps and disparities between aspirations and capabilities. Gaps cannot be too wide, however, as this is a sign of serious miscalculations and errors in strategy formulation. But if there are, steps should be taken to narrow the gaps. Such steps could entail developing training programs and/or being involved in acquisitions, alliances, and partnerships.

ORGANIZATIONAL ALIGNMENT AND EXECUTION IN OUR DECISION-MAKING FRAMEWORK

During the execution of a strategy, rewards and performance metrics should all be balanced and work together to ensure that corrective action is activated when there are deviations in performance. In addition, execution should be integrated tightly into a financial model that gives investors a very clear picture of what returns they can expect and how they will hold the management team accountable for those returns. Along with the financial model, it is imperative that compensation lines up with performance. Measuring performance and compensating employees should be consistent with the goals being accomplished and in agreement with the financial model of the strategy.

Generally, establishing processes allows CEOs to have some degree of control over the operations of the company during the execution phase. It is necessary not to overdo a process because the proliferation of processes may not produce any results and instead provide confusion due to the development of an environment that is bureaucratic and not conducive to flexibility. In practice, the CEO should identify the four or five processes that are critical to managing the company. For example, such processes may include a process that measures cash flows linked to the financial model, a process that monitors proposals to secure future clients, a process to acquire talent, a process to develop a multi-pricing method for services, and a manufacturing process to monitor efficiency.

However, the customer relationship management process is of critical importance as it leads to revenues and profits. The way the company interacts with customers, including its website or the call centers or its sales force, is important in retaining current customers and creating future clients. All these aspects need to be coordinated into a process so that employees have readily accessible information, and then through advanced AI analytic and cognitive tools, begin to discern patterns and adjust decisions to maximize output. Along with the relationship management processes, HR processes are critical. How the firm recruits, hires, and retains employees, as well as how it trains people, conducts performance evaluations, and compensate employees are all critical elements that help establish an effective human resource approach to managing a company.

Many companies get some of the above issues right, but not all companies get them right. And getting them all right is what provides the alignment. Then it becomes a matter of the execution, discipline, and stick-to-itiveness to begin to get results. Once the firm begins to get results, it creates the momentum that leads to a journey, not to a destination. An alignment should take place over a longer period, not just six or twelve months, because strategies are usually executed not over a couple of quarters but over multiple years. Many other activities may take place that bring attention to other issues that the executives must dealt with. The CEO must always maintain that alignment across those five components in the decision-making framework to achieve results that are better than mediocre.

Processes are important, but it is critical that you identify the end-to-end processes that are truly important in managing the business. It must be ensured that those processes are properly architected, properly engineered, and then properly automated so that everyone has access to the appropriate information, and more important, that they deliver the outcome for which you are striving. For example, if you have a process to train several people, and the metric there is the number of certified people, ultimately you have to evaluate the extent to which the process is delivering that outcome. It is expected that a process is about delivering outcomes. And you must ensure the clarity of the process that you are engineering and reengineering, what that outcome is, and scrutinizing that you are getting that outcome.

Alignment across the five components in decision-making becomes important in the execution process. This alignment requires patience, persistence, and discipline. As CEOs execute a strategy, changes are inevitable but do result in payoffs. As changes are implemented, time is required for the parts of the 5-components framework to root themselves so they can grow. Occasionally CEOs become impatient because they are not getting the immediate results they want. When changes take place, temporary instability is created in the management system. And the instability then begins to change the direction the organization is moving in, and that is what creates lack of alignment. As a result, the final outcome is not the one the CEO would have hoped in the near future. In fact, it may not resemble what the CEO committed to deliver against the plan of action. In this case, the patience and the discipline come into play.

EXECUTION AND MANAGEMENT CHANGE

Deviations from projections invite changes in management systems and processes. Changes should be impeded to produce better outcomes. Academics have identified factors and precipitating circumstances that, when applied during the execution of a strategy, will certainly solidify changes and make resistance to change insignificant.[109] These include:

+ Establishing a sense of urgency within the organization.
+ Forming a coalition that includes leaders committed to change.
+ Creating a vision to guide the process.
+ Communicating the vision through the appropriate channels consistent with the organization's culture.
+ Empowering many others to act on the vision.
+ Creating short-term wins to generate momentum and a sense of success to be followed by more successes.
+ Consolidating improvements to demonstrate credibility and produce permanent changes in management systems and processes.
+ Institutionalizing new approaches to be flowed in future decisions as the outcome changes.

When changes occur and solidify management processes, they then become permanent within the organization. When those changes are supported by the culture of the firm and become part of shared experiences and norms of employees, they are transformational. Transformational changes reposition the company in the marketplace.

DEVELOPING OBJECTIVES AND MEASURING PERFORMANCE DURING THE EXECUTION OF THE STRATEGY

A simple management system may be used to identify and measure performance gaps and to detect potential opportunities. Opportunities may be

---

[109] John Kotter. "Leading Change: Why Transformation Efforts Fail," *Harvard Business Review*, 73, no. 2, March–April 1995, pp. 59–67.

associated with acquisitions that can be filled by using the firm's capabilities in human capital or acquisitions to bring the necessary skills to bolster the company's position. The management system should have an in-depth process to evaluate those opportunities that offer adequate return on capital investment. The operating aspect of the management system that focuses on performance gaps is different from the system that identifies opportunities, particularly around asset deployment such mergers and acquisitions. It is not uncommon that the two management systems are organized differently to avoid overlapping and complexity. The separation is necessary, especially if the opportunity gap is large, meaning that there are several opportunities available for consideration but may be inconsistent with the strategy in place.

Performance measures typically are matched with objectives and goals over a discrete period, usually one year. Objectives are essential in the execution of strategy since they (a) represent the basis for allocating resources, (b) are primary mechanism for evaluating managers, (c) are the tools for monitoring progress and deviations from results, and (d) establish organizational, divisional, and departmental priorities, which all inform the pecking order of activities and the significance of one set of tasks versus others.

To be effective in measuring success in the execution of strategy, objectives should be measurable, consistent, reasonable, challenging, clear, communicated throughout the organization, characterized by an appropriate time dimension, and accompanied by commensurate incentives and rewards. Unfortunately, too often objectives are stated in generalities with little operational usefulness. Annual objectives, such as, "to improve profits," or, "to improve consumer visibility," are not clear, specific, or measurable. Objectives should state quantity, quality, cost, and time. Also, they should be verifiable. Terms and phrases such as "maximize," "minimize," "as soon as possible," and "adequate" should be avoided. Finally, objectives should be supported by clearly stated policies. It is important to tie rewards and sanctions to objectives so that employees and managers understand that achieving objectives is critical to successful strategy implementation.

There are different ways to measure performance during the execution phase. One of them is a variation of the balance scorecard.[110] A balance

---

[110] Robert Kaplan and David Norton. "Using the Balanced Scorecard as a Strategic Management System," *Harvard Business Review*, August 2007, pp. 2-13.

scorecard includes all critical elements required to deliver the outcomes. These elements include financial, product, organizational, and operational factors all summarized in one score. While a great tool, the balance scorecard tends to provide a plethora of elements requiring measurement and assessment. Much thought needs to be placed into what to measure and how to compensate for what is measured. In the typical management jargon, "If you do not measure an activity, you cannot manage it." In other words, metrics, data, and other information are required so that there is no doubt about the measures of performance. While the balance scorecard is an appealing metric to measure the success of the strategy execution, it lacks simplicity as it tends to be comprehensive and holistic. The balance scorecard measuring performance against projections becomes a complex and labor-intensive process that tends to be bureaucratic in nature. For small firms with a simple product or service portfolio, the balance scorecard is useful in measuring performance during the execution phase. However, for large, multidivisional firms with complexity in their service and product portfolios, the balanced score card becomes a complex, albeit comprehensive process for measuring performance, where its adoption should be evaluated on the merits of costs and benefits.[111]

Also during the execution phase, CEOs are cautioned about, "You get what you measure," and consequently, "You get what you pay for." Ambiguity in measuring factors that impact performance will lead to ambiguity in measuring performance. As a result, management while willing to compensate for measures of performance, fails to provide incentives clearly aligned with performance results. For example, it has been suggested the customer is important for any organization and that customer satisfaction is critical to repeat sales and, consequently, revenue growth. However, it is ironic that in organizations where customer satisfaction is an objective measure of performance, customer satisfaction is not measured, or if it is measured, it is done in ambiguous terms. How is it possible that customer satisfaction is important in the execution of a strategy when the management is unwilling to measure it objectively with a result of compensating employees for improving customer satisfaction?

---

[111] Robert Kaplan and David Norton. *Alignment: Using the Balanced Scorecard to Create Corporate Synergies* (Boston: Harvard Business Press 2006).

Some measures, however, work better than others. A simplified performance scorecard for managers may be more effective than a balanced scorecard. Simplified scorecards can be broken into three components: (a) financial measures, including revenues, profitability, and margins, (b) strategic priorities that allow for the measurement of how people execute against the strategy, and (c) personal development, which includes the extent to which managers adhere to the values, are team players, are argumentative or collaborative, and to what extent they work to improve their intellectual and technical skills.

THE ROLE OF ORGANIZATIONAL STRUCTURE IN THE EXECUTION

The organizational structure dictates how the execution of the strategy will take place and consequently, how the other parts of the decision-making framework will be facilitated. The reason organizational structure is important in strategy execution is because a firm's design dictates how objectives will be established and how resources will be allocated. In addition, the organizational structure determines the flow of information in regard to the operations of the firm; the way funds are distributed within the firm; and how information about operations, such as production, marketing, and other processes, is collected and analyzed within the firm. As organizations become larger and more complex, information-processing requirements exceed individual capacity. Two typical outcomes of this problem are (a) satisfying, not maximizing behavior in decision-making, and (b) bounded rationality exhibited by CEOs and key operating executives. The former suggests that during execution more often managers, due to complexity and large information flows requiring detailed analyses, prefer to satisfy, not maximize outcomes when confronted with objectives requiring lots of information. This means that the decision-making capacity of any CEO cannot be fully rational because of limits associated with the time and effort required to analyze objectively a large flow of data and information. Since it is not humanly possible to handle the processing of every detail, CEOs tend to be mostly rational, but with limits. If we accept that information flows are facilitated by the structure of the firm it follows during the execution of a strategy, the firm's structure determines how information flows to various decision makers and how this information may be used to influence the behaviors of people to align the interest of employees with the interests of the firm.

The structure reveals how the firm is organized. Being well organized in centralized or decentralized mode can represent a great competitive advantage or disadvantage for a firm. For example, in a structured global organization, objectives are stated in geographic terms, and resources are allocated by region. For a firm with a centralized management system, strategy becomes more of at the top sort of exercise, and execution becomes the most important characteristic or skill that required within the management team. In contrast, in a highly decentralized organization, it is important for the company to have some strategic capability as well as operational capacity. Strategy is executed at the divisional level. For a highly decentralized structure like GE, the CEO should rely on someone with strong skills in running, for example, the GE engine business who can execute. Also, the operating executive who runs the energy business for GE should be competent with strategy because it is a different business. Therefore, the structure of the firm and the type of markets within which the firm operates dictates where execution of strategy takes place and what type of operational and strategy skills are required by executives to execute the firm's strategy.

However, the relationship between organizational structure and execution is more dynamic. Organizations tend to follow a repeated cycle of changes in organizational structure when strategy is implemented. The cycle begins with a new strategy. Once a new strategy is formulated, it is not unusual for the execution of the strategy to reveal performance and opportunity gaps. Based on new information and facts, to respond to performance deficiencies, resolve problems, and improve outcomes, the CEO must adjust the administrative structure. A modified organizational structure temporarily resolves performance gaps as performance and profitability are restored in the short term and profit targets are achieved. However, opportunity gaps offer the temptation for profit growth by expanding into new markets and/or services. As the firm takes advantage of the new opportunities and pursues them, the cycle of changing the structure to accommodate performance gaps repeats itself. The execution-structure relationship reflects a continuous quest for achieving targeted performance with the adjustment of organizational structure and pursuit of new businesses for growth. As a result, execution adapts to new opportunities. Consequently, organizational structure will change to reduce performance gaps. In summary, the relationship between execution of a strategy and organizational structure tends to be dynamic with feedback loops.

CHAPTER NINE

Globalization 2.0

Our decision-making framework presents CEOs with a disciplined process to formulate a strategy, follow up with an asset deployment program based on a financial model that considers capital allocations and profitability supported with a positive cultural environment and leadership capabilities. In the previous chapters, we discussed specific aspects for each element of the framework and outlined conditions under which the CEO will be successful in implementing the process. However, the business environment within which CEOs operate is in constant flux and always changing. Changes in the business environment may be attributed to short-term adjustment in the microcosm of companies competing for dominance and profitability in their industries. Changing consumer preferences for online purchases or changes in the competition within an industry due to new entrants or tightening of distribution channels are examples of changes that impact each firm differently. These changes tend to be idiosyncratic and firm-specific, not market-wide, and they require short-term adjustments in the execution of our 5-components framework. Operating investment and financial plans will be realigned to allow the firm to adopt to new sets of competitive conditions. Alternatively, changes in the business environment may reflect long-term trends that influence the climate within which a company operates. These changes tend to be systematic and impact all firms across the board. Systemic and market-wide changes in the environment include changes that are beyond the control of companies and influence all companies simultaneously, although to a different degree. Examples include changes in interest rates, inflation,, and taxation of overseas profits.

One systematic and fundamental change that has been observed in the business environment in the last century is globalization, which reflects a shift in economic and business activities. We have been moving away from national-centered economies toward more interdependent national economies. Previously, self-contained companies—isolated from each other by barriers to cross-border trade and investment, by distance and time zones, and by differences in regulation, culture, and business systems—have been replaced with the emergence of global markets of products. Limited barriers to cross-border trade and shrinking of distances due to the internet, communication, and transportation advancements have all contributed to the creation of global markets. The process by which this slow but decisive transformation has occurred and is stills evolving, commonly referred to as globalization, has accelerated in the past twenty years. Globalization is hardly a new concept. However, the speed with which globalism has impacted the world has been due to technology. Certainly the internet and mobile phone technology, microchips, and some other key technologies have greatly accelerated globalization.

WHY GLOBALIZATION?

The interdependence of national economies and, consequently, the expansion of business activities across the world have increased over time. Two commonly held theories explain the motivation for global business activities and the interdependence of nations. It is well understood that factors of production such as labor, capital, land, and technology are not equally endowed by all nations. Some nations have abundant labor resources and others ample capital. In addition, because of costs or other considerations, there may be no mobility in the factors of production. The theory of comparative advantage suggests that business activities among nations expands when countries specialize in the production of those goods or services that they produce relatively more efficiently. By using factors of production that are relatively more efficient and importing goods that maintain low comparative advantage, business activity expands.

Another theory that explains increased business activity is the theory of market imperfections. Since factors of production (for example, labor) are not transferable or are costly to be transferred from one country to another, businesses step in to take advantage of these imperfections and create opportunities. Asymmetric access to these imperfect markets creates opportunities for business activities to expand across the globe to take advantage of these market imperfections.

SHIFTING BUSINESS ENVIRONMENT IN MARKETS AND PRODUCTION

While these theories provide an intellectual foundation for explaining globalization, the shift toward a more globally interdependent world impacts businesses in two ways. First, it makes markets global, and second it makes production of goods and services global. The globalization of markets and production makes the application of the 5-elements framework more challenging due to pressures to adapt to a changing global environment, thus shifting corporate priorities or objectives.

The globalization of markets refers to the merging of distinct and separate national markets for products and/or services into one huge global marketplace. Falling barriers to cross-border trade have made it easier to sell internationally. It has been argued for some time that the tastes and preferences of consumers in different nations are beginning to converge on some global norm, thereby helping to create a global market. Consumer products such as Citigroup credit cards, Coca-Cola soft drinks, video games, McDonald's hamburgers, Starbucks coffee, IKEA furniture, and Apple iPhones are frequently held up as prototypical examples of this trend. The firms that produce these products are more than just benefactors of this trend; they are also facilitators of it. By offering the same basic product worldwide, they help create a global market.

The globalization of production refers to the sourcing of goods and services from locations around the globe to take advantage of national differences in the cost and quality of factors of production (for example, labor, energy, land, and capital). By doing this, companies hope to lower their overall cost structures or improve the quality or functionality of their product offerings, thereby allowing them to compete more effectively. Early outsourcing efforts were primarily confined to manufacturing activities, such as those undertaken by Boeing, Apple, and Vizio. Increasingly, however, companies are taking advantage of modern communications technology, particularly the internet, to outsource service activities to low-cost producers in other nations. Many software companies, including IBM and Microsoft, now use Indian and Chinese engineers to perform specific functions on software designed in the United States. For example, the time difference allows Indian engineers to run debugging tests on software written in the United States when US engineers sleep, transmitting the corrected code back to the United States to be ready for US engineers to work on the following day. Dispersing value-creation activities in this way can compress the time and lower the costs required to develop new software programs.

THE DRIVERS FOR GLOBALIZATION

Drivers for globalization and contributing factors for the process of interdependence and integration of markets and production include:

1. *Declining trade and investment barriers.* Following WWII, advanced economies committed themselves to reducing barriers to the free flow of goods, services, and capital among nations.[112] Agreements under the General Agreement on Tariffs and Trade (GATT) and subsequent work by the World Trade Organization (WTO), followed by several other regional agreements, reduced substantially the tariffs of products and traded goods. In addition, restrictions on mobility of capital and foreign direct investments were removed, resulting in a more favorable investment environment.[113]

2. *Changing technology.* Advances in telecommunications, the internet, and transportation technology revolutionized business activities and transformed business practices, making it more cost-efficient

---

[112] J. A. Frankel. "Globalization of the Economy," National Bureau of Economic Research working paper no. 7858, 2000.

[113] United Nations. *World Investment Report,* 2014.

to source products from countries with lower costs of labor and raw material.

3. *Changing composition of global trade.* As the United States dominated international trade and foreign direct investments in the 1960s, almost half the world was not exposed to Western products until the fall of communism in the USSR. In 1960s, the United States, with a prosperous corporate sector, accounted for 38 percent of the world output measured by gross domestic product (GDP), while in the 2019 declined to 24 percent.[114]

4. *Changing world order and the openness of politics and democracy.* The opening of China and the fall of communism from 1960 to 2013 made China's share of world output increase from a trivial amount to 12.2 percent, making it the world's second-largest economy. Other countries that markedly increased their share of world output included Japan, Thailand, Malaysia, Taiwan, Brazil, and South Korea. As emerging economies such as those of China, India, Russia, and Brazil continue to grow, a further relative decline in the share of world output and world exports accounted for by the United States and other long-established developed nations seems likely. The World Bank has estimated that today's developing nations may account for more than 60 percent of world economic activity by 2025, while today's rich nations, which currently account for more than 55 percent of world economic activity, may account for only about 38 percent.[115] Forecasts are not always correct, but these suggest that a shift in the economic geography of the world is now under way, although the magnitude of that shift is not totally evident. For international businesses, the implications of this changing economic geography are clear: Many of tomorrow's economic opportunities may be found in the developing nations of the world, and many of tomorrow's most capable competitors will probably also emerge from these regions.

5. *Changing nature of business activity and the rise of firms with global exposure.* Advances in the internet have changed business activity

---

[114] US Department of Commerce, *Bureau of Economic Analysis Report,* 2021
[115] World Bank, *Global Economic Perspectives,* January 2021.

as many traditional businesses experienced digital transformation and offered services across the world. While many multinational firms continue to thrive, small and medium companies became more exposed, not to local or regional opportunities, but global ones for sourcing and sales. One consequence of this trend has been the emergence of many small firms that prosper in the global environment as their business models are adaptable to changing demands and costs across the globe.

BENEFITS FROM GLOBALIZATION

For businesses, the globalization process has produced tremendous opportunities. Firms can expand their revenues by selling around the world and/or reduce their costs by producing in nations where key inputs, including labor, are cheap. The global expansion of enterprises has been facilitated by favorable political and economic trends. Since the collapse of communism a quarter of a century ago, the pendulum of public policy in nation after nation has swung toward the free-market end of the economic spectrum. Regulatory and administrative barriers to doing business in foreign nations have been reduced. Those nations have often transformed their economies, privatized state-owned enterprises, deregulated markets, increased competition, and welcomed investments by foreign businesses. This has allowed businesses, both large and small, from both advanced nations and developing nations, to expand internationally.

The context within which we can explore the benefits and adverse consequences of globalization is based on broad cycles of politics, society, culture, and business. We have always had the forces of globalization in business and economic activity.

As mentioned earlier in the book, the latest phase of globalization was kicked off by President Ronald Reagan and Prime Minister Margaret Thatcher as political, societal, and cultural shifts took place during their times. It was accelerated by major technological changes that have taken place since early 1980s, lasting until the second decade of the twenty-first century. Globalization allowed the movement of virtually everything: movement of financial transactions, movement of intellectual property, movement of people, movement of goods and services. It triggered a complete change in supply systems. It ushered in a labor arbitrage, where jobs could be moved to other countries that had lower wage rates, and the supply change was sourced there with the lower labor cost. The 1992 European integration and the creation of the euro also helped to accelerate globalization in what appeared to be a European experiment in unifying cultures, while allowing for mobility of capital and labor and no restrictions in establishing cross-European business enterprises. Overall, not only in Europe but across the globe, this openness brought about significant productivity improvements and a significant improvement in global living standards. Over that last forty years, we have seen more people come out of the ranks of poverty than in any other time in the history of the world. This is the good news.

DE-GLOBALIZATION: IS IT REAL?[116] THE NEW CONTEXT OF BUSINESS ACTIVITIES

Is the shift toward a more integrated and interdependent global word a good thing? In the 1990s, many influential economists, academics, politicians, and business leaders seemed to think so. Globalization stimulates economic growth, raises the incomes of consumers, and helps to create jobs in all countries that choose to participate in the global economy.[117] However, despite enormous benefits, mostly observed in the post-WWII till the late 1980s period, there is a rising tide of opposition to globalization. In fact, recent developments cast doubt on the importance of globalization and question the benefits associated with open markets and free trade. While academic research has documented benefits from free trade, some skeptics have recently argued that globalization has gone too far, causing dislocation of jobs, thereby amplifying inequality and creating vulnerabilities in the global financial system. In response, it is proposed that the fast pace of interdependence should be reversed to preserve employment, improve national prosperity, and stimulate demand through investing in local, not global, business opportunities.

---

[116] "De-Globalization: Is it Real?" Conference organized by the Global Interdependence Center (GIC) and LeBow College of Business, Drexel University, April 21, 2017. Conference presentation materials appear on the web site of GIC.

[117] Jagdish Bhagwati. *In Defense of Globalization* (Oxford: Oxford University Press, 2004).

More specifically, the criticisms include the following:

1. The fear that globalization is forever changing the world in a negative way and trade seems to be unfair among countries, and companies create excessive profits by taking advantage of cross-country differences in labor wages.

2. In developed countries, labor leaders always argue about the loss of good-paying jobs to low-wage countries. The wage gap between developed and developing countries motivates businesses to produce in countries with lower wage costs.[118]

3. Globalization encourages "immoral" CEOs to relocate manufacturing facilities offshore to countries that lack adequate regulations to protect labor and the environment.[119]

4. Globalization has caused national governments to lose economic power to multinational companies and transnational organizations such as the European Union, WTO, and the United Nations. The loss of national sovereignty is of concern to democratic institutions of many countries, as decision-making is shifting from elected governments to unelected bureaucrats.

5. Investment flows tend to move to emerging countries with large wage gaps relative to developing countries. Flows help build manufacturing facilities or specialized services only to be reversed when products become uncompetitive. Investment outflows from emerging countries generate unfavorable economic conditions and lead to crises and employment problems for those countries.

6. Globalization has created enormous imbalances in developed and emerging countries' trade balance of payments. Large imbalances create vulnerabilities for the global financial system that may lead to global currency crises.

---

[118] Supporters of globalization point out that globalization, due to comparative advantage, will result in countries specializing in the production of those goods that they can produce most efficiently, while importing goods that they cannot produce as efficiently. Despite some job dislocation, the whole economy is better off with globalization.

[119] Academic studies show this is temporary and that economic progress yields tougher environmental regulations and stricter labor standards. In general, as countries get richer with more business activity, they enact tougher environmental and labor regulations.

These criticisms led anti-globalization advocates to suggest that countries should reexamine their trade policies by promoting domestic production in key economic sectors to preserve jobs.

The Impact of Globalization on Workers

There are concerns over low wages in poor countries and wage suppression or loss of jobs in developed countries. According to the theory of comparative advantage, trade should help poor countries to the extent there is an abundance of labor in those countries. Trade should help the purchasing power of all workers, and if anyone is hurt, it is the workers in labor-scarce countries. The low wages in export sectors of poor countries are higher than they would be without the export-oriented manufacturing, and although the situation of these workers may be more visible than before, that does not make it worse. Practically, the policy issue is whether labor standards should be part of trade pacts. Although such standards may act in ways similar to a domestic minimum wage, developing countries fear that such standards would be used as a protectionist tool. A case study on the 2013 collapse of a garment factory in Bangladesh highlights this tension. The Bangladeshi garment industry would not be globally competitive if it had to raise labor standards to rich-country standards. Bangladeshi garment workers, though very poorly paid by rich-country standards, earn more than workers in non-export sectors. A potential solution would be for consumers in rich countries to pay more for goods certified to have been produced under improved labor standards, thereby giving producers in poor countries both the means and the incentives to improve labor standards.

The Impact of Globalization on the Environment

There are concerns that export manufacturing in developing countries is bad for the environment. Many advocate that any trade negotiations should involve discussions and agreements on environmental standards. Others advocate that while essential, environmental standards should not destroy the export manufacturing sector of developing countries by making business activity costly due to added regulations. In general, production and consumption can cause environmental damage. However, as a country's GDP per capita grows, the environmental damage done first grows and then eventually declines as the country becomes prosperous enough to initiate measures to protect the environment. As business activity through trade lifts incomes of some countries, it may be bad for the environment, but by making poor countries richer, it is an otherwise good thing.

In practice, the concern is about the existence of "pollution havens"; that is, countries with low environmental standards that attract "dirty" industries. While many speculate that China and a few other Asian countries encourage pollution, there is relatively little evidence of this phenomenon, and dirty industries may be localized. However, there may be business activities that carry international consequences on pollution levels. An example of pollution that crosses borders is greenhouse gases. In the United States, in an effort to reduce carbon emissions, regulators have imposed carbon tariffs on imports from countries that do not have their own carbon taxes. Proponents argue that such tariffs are necessary to prevent production from shifting to pollution havens and to reduce the overall level of carbon emissions. Opponents argue that these tariffs are simply more protectionism masquerading as environmental regulations.

GLOBALIZATION 2.0: AN ECLECTIC APPROACH

Despite benefits, globalization has been challenged both at the local and regional levels. We are now shifting into a new area in which globalization is an *eclectic*, not a *holistic* approach. Named Globalization 2.0, it allows countries or regions to accept the parts of globalization they like and reject the parts of globalization that they dislike. As globalization has been morphed toward an eclectic preference of nations to conduct business and trade with other international partners, it is hardly a repudiation of the benefits from open trade and global businesses. Instead, it reflects a country's realities from the evolution of business practices and trade experiences with other nations.

Eclectic globalization is the result of (a) changes in the nature of business in the 1990s and beyond, (b) the emergence of trading with countries in close proximity, and (c) the concerns arising from global gaps in wealth. All these issues have brought more attention to the blanketed benefits of globalization.

The Changing Nature of Business

A century ago, more trade was in primary products as nations tended to trade for things that literally could not be grown or found at home. Today the motivations for trade are varied, and the products we trade are increasingly diverse. Despite increased complexity in modern international trade, the fundamental principles explaining trade at the dawn of the global era still apply today. Most of the business activity involves trade in manufactured goods, with agriculture and mineral products making up less than 20 percent of world trade. Developing countries tend to have businesses primarily exporting manufacturing goods and services. The focus of international trade and business activity has been on services as modern information technology has expanded greatly. Examples include technicians located halfway around the world providing reports on OCR scanning, persons staffing a call center, or accountants located in emerging countries. Although service outsourcing represents a small fraction of business activity, steady, gradual expansion and the potential for large increases are an important part of how trade will evolve in the coming decades.

Gravity

An emerging trend in business activity is regionalism, which stems from the economic benefits of countries that tend to conduct businesses with nearby economies. Studies have showed that trade is most cost effective when countries trade with nearby nations, and the volume of trade is proportional to country size. The concept behind these studies is the so-called gravity model as it is similar in form to the physics equation that describes the pull of one body on another as proportional to their size and distance. Gravity, for example, explains the large benefits from collaboration in trade and business activities between the United States, Canada, and Mexico. The logic supporting the gravity model in trade is that consumers in large countries have large incomes to spend on imports; at the same time, large countries produce a large quantity of goods available to sell as exports. This means that between countries, the larger either trade partner is, the larger the volume of trade between them. At the same time, the distance between two trade partners can substitute for the transportation costs that they face and serves as proxy for more intangible aspects of a trading relationship, such as the ease of conduct for companies. This model can be used to estimate the predicted trade and business volume between two or more countries and to look for trade patterns.

The gravity model is also used to demonstrate the importance of national borders in determining trade flows and business activity. According to many estimates, the long border of 5,525 miles between the United States and Canada provides for $1.6 billion in goods crossing the border each day. Other factors such as tariffs, business and trade agreements, and common language can all influence the volume of trade and can be incorporated into the gravity model.

The gravity concept is consistent with current business practices. For example, countries tend to trade and conduct business with nearby economies. Transportation costs and perhaps regional cultural preferences, along with proximity to business partners, make commercial activities and trade preferred relative to far distant countries. In addition, the magnitude of business activity (that is, the volume of sourcing or volume of sales) is proportional to the size of trading counties.

Polarities and Wealth Inequality in America

Despite several positive outcomes from the globalization, there are unfortunately negative consequences with the latest phase in globalization, which has impacted mostly the middle class by weakening its economic prosperity. As globalization has accelerated and marched forward, we have observed polarities where much wealth has been created at the very high end of the income scale, while wealth has increased marginally or not at all for people in middle or lower-middle class. What globalization has done unwittingly is to have weakened the middle class, and this is largely due to many jobs that have gone overseas and/or the automation of production processes as a result of technological changes. Many of the people who have been displaced did not have the skills, and no one has helped them learn the skills to compete for the new jobs that have become available as a result of this rapid change in technology and the inexorable march toward globalization.

These conditions began to unravel probably in the early 2000s, but certainly around the financial crisis in 2008 and 2009, during which we developed a significant bubble in the financial industry with the subprime mortgage crisis. Again, these mortgages were all done for a good reason, which was to give people a chance to acquire a house. For most households, a house is the largest asset they would buy, and at that time, housing prices had at least kept up with inflation, so it was a reasonably good investment in terms of helping people acquire net worth. Nevertheless, this blew up in 2008 and 2009. This episode destroyed much of the wealth that had been created in the middle- and lower-middle classes. It further exacerbated this polarization in income and wealth accumulation. Moreover, we had significant debt that most the Western countries had to assume to get the economy moving again.

One result of these developments is questioning the extent to which this acceleration of globalization really helps broaden society or makes the political divisions and fragmentation of our societies and our cultures even more extreme than they were in the past. In a free society, we have always had liberal and conservative views, but when people lost the moderate middle and globalization hollowed out the middle class, the extreme left and the extreme right became bigger and were able to elect people to government and leadership positions. This has further exacerbated the polarization between the far left and the far right. As a result, these trends have opened the door for regions to emerge once again.

In the 1980s the United States was the unquestioned power after it won the Cold War. However, after the Cold War, the United States observed the emergence of a multipolar world. The rapid emergence of China has had major economic implications that involve mixed outcomes. On one hand, due to labor arbitrage, US citizens have benefited enormously from low-cost products imported from China that have allowed inflation to stay at bay. On the other hand, the United States outsourced the supply chain for products they previously manufactured or produced domestically. As a result, jobs that previously offered households good middle-class wages and high standards of living disappeared.

On the geopolitical front, Russia reconstituted itself as a regional power in the former Soviet Union. At the same time, the United States engaged in multiple wars in the Middle East and elsewhere, and we have observed a power shift in the Middle East with the emergence of Iran and other regional allies.

THE CURRENT STATE OF GLOBALIZATION 2.0

Recent practices in international trade by many nations suggest that the eclectic model to globalization is currently in effect. For example, when China joined the WTO, we thought it would become an active member of the world trading community. Instead, what this country really did was put a mercantilist system in place that really exacerbated the loss of jobs and middle-class income in developed countries, such as the United States. Thus, they really did not adhere to the standards of the WTO. China has used part of the rules of the WTO to its advantage and has ignored others, especially those rules related to intellectual property, which are not in its best interests.

We have also observed a rise of business activity and trade in different regions around the world. South America, China, India, and Southeast Asia have all taken on different roles in globalization. Trade has become more regional and less global. It might be geopolitical similarities, transaction costs, and reduced transportation expenses that motivate trade to be conducted at the regional level, despite the technology that has been introduced and the means of transportation that exists. The regional approach to globalization was not an issue thirty years ago. It is now, as regions increasingly have a bigger leadership role and will eventually determine how globalization moves forward. However, nothing will derail globalization. The supply chains, communication technologies, and financial infrastructures, for example, all are so embedded globally they will not change. What may change is that certain regions will begin to opt out of parts of the globalization model, which will then tend to fragment the way globalization has been practiced the last fifty years. This will impact how we practice capitalism. It will have an impact on the role of our government. And it will certainly have an impact on the interregional conflicts and cooperation on a global basis. Every day, the media shows that the Soviet Union is trying to reach out the parts of the former Soviet Republic and expand its sphere of influence. China, with its "belt and roads" initiative and investment exercises, is influencing Africa to access raw materials. All these are characteristics of Globalization 2.0. It will be different from how we have practiced globalization and capitalism in the last twenty years.

CAPITAL IN THE ERA OF GLOBALIZATION 2.0

The role of capital in economic activity has evolved. In the 1980s, nations had not had enough capital to invest in business, and consequently, the cost of capital was very high. Indeed, there was not enough capital to invest in harnessing, utilizing, and leveraging the accelerating change in the technology base and in improving productivity. As a result, the cost of capital was high. In order to offset these costs, during the expansion in the twentieth century, capital returns were taxed at a much lower level relative to tax levels on individual income, thus providing incentives for wealth accumulation. However, in the 2010s, we had exactly the opposite problem. Due to subprime crisis of 2008 and the intervention of the Federal Reserve and other Central Banks around the world, there was enormous liquidity in the money supply system with inexpensive credit, to the point more money was available to invest than good ideas in which to invest in. In addition, another much larger wave of liquidity was injected through central banks across the world due to COVID-19. The result is that today, we have more capital chasing fewer productive ideas. It is showing up in increased valuations and the cannibalization of companies through, for example, private equity and other private pools of capital. The ultimate outcome is that this is creating tension in our political system as well. As a result of this tension, we may begin to focus on productivity improvements and societal impact to globalization as opposed to just focusing on shareholder returns within capitalism.

GLOBALIZATION 2.0 AND NEW BUSINESS THINKING

All these developments create a whole new way of thinking for business leaders. In the past, leaders were always looking for opportunities to reduce costs and improve profitability by moving work to the lowest possible cost area in the world. Now, however, they must consider the impact on the workers, on the communities, and on the broader society and cultural dimensions of the countries within which these companies operate. Globalization 2.0 may be more regional, as the gravity model has suggested. There may be more conflicts between these regions. We may begin to have the debate and perhaps move away from capitalism, a system dedicated to shareholder returns. Companies and CEOs may begin to focus discussions on the contributions of other constituents, not just shareholders, as they make decisions.

GLOBALIZATION 2.0 AND THE BOARD

Perhaps an area where the role of globalization has the most influence is corporate governance. The board of directors represents the interests of shareholders and serves as monitors of management decisions. The board also acts in an advisory role to the CEO on matters related to strategy and operations. The board ratifies distributions to shareholders. Stock returns represent the ultimate, easily observable, and objective measure of performance of the company. As they focused on maximizing shareholders' wealth, anecdotal evidence suggests that many American companies have performed better than their counterparts in other economies. US companies dominate in many fields because they have been tied to very measurable results. The singular focus on stock returns has made many American companies and the US stock markets highly valuable compared to corresponding companies and stock exchanges in Germany, the United Kingdom, and other developed securities market.

Is capitalism as practiced in this way the best model given where we are in the global development of the world? Is this model of capitalism producing the best results? In fact, there are concerns about this model of capitalism as matters related to the environment, sustainability, and growth preoccupy business leaders. Critics of the current model point to issues about climate change and the environment, and advocate that boards develop a framework that incorporates society's concerns. Advocates of the current model point to the ambiguity of goals if objectives other than shareholders' wealth maximization are introduced and the difficulties associated with holding managers accountable for their decisions that cannot be measured objectively.

There are strong arguments on both sides. America's capital markets are the most efficient capital markets in the world. They are the deepest and the most efficient because of the transparency and the focus on shareholder returns. On the other hand, while we have had this tremendous focus on shareholder returns, we have also substantially hollowed out the middle class. This has profound implications and has led to the polarization of our political system. It seems that the middle ground in the United States is disappearing. Historically, the middle class was huge and served as the ballast in the ship, keeping it from lurching left or right.

One critical question is what the role of capital markets is and what role companies within capital markets play for the betterment of society. At the extreme, some would argue whether they should have a role at all. However, it is not clear cut. There is no black or white. It is all gray; it is all nuanced. And this is why boards are going to have to grapple with these issues in the future. However, companies cannot operate in total isolation from the cultures and the societies within which they exist. Also, as societal norms change, companies will have to adapt, not the other way around. In addition, for the last twenty years, companies have acted more in isolation to the environments in which they work. It seems the pendulum is going to begin to shift a little bit more to the middle. Indeed, this is controversial. At the height of capitalism, most of the companies were in the United States, most of the employees were in the United States, and they headquartered themselves in another tax jurisdiction to be outside the rules and regulations in the US tax regime. In other words, the individual is an entity unto himself or herself because companies are organisms. They are living, breathing organisms. Thus, when the organism takes itself so far outside the body, something is going to happen. Either the body is going to miss it, and it does not do as well, or if the individual isolates himself or herself so far, the person/she may not be able to exist without being inside the body. This is the future debate with mostly unknown consequences; it will be more nuanced with more shades of calibration.

GLOBALIZATION AND ENVIRONMENTAL, SOCIAL, AND GOVERNANCE PRINCIPLES[120]

For many, the term "ESG" (environmental, social, and governance) brings to mind environmental and sustainability issues such as climate change and resource scarcity. These are elements of ESG, but in practice, the term means much more as it covers social issues such as a company's labor practices, talent management, product safety, and data security. It covers governance matters, such as board diversity, executive pay, and business ethics. These are topics that can materially impact a company's long-term value.

The genesis of ESG is traced in August 2019, when nearly 200 CEOs from the Business Roundtable, including the leaders of some of the US's largest companies, indicated a shift in how they defined the purpose of corporations in society. In a statement that was included as part of the *Principles in Corporate Governance*, the Business Roundtable argued that companies should no longer seek to advance only the interests of shareholders. Instead, corporations should consider a broader stakeholder approach that includes the interests of employees, customers, suppliers, and the communities in which they work.

The Business Roundtable has devised several guidelines for boards to take into consideration in building relationships with stakeholders and a mandate to adhere to the ESG principles. It is expected that companies should be supportive of the communities in which they do business, to be responsible stewards of the environment, and to consider sustainability as one of the key issues in operating their businesses. Directors play a key role in helping bring ESG issues into focus for the company and thinking about the risks and opportunities that these issues pose.

With respect to citizenship, companies should strive to be good citizens of the local, national, and international communities in which they do business, to be responsible stewards of the environment, and to consider other relevant sustainability issues in operating their businesses. Failure to meet these obligations can result in damage to the company, both in immediate economic terms and in its longer-term reputation. Because sustainability

---

[120] The section is based on "Principles of Corporate Governance," *Business Roundtable*, 2016, pp 26–27.

issues affect so many aspects of a company's business, from financial performance to risk management, incorporating sustainability into the firm in a meaningful way is integral to a company's long-term viability.

With respect to community service, a company should strive to be a good citizen by contributing to the communities in which it operates. Being a good citizen includes getting involved with those communities; encouraging company directors, managers, and employees to form relationships with those communities; donating time to causes of importance to local communities; and making charitable contributions.

With respect to sustainability, a company should conduct its business with appreciation for environmental, health, safety, and other sustainability issues relevant to the company's operations. The board should be cognizant of developments relating to economic, social, and environmental sustainability issues, and should understand which issues are most important to the company's business and to its shareholders.

The ESG Debate in the Boardroom

For an agenda that includes ESG principles, the board of directors should address any potential risks associated with ESG, ascertain that ESG is backed into long-term strategy, develop a set of matrices to assess efforts for implementing ESG initiatives, facilitate information disclosures about ESG outcomes to shareholders, and ensure the transparency of measures required for the implementation of ESG.

ESG principles were well published, and the popular press covered in considerable details the new shift in corporate governance. At the same time, institutional investors have put a strong focus on ESG issues in recent years. They are increasingly looking for reporting from companies on how they take material ESG-related risks into account and what sustainability efforts they are undertaking. They also encourage companies to take a long-term approach to thinking about how the company will thrive in a changing world that involves systematic engagement with a diverse group of stakeholders, not just shareholders. However, recent surveys of corporate directors suggest that the concept of ESG perhaps is exaggerated.

In a survey of 710 corporate directors conducted by PwC in 2019,[121] while many business leaders offered their support for this stakeholder-centric approach, directors were mixed. Only 58 percent agreed that companies should prioritize a broader group of stakeholders when making company decisions. When it came to the idea of corporations having a social purpose, however, directors were very supportive. Almost 73 percent of the directors who were surveyed agreed that companies should have a social purpose, and 83 percent believed that a social purpose and company profitability were not mutually exclusive.

Many would have thought that boards of directors are very responsive to the expectations of investors, especially institutional investors, when it comes to ESG initiatives. Yet results of the 2019 PwC's survey of boards of directors showed that directors believed that the investor focus on ESG was excessive and overblown, and that investors were giving too much time and focus to issues such as board diversity, environmental or sustainability issues, and corporate responsibility. As with the pushback against diversity mandates, this may in part be directors' desires to feel that they were in control of their own boardrooms rather than letting external factors set their agendas. Almost 56 percent of directors believed that investors' focus on environmental and sustainability issues was excessive, and 63 percent of directors surveyed thought that investors' emphasis on board gender diversity was overblown. One area where directors thought investors' attention was appropriate was their focus on long-term stock performance. Seventy-five percent of directors agreed that investors were giving it the right amount of attention.

Even if shareholders continue to emphasize the importance of ESG issues, directors are less focused on the topic. Out of 660 responses, only 57 percent of directors confirmed that ESG is a part of their risk management discussions, despite the calls from investors to think of ESG in terms of risks and opportunities.[122] In addition, only 50 percent of the directors agreed that the board had a strong understanding of ESG issues, that ESG was important to the company's shareholders, and that ESG issues were linked to the company's strategy. With these views, it is not surprising that only 34 percent

---

[121] PwC. *Annual Corporate Directors Survey,* October 2019.

[122] PwC. *Annual Corporate Directors Survey,* October 2019, pp. 19–20.

affirmed that ESG was regularly a part of the board's agenda. However, as ESG issues continue to grow in importance for investors, it falls to board leadership to ensure that the topic and related risks and opportunities are given enough attention in the boardroom. One important area is the role of specific environmental and social issues in the EFG framework in strategy formulation. Surprisingly, only 26 percent of the directors agreed that issues such as health care, resource scarcity, and human rights should be considered when developing company strategy.

Considering the recent survey responses from the boards of directors, it seems directors believe the ESG agenda is overstated in its significance, despite it is part of the dialogue. In particular, the directors appear to be lukewarm on a stakeholder approach to governance, and they believe that the ESG agenda fails to find full support in the boardroom and in becoming a valuable input in strategy formulation. All these findings do not, by any means, suggest that the ESG issues will disappear. Given the state of evolution of these issues, it seems that it will take a longer time for ESG issues to be central to discussions in corporate governance. From the investors' perspectives, however, we see more acceptance of ESG, with investments being made in companies that adhere to ESG principles. We see investments made in companies that are decarbonizing. Thus, this is an entirely different environment in which business CEOs have to operate, a different environment within which they have to position their companies so that they can continue to thrive. In essence, it is creating a new investment model.

MORE TURBULENCE

Issues of health due to the pandemic and race will fundamentally change the equation under which we have been working for the last forty years, just as Iran seeking nuclear power has changed the balance of power in the Middle East. Demographic changes and how Asian and European populations are rapidly aging, regional conflicts, and globalization will be impacted as we move into this next era. Nevertheless, now we are beginning to see the climate change. In our view it will affect capitalism and private investments. It is going to impact how governments must respond to protect their countries and their citizens.

We have been talking about pandemics for more than thirty years. But now, with globalization, the transmissions of pandemics spread almost instantaneously on a scale that has been unprecedented. Undoubtedly, we are not geared to be able to manage this because pandemics are largely managed within the country; they are not managed globally. As a result, we have seen globally many different responses to the 2020 COVID pandemic. Some have worked much better than others.

SUMMARY

In today's world, nations collaborate and compete. Business activity follows this model, and over time, the law of comparative advantage has made countries specialize in business activities in which they exhibit a relative advantage over other nations. However, in today's environment, countries want to do what is in their best interests globally, but only if it makes sense for them regionally. Then they only want to do it regionally. In summary, Globalization 2.0 has created polarities. Thus it is going to be a very difficult model to manage because we will wind up with very few agreements as to what we ought to act on globally.

Though the benefits of trade have likely been larger than the costs, these costs have been concentrated within specific industries and within certain communities. Industries tend to be geographically concentrated, taking advantage of external economies of scale, so when an industry collapses due to trade, the losses are heavily concentrated within certain communities. These losses have been magnified by a reluctance of US workers to move away from economically depressed regions. These concentrated losses from trade may help to explain the recent success of protectionist political movements.

CHAPTER TEN

Leadership in Turbulent Times

COMPLEXITY IN DECISIONS

Decisions at the top of the organization represent complex choices about corporate goals and the means to achieve them, choices that outline the strategic direction of the organization. Indeed, strategy is the stream of decisions that over time reveal management's goals for the corporation and the means they choose to achieve them. These choices define the rate at which companies may grow in sales and profits. They determine how earnings will be divided between dividends for shareholders and funds to be retained for future internal investments. They define the products and markets in which the company will compete, whether and how to enter new business domestically, how much to spend on research and development, whether and how to expand internationally, and whether to grow and diversify through acquisitions.

Decisions are especially complex when the organization is exposed to a turbulent business environment. Crisis-driven or even anticipatory changes because of a turbulent environment intensify complexity in decision-making. However, changes create new opportunities for corporate growth and value, but at the same time, they challenge the core competences of any company as they exposure the firm to vulnerabilities and competitive threats.

If addressed effectively, these challenges produce innovations and renewed focus on the firm's focus.

Obviously, decisions at the top have a major impact not only on the company itself and the industry within which it operates but also on the local, regional, and many times national economies. This is especially true when these firms are large and mature. In 2019, Fortune 500 firms represented two thirds of the US GDP, generated $12 trillion in revenues, had $19 trillion in market value, and employed 29 million people.[123] Management decisions for these big firms not only impact the customer base but also shape the well-being of the communities within which they operate. Inevitably, executive decisions that involve complex choices and trade-offs about strategy, investments, and financing influence the economy at the local and often national levels.

While these decisions sometimes are considered mysterious and in extreme circumstances are attributed to charismatic leadership or pure luck, we have advocated a process for undertaking these decisions that, when applied, creates conditions for better outcomes and success. The process involves a decision-making model that consists of five components: (a) strategy, (b) asset deployment, (c) the financial model, (d) leadership, and (e) culture, which includes a system for compensation and components of measurement. The strategy element aims in identifying how a company is positioned in its industry and whether it has a favorable presence in promising subsectors within its industry. The asset deployment element evaluates whether a company has requisite assets and partnerships to execute on its strategy and if there is a need to divest, acquire, or restructure current assets, including intellectual property and proprietary assets. The financial element of the model focuses on aligning the business activities with revenues to improve the quality of earnings and requires a well-communicated and transparent financial model as well as an approach to capital allocation. The leadership element of the model seeks to ensure that there is a capable management team in place with a breadth and depth of motivated senior executives capable of leading the company. Finally, the culture element of the model assesses the extent to which management and compensation systems provide needed incentives to continuously improve key performance metrics consistent with

---

[123] www.Fortune.com/fortune500/2019

business and financial goals while an open and transparent culture embraces ethical business practices.

The model we have advocated helps business leaders undertake complex decisions in an organized fashion. The process in making these decisions has been tested in practice over a long period in several companies with successful outcomes. The process, however, is not free of constraints. Many believe that these constraints are based on the discipline of capital markets as they think that ultimately executives maximize shareholders' wealth. Others contend that an executive's choices are constrained by short-term orientation as corporate leadership is transitory. However, the realities as we understand them from the many years of executive positions in companies and in studying business management reveal that, contrary to popular myths, business leaders respond also to the needs arising from societal changes. These external societal changes have been a constant reminder of the evolution of our societies and their adaptability to technological and environmental changes. These changes reflect normality in a turbulent business environment. Executives are committed to enhancement of corporate wealth and deeply care about improving value by creating conditions for competitive advantage to ensure the firm's continuity and survival. Indirectly this value flows to society and measurably improves the world. What is not clear is how markets and institutional investors price in the capital markets corporate social responsibility, and to what extent business executives making these decisions are, "Doing good by doing well."

LEADERSHIP IN A NEW ERA

Managing a firm requires attention to an ever-changing environment. The world we now live in is changing as we experience turbulence and uncertainty that place greater demands on leaders to manage the firm. Business leaders face pressures to navigate the internal and external affairs of the firm through the complexities of a changing world and often balance conflicting actions internal to the organization. Corporate purpose is now the focus of a fundamental and heated debate, with rapidly growing support for the proposition that corporations should improve the welfare of all constituencies they serve, not just the welfare of shareholders. While there are plenty of examples that make the work of business leaders increasingly complex, we point to at least three recent developments that provide challenges to executives in navigating the difficulties ahead. First, even prior to the global financial crisis of 2008, the Anglo-American capitalist system has been challenged in terms of its contributions to society. Second, a new era of protectionism has provided a healthy debate on the benefits arising from globalization and free trade. Third, the recent COVID-19 pandemic, which practically shut down global economic activity, despite its devastating disruptions offers opportunities for innovation while challenging traditional business models. These three developments have created turbulence and added complexity in decision-making. There is a healthy debate about the future of capitalism, the role of corporations in advancing corporate social responsibility, and the role of globalization in improving social welfare.

In the segments that follow we will turn our attention to discussions about (a) stakeholder capitalism as an alternative to Anglo-American capitalist system, and the role of ESG in advancing the debate for boards and executives to address social corporate responsibility and sustainability; (b) the pressing issues of inequality partially due to globalization that require the attention of business leaders; (c) the future of business leadership when executives operate in a constantly turbulent environment with crises or even anticipatory changes and posit how our methodology helps advance the quest for value and successful outcomes. Finally the Appendix of this chapter we address the impact on businesses of the epic 2020 COVID-19 pandemic and implications to decision making and leadership.

DOES THE ANGLO-AMERICAN CAPITALIST SYSTEM REQUIRE AN ADJUSTMENT?

The Anglo-American system of governance is based on the philosophy that a firm's objective should follow the rule to maximize the wealth of shareholders, which is translated in practical terms to maximizing the stock price of a publicly traded firm. By maximizing the financial returns to shareholders, as measured by capital gains and dividend distributions, the Anglo-American model compensates for the risks assumed by all capital providers. Indirectly employees, the government, and local communities benefit from the firm's activities, but this comes as a consequence and an afterthought of share-holder maximization. The Anglo-American model of capitalism has been adopted since the WWII as the prevailing model for managing corporations. Without doubt, capital mobility and free markets have been a positive social force by advancing economic growth across the globe. This in turn has brought dramatic advances in health, longevity, and general prosperity around the world.

In addition, two circumstances propel the success of the Anglo-American model. First, as many countries after the fall of communism privatized companies, a shareholders' wealth maximization (SWM) model was required to attract international capital and technology from foreign investors. Second, around the world, shareholder-based multinational firms have increasingly dominated their global industry segments, and their success attracts more success. Funding continuous expansion, equity capital raised from various countries, not just the United States, these multinationals globalized the message of shareholders' wealth maximization as the ultimate goal for capitalism.

The SWM model embraced by academics assumes as a universal truth that the stock market is efficient and that share prices always correctly capture all expectations about returns and risks as perceived by investors. Absent of costs, efficient markets quickly incorporate information into share price. In turn, stock returns make capital to be allocated efficiently in an economy to support growth and development needs of society.

In addition, the SWM model treats risk as the probability of varying returns that the firm's share brings to a well-diversified portfolio. From the supplier of capital perspective, the investor, risks associated with the management of a company—like business risk, financial risk, and operating risk—all could be diversified to reduce idiosyncratic risk that is risk specific to a company. This approach, it has been argued, tends to be opportunistic and only focuses on reducing the risk to providers of capital while maximizing returns. Executives should not be concerned with the management of the risk of the shares of the firm they manage. That is unsystematic risk unless it increases the probability of bankruptcy. Rather, they should focus on maximizing the distributions to shareholders and undertake actions to maximize the price of the shares.

Anglo-American capitalism promotes the idea that businesses serve primarily the interests of the supplier of capital, the investors, who select professional managers to maximize returns to capital. There are at least three complications with the SWM model. First, constituencies of the company, such as employees, customers, and the community at large, are secondary to the returns obtained by shareholders. The pecking order of significance is the capital that provides the resources for the launch and continuation of business activity. However, as it has become apparent in the last two decades with the subprime crisis and the pandemic, other constituencies are important as well. The second complication with the SWM model is that managers as agents of investors/shareholders often undertake decisions to improve their personal welfare by consuming perks on the job, approve less-risky projects with low returns to avoid explaining possible failures from implementing high-risk high-return investments, and usually make decisions to ensure their personal successes since they hold superior information relative to outside shareholders. These well-documented costs, called agency costs, in the modern corporation have been alleviated with an incentive compensation plan for executives and other mechanisms that align the interests of shareholders and managers.

Yet, the third complication with the SWM model is based on the horizon of decision-making. In the past, short-term focus on decision-making in an effort to maximize returns has created distorted management incentives and the pressure for continuous growth in earnings and returns to meet inflated shareholders expectations. These conditions resulted in several companies undertaking risky, descriptive, and sometimes dishonest practices that ultimately led to their demise. Companies like Enron, Tyco, Health South and WorldCom in the 1990s, by adopting these practices, at the end destroyed shareholders' wealth and became examples to be avoided. The disruptive forces of short-term focus on the part of the management have been labeled as "impatient" capitalism. This point of debate is also sometimes referred to as the firm's investment horizon in reference to how long it takes the firm's actions, investments, and operations to result in earnings. The contrast to impatient capitalism is patient capitalism, which focuses on long-term returns.

With the deepening of the capital markets in the United States and ascent of institutional investors, the SWM was further embraced until skepticism started settling in with the subprime crisis of 2008 and the impact of the 2020 pandemic on the population. These two recent crises revealed weaknesses of the system in addressing inequality and equity among people when the impact has been asymmetric across the population and the subsequent economic recovery. As a result, a healthy debate among corporate executives, policy makers, and institutions and organizations representing diverse constituencies currently has offered consideration of two alternatives to shareholder capitalism: stakeholder capitalism and the ESG movement. While this debate is far from over, executives are required to navigate through often conflicting views and make decisions to improve value.

Stakeholder Capitalism

As an alternative to the Anglo-American model, *stakeholder capitalism* has been advanced. According to stakeholder capitalism, corporate leaders should focus on the well-being of stakeholders, not just of shareholders. The Business Roundtable issued a statement that was presented by its authors and characterized by many commentators as a major milestone: "We share a fundamental commitment to all of our stakeholders. We commit to deliver value to all of them, for the future success of our companies, our communities and our country."[124] This statement was described as a major departure from the 1997 report of the Business Roundtable that embraced shareholder importance. The statement was joined by 188 CEOs leading companies with aggregate capitalization exceeding $13 trillion and representing over a third of total capitalizations in the US equity markets. In addition, the CEO of BlackRock, the world's largest asset manager, issued a letter to all CEOs urging them to be, "committed to embracing purpose and serving all stakeholders." Finally, in a clear effort to promote stakeholder's capitalism, in January 2020, the World Economic Forum in Davos published a manifesto urging companies to move from the traditional model of shareholder capitalism to the model of stakeholder capitalism.[125]

---

[124] The Business Roundtable declaration provides ambiguity for decision-making based on the follow-up statement, "while we acknowledge that different stakeholders may have competing interests in the short term, it is important to recognize that the interests of all stakeholders are inseparable in the long term."

[125] The Business Roundtable statement, while accepted by many executives, has been criticized as being vague, overlooking trade-offs in considering the interests of a diverse group of constituencies, and lacking tangible guidance for "optimum" decision-making.

Stakeholders' capitalism is hardly a new idea. It is based on the assertion that businesses should seek to serve the interests of consumers, suppliers, workers, and society, as well as shareholders.[126] What made it reappear in the late 2010 was a widespread distrust for business as usual, as several surveys and elections have shown, especially after the global financial crisis of 2008. Stakeholder capitalism serves as a bridge between businesses and the communities of which they are a part. The interdependence and interconnectedness of business and society is obvious.

The notion of interdependence of all constituencies is especially strong in continental European and Japanese markets, which are characterized by a philosophy that all of a corporation's stakeholders should be considered, and the objective should be to maximize corporate wealth. Thus, a firm should treat shareholders on par with other corporate stakeholders, such as management, labor, the local community, suppliers, creditors, and even the government. The goal is to earn as much as possible in the long run but to retain enough to increase the corporate wealth for the benefit of all.

The stakeholder capitalism model is agnostic about the efficiency of the markets since the firm's financial goals are not exclusively shareholder-oriented because they are constrained by the other stakeholders. In this model it is assumed that long-term loyal shareholders, often controlling shareholders, influence corporate strategy rather than the transient portfolio investor. Unlike the Anglo-American model, the stakeholder capitalism model advocates that the operating risk of a firm does count. It is a specific corporate objective to generate growth earnings and dividends over the long run with as much certainty as possible given the firm's mission statement and goals. Risk measurement is based more on product market variability than on short-term variation in earnings and share prices. Regardless of these modifications, the stakeholders model has its own flaw. Trying to meet the desires of multiple stakeholders leaves management without a clear signal about trade-offs. Instead, management should influence these trade-offs through complex disclosures. Instead of

---

[126] The idea for stakeholder capitalism is hardly new. Milton S. Hershey advocated in late 1880s that "business is a matter of human service," while Adam Smith noted in *The Theory of Moral Sentiments* that the individual is, "sensible too that his own interest is connected with the prosperity of society, and that the happiness, perhaps the preservation of his existence, depends on its preservation."

a single goal, there are multiple goals that may be measured by scorecard or related mechanisms.

It is widely recognized that companies are unlikely to be successful if they treat stakeholders badly and without any consideration of their input in the decision-making process. In 2006 the UK Companies Act urged corporate leaders to pay close attention to how stakeholder factors affect long-term value maximization.[127] This suggests that the stakeholder capitalism idea is mostly based on the consideration of stakeholders' interest as a means to the end of shareholder value maximization, not a decision-making rule. Supporters of stakeholders' capitalism have generally avoided providing a methodology or criteria for aggregating the interests of diverse constituencies in an organization. Nor have they provided guidance for decision-making. Absent of concrete steps in implementing stakeholders' capitalism, executives and boards are left at their own discretion to implement a decision-making framework to address diverse interests of the constituency.

Stakeholder capitalism is not free of criticisms.[128] It has been argued that it is a PR move for CEOs that allows them to avoid unfavorable laws and regulations. Incentives, such as cash and equity bonuses, come from applying the SWM approach and increasing the company's stock value. By advocating the idea of protecting the interests of stakeholders, especially when the stakeholders themselves are not well defined, CEOs continue to benefit shareholders while pretending to participate in a new approach in leading corporations. Therefore, CEOs have been backed into a corner, on one hand maximizing stock prices using the SWM model and on the other hand, making statements consistent with moral norms. In the end, customers and shareholders alike desire a financially strong company with the best products and services in the market. Stakeholder capitalism, in addition to its ambiguous recommendations for decision-making, carries costs to both the stakeholders and the company. The framework should, therefore, be rejected by anyone who cares about either stakeholders or shareholders.

---

[127] The UK law advocates the concept of "enlightened shareholder value," which is a form of corporate social responsibility.

[128] The most comprehensive review of the arguments against the corporate stakeholder's model appears in "The Illusory Promise of Stakeholders Governance" by L. Bebchuk and R. Tallarita, published by *Cornell Law Review*, vol. 106, December 2020, pp. 91–178.

The ESG Movement

Another area that requires the attention of business leaders and corporate boards is the heated debate about ESG, with rapidly growing support for the proposition that corporations should improve broad social and environmental conditions. Primarily raised by institutional investors in the late 1990s, the ESG framework examines how management actions may impact the environment (for example, carbon emissions), the society (for example, employee satisfaction, employee rights), and governance (board structure, business ethics). The framework was developed based on the notion that institutional investors act as agents on behalf of investors who care for long-term value and, at the same time, believe in the sustainable long-term impacts of their investments in the environment. Through their savings and pension plans, shareholders/investors want to invest their capital, not just to maximize returns, but to have a lasting and sustainable impact over the long-term. After the Enron scandal and the subprime crisis of 2008, the development of prudent regulation, disclosures, and stewardship guidelines all contributed to adopting ESG criteria as part of active investment management practices. These practices, while informal at the beginning, now have been articulated in professional organizations and advocate that managers should, "Do good," and at the same time, "Do well," for their shareholders.

Responding to pressures by institutional investors, many executives and organizations like the CEO Roundtable have recognized that the value created by companies is delivered to society, not exclusively with the infusion of capital by shareholders, but it is created though joint efforts among several constituencies, including suppliers, customers, employees, and the communities in which firms operate. Implicitly, executive decisions that impact the firm's ecosystem and its environmental exposure, social practices, and governance issues materially affect corporate value. For example, Volkswagen's 2015 Dieselgate shows how management decisions that involved environmental risks, fraud, and deception destroyed value for shareholders.[129] Taxes and subsidies imposed by government may mitigate negative impact on the environment and provide guidance to managers.

---

[129] Many other examples of negative externalities include the 2001 Enron accounting fraud, the 2010 Deepwater Horizon oil spill, and the 2018 Facebook data privacy scandal.

More specifically, the ESG framework includes qualitative measures across three pillars that involve the interactions of the company with its constituencies. The environmental pillar measures a firm's emissions in the environment, the efficient use of natural resources in the production process, pollution and waste, and design of produces that are eco-friendly.

The social pillar covers the company's efforts to maintain loyal employees by improving safety, health, and training programs; satisfy customers by producing quality products; and being a good citizen to the community that it operates in. The governance pillar includes the adoption of safeguarding shareholder rights, having an effective board with independent directors, and adopting executive compensation plans to ensure accountability, and avoiding fraud and illegal practices.

The ESG framework is still evolving, and its key drivers are mostly qualitative in nature. In fact, there is no consensus among academics or practicing executives on the key measures of ESG and its impact on company value in the long-term. But it is well understood that those issues relate to intangibles that are not reflected in traditional accounting or financial measures of corporate performance. Those who advocate responsible and sustainable investing are mostly concerned with nonfinancial criteria.

The role of institutional investors should be recognized in the ESG movement as they are the largest holders of public companies not only in the United States but worldwide. Institutional investors play key roles in allocating pools of capital across the world and in 2017 controlled more than 40 percent of public equity market capitalizations.[130] In the United States, institutional investors hold around 72 percent of public shares of the US stock market.[131] There is no consensus among institutional investors on the exact list of ESG issues. However, most attention with respect to the environmental dimension is placed on climate change and involves around the idea to assess the cash flow risks of firms' exposures to carbon and the risks associated with climate change. It has been advocated those environmental externalities resulting from the firm's operations (pollution, emissions, and so on) should be addressed with government regulations

---

[130] OECD. "Investment Governance and the Integrations of Environmental, Social and Governance Factors," 2017.

[131] Conference Board, "The 2010 Institutional Investment Report: Trends in Asset Allocation and Portfolio Composition," 2010.

while executives should identify, measure, and contain corresponding exposures.

Institutional investors have been more vocal on matters related to governance as the value of good corporate governance is at the top of their priorities. The period of 2000–2020 has been especially productive for hedge fund activism on corporate governance. Activism includes actions on behalf of institutional investors to eliminate provisions and tactics to delay hostile takeover bids (for example, classified boards), voting rights (for example, supermajority provisions), golden parachutes, and takeover defenses (poison pills). Extensive academic research synthesized the results of more than seventy studies and documented that the activism in the 2000s has been more effective and material as it resulted in increases in firms' market values.[132] The creation of the Council of Institutional Investors by public pension funds in the mid-1980s accelerated shareholders' activism, and actions were translated to the interests of all shareholders. The evolution of shareholder proposals and the publicity of activists' successes on matters related to board structure, change of control transactions, and executive compensation, contributed to major changes in the works of boards.

One interesting development in recent years has been the trend toward passive investing and the growth of the index fund market. Vanguard, BlackRock, and State Street are the "Big Three" firms that manage the overwhelming majority of index funds. Index investors provide long-term capital and presumably stick with the firms that comprise the index. In theory if a firm is part of the index, investors should care about governance and influence changes when operating performance, and consequently, returns suffer.[133] Some research found that increased passive ownership is associated with greater tendency by activist investors to obtain board seats, remove takeover defenses, and facilitate a merger. Other studies suggest that passive investors tend to be passive monitors.[134] With the rise of institutional own-

---

[132] M. R. Denes, J. M. Karpoff, and V. B. McWilliams. "Thirty Years of Shareholder Activism: A Survey of Empirical Research," *Journal of Corporate Finance*, 44, 2017, pp. 405–424.

[133] I. R. Appel, T. A. Gormley, and D. B. Keim. "Standing on the Shoulders of Giants: The Effect of Passive Investors on Activism," *Review of Financial Studies*, 32, 7, 2018, pp, 2720–2774.

[134] E. Iliev, J. Kalodimos, and M. Lowry. " Investors' Attention to Corporate Governance," *The Review of Financial Studies*, 40, 1, 2021, pp. 201–229.

ership in foreign stocks, corporate practices of firms around the world have the tendency to converge to a US shareholder-centric model.

Despite the hotly debated topic of performance of indexed investment strategies relative to active management of funds, the trend is clear. Not only have many institutional investors asked companies to show evidence of responsible and sustainable investing, but many executives voluntarily adopted disclosures about the contributions of their firm toward ESG practices by reporting annual sustainability reports. For example, in 2017 85 percent of S&P 500 index companies and 60 percent of the Russell 1000 Index companies published sustainability reports. The number of companies will increase, and the executives will adhere to an additional pressure of decision scrutiny.

In this new environment, board directors and executives will be called to address key challenges in handling ESG initiatives that may involve the following:

- *Clearly define ESG dimensions.* The CEO typically uses the company's products and services to anchor the company's definition of ESG. Products and services serve as focal points to explore possible risks due to environmental concerns, societal changes, and governance oversight.
- *Integrate ESG into the corporate strategy.* The CEO should identify the most material risks and opportunities, and link ESG to financials.
- *Practice active oversight.* Clarify boards' ESG oversight responsibility and roles, and ensure effective management report to the board.
- *Manage external expectations.* Engage with investors, especially institutional investors to understand their perspectives. Understand critical stakeholders' perspectives. Externally report the current state of the company's ESG oversight.

The most difficult task for the CEO is to integrate the ESG framework into strategy. While there is not a specific approach used when formulating a strategy, it is suggested that the CEO develops the current ESG company profile and key exposure areas for the company.[135] As a next step,

---

[135] *Strategic Oversight of ESG: A Board Primer.* National Association of Corporate Directors (NACD), 2002.

the company can undertake an assessment of material risks at the time of strategy formulation with respect to environmental, societal, and governance dimensions. Material risks may be operationalized and typically include areas such as privacy and data security breaches, extreme weather conditions disrupting operations, workplace injuries, fines and penalties arising from ESG violations, impact from the growth of artificial intelligence on job creation, the impact of nanotechnology on product development and human health, linking executive compensation to ESG factors.

Since institutional investors have perceived power in allocating capital across sectors, can they play a role in influencing executives on matters related to corporate social responsibility, the environment, and sustainability? It is hypothesized that institutional investors representing the interests of diverse pension and savings plan participants believe that firms that "Do good, do well." There is an active theoretical debate on the value of ESG and corporate social responsibility for firms, but there is no clear evidence that firms that "Do good, do well." Often the causation is that firms that "Do well, do good" as well.[136] Unfortunately, there is no clear evidence that investors (shareholders) can receive good returns when executives follow decisions to do good for the society and the environment. The context within which executives make decisions matters as the corporate social responsibility initiates are treated in a variety of ways by the capital markets. For example, investors react in a neutral way to announcements of new initiatives for sustainability and the environment. When considering firms with high and low agendas on corporate social responsibility initiatives, there are no differences in returns, meaning that higher exposure to initiatives that deal with corporate social responsibility is not recognized with higher returns in the stock market. Also, funds with clear mandates to invest in companies with track records on matters related to corporate social responsibility exhibit performances that are no different than conventional funds. Other studies have found that when executives do not blindly develop environmental and sustainability investments, but rather pursue strategies that reduce the risk of costly environmental incidents and have higher risk-adjusted returns.[137]

---

[136] Pedro Matos. *ESG and Responsible Institutional Investing Around the World: A Critical Review.* CFA Institute Research Foundation, 2020.

[137] S. Glossner. "Investor Horizons, Long-Term Blockholders, and Corporate Social Responsibility," *Journal of Banking and Finance*, 203, June, 2019, pp. 78–97.

Regardless of this mixed evidence, the popular press in the 2010s reports often on stories highlighting a growing client demand for institutional investors to care about corporate social responsibility.

The interest in ESG issues, however, is beyond investing. In 2006, the United Nations developed the Principles of Responsible Investment (PRI) and invited institutional investors to become active in supporting ESG at target companies. More than 2,600 signatories around the world responded to the call by the end of 2020. Evidence shows that a large percentage of signatories is fully engaged with companies and try to implement ESG initiatives or disinvest in firms by screening companies that do not follow ESG initiatives. Studies also found that success in ESG investments are higher when there is a lead investor based in the same country as the targeted firm. Support is also significant for lead investors with large size of assets under management (AUM) and control large investment stakes in a targeted firm. The support of ESG initiatives by major institutional investors overall is reflected in good firm performance.[138]

There is limited evidence on how ESG investing affects returns and how much clients of institutional investors are willing to sacrifice in returns and impact investing. One legal complication is that most of large NYSE-listed firms have been incorporated in the state of Delaware, and state statutes enforce the shareholder "primacy" rule, which requires executives and directors to advance the welfare of shareholders, not stakeholders. Therefore, many touted initiatives of Delaware-incorporated firms focused on corporate social responsibility, if they sacrificed stock returns may deviate from the shareholders' wealth-maximizing objective. This puzzling contradiction adds complexity in handling decisions and creates challenges to executives in managing investments and financing choices in a world of conflicting goals.

Investment Trends in ESG

There is a continued commitment by many governments around the world and great investor interest in ESG issues. This defied initial concerns that during periods of harsh operating environments, as firms desperately try to

---

[138] E. Dimson, O. Karakas, and X. Li. "Coordinated Engagements," Working paper, appeared at SSRN, October 2019.

reduce costs and survive ESG standards would be abandoned. This has not happened, as shown by continued strong inflows into ESG-managed assets throughout the year: Morningstar, for example, recently estimated that sustainable fund assets now accounted for 9.3 percent of total fund assets. ESG funds in the United States have reached $225 billion in 2020, spectacular growth from $50 billion in 2015. We expect the share of ESG investments to continue because of primarily to three factors.

1. The realization that an erratic operating and living environment may be partly due to failures in environmental management. Over the past four decades, drastic climate changes contributed to many losses from disruptions in business operations.

2. Younger, educated professionals show interest in ESG, which is translated to more investments in these projects supporting climate and environmental initiatives. Their political engagement, along with social media coverage, shows that this generation makes not only investment but consumption choices to help improve climate and the environment.

3. An increasing body of ESG legislation and compliance requirements exists around the world. The emphasis has been placed on providing guidelines for sustainability and on changing operating models (for example, pollution) to improve environmental conditions.

Despite all these developments, investing in ESG and socially focused funds has not been widely adopted by US money managers of 401(k) retirement plans. According to the Plan Sponsor Council of American, only 2.6 percent of US corporate plans offered ESG funds as part of several investment options in employee-benefit plans.[139] This is primarily due to a US Labor Department rule issued in October 2020 that imposes restrictions on options and criteria used for available investment vehicles for a company's 401(k) funds. While it does not rule out a retirement plan's investment in ESG funds, it imposes conditions under which retirement plans may select ESG funds. One condition is that the plan administrator cannot sacrifice worker 401(k) returns for nonfinancial reasons. Plan administrators can

---

[139] Dawn Lim. "Wall Street Pushes to Reverse 401(k) Rule." *Wall Street Journal*, March 4, 2021.

consider ESG plans if they determine competing investment options would have equal financial merits. While the rule will be revisited in the future, almost $51 billion of new inflows were allocated in US 401(k) plans toward ESG funds in 2020, albeit a very small fraction of total inflows.

One interesting development is that ESG principles are increasingly vital for the alternative assets industry, not just public companies. Fund managers in private equity, hedge funds, private credit, and infrastructure private investments are responding to growing demand from institutional investors seeking to allocate to ESG-committed funds. Preqin[140] reports that since 2011, more than 4,400 ESG-committed private capital funds have raised $3.06 trillion in combined assets worldwide. Almost two-thirds (61 percent) of institutional investors surveyed by Preqin said that ESG will become a bigger part of the industry by 2025. However, as new demand for ESG-committed mandates grew, so did questions and skepticism from investment managers. Concerns arose from lack of an objective definition of ESG with key metrics and practical difficulties in managing portfolios under additional constraints while increasing performance returns. Pricing environmental-, social-, or governance-related risks may be difficult. For the ESG factors that have been quantified or qualitatively scored, standardization of these has also raised questions when trying to compare investment opportunities. Public markets have struggled with this despite greater transparency, but these concerns compound with the complex and opaque nature of private assets.

Regardless of the difficulties in implementing ESG rules in public and private market investments, the trend is clear. Institutional investors expect more ESG-initiatives for companies they invest in, and annual capital mandates supporting ESG goals have been increased steadily in the last two decades.

GLOBALIZATION AND INEQUALITY

The debate about the distribution effects of globalization across countries and industries has intensified in recent years, and CEOs of large companies unliterally are in the middle of the conversation. There is plenty of evidence

---

[140] "Preqin Impact Report: The Rise of ESG in Alternative Assets," London November 2020.

that the free movement of goods, services, capital, technology, and labor among countries integrates markets and economies and produces greater efficiency of resource allocation, higher productivity, and more investment opportunities. This has brought economic prosperity and created opportunities for companies to compete in the global marketplace. However, competition has brought social inequalities and undermined cultural customs. It has often been perceived as a potential threat for social and cultural cohesion.

Most important, executives, while competing globally, are confronted with local and domestic issues including inequality, marginalization of economically vulnerable groups, and possible loss of cultural diversity. As business leaders responsible for creating value to the organizations they lead, executives are challenged with promoting the principles of free trade to compete globally while asked to manage the demands of stakeholders in the local and domestic environment. One of the many demands in the local and domestic environment, where large global companies maintain operations, is to reverse income inequality. Considered the most contentious issue and the one of the negative side effects of globalization, income inequality is a puzzle to executives due to apparent contradictions in providing a solution. To bridge the gap of income inequality, business leaders understand that adjustments in labor wages should take place. These adjustments, in turn, increase labor costs, weaken profit margins, reduce stock returns, and create conditions for corporate disinvestments, which in turn reduce prosperity to the community where the company operates. In the long-term, impact of efforts in reducing income inequality diminish the firm's competitive advantage. These contradictions from leading efforts to compete globally while taking actions to reduce income inequality present additional challenges to executives, even more so in recent years with concerns about increased tariffs and supply chain discontinuities.

Income inequality is typically measured by the ratio of the income of the top 10 percent to the bottom 90 percent of earners in a country. It reflects both internal government policies as well as external/global economic considerations that influence a country's prosperity. Internal government policies involve fiscal decisions, taxation, and government actions related to redistribution of wealth in the country. External/global economic considerations deal with the country's export and import capabilities, attractiveness to foreign investments, adoption of new technology, and the degree of openness to migration/immigration.

Domestic government policies impact a country's income inequality. Global economic conditions, however, may reduce or amplify inequality of one country relative to the rest of the world. One should, therefore, distinguish between inequality within a country and inequality across the globe. Regardless of the perspective, three key factors explain inequality in broad terms: globalization, technological changes, and migration. The leading factor, globalization has caused both positive and negative outcomes in inequality.

Globalization started with China's ascent in the world economy. As the most significant economic development from 1990 to 2018, it has whetted the enthusiastic appetite of American businesses to trade with China. This was the result of the full integration of the Chinese economy into the world trade with the eventual inclusion of China to WTO in 1997. The integration of China into the global manufacturing more than doubled the available labor supply for the production of tradeable products worldwide. Between 1990 and 2017, the Chinese economy added 240 million workers to the global labor force, while the United States added less than 45 million workers during the same period.[141] In addition, after the fall of the Berlin Wall in 1989, Eastern European countries and their labor forces were integrated with EU economies and added to the global trading system. The combined effect of the rise of China and the integration of Eastern Europe to the global markets produced an oversupply of labor with marginal wage increases, thus very low inflation. Reduced trade barriers as negotiated with advanced and developing economies. In Doha in 2001, additional conditions were established to increase the acceleration of globalization.

These developments, however, created spillover effects to both advanced countries, like the United States, and developing economies, like China and other Asian countries. First, the oversupply of labor created dislocations for high-wage earners and substantially increased inequality in the United States. Second, as developing countries began integrating into the global economic system, their labor wages started converging to those of advanced countries. The result was a reduced gap in inequality between advanced or

---

[141] Charles Goodhart and Manoj Pradham. *The Great Demographic Reversal* (New York: Macmillan Palgrave, 2020).

developed and developing countries. Income inequality between countries and in the rest of the world has improved, but income inequality, especially wealth inequality, has worsened within most countries. The negative outcome of globalization on inequality has been amplified in recent years in advanced countries, especially in the United States.

When considering the impact of globalization on inequality, the following stylized facts provide a useful background to practicing executives.

- Inequality in the late 2010s has dominated the political debate in various counties, especially countries that are still characterized by modest economic recovery and high unemployment after the great financial crisis of 2008.
- The integration of emerging economies into the global economic system has allowed aggregate income levels to converge to those of advanced or developed economies, thus reducing poverty. Despite positive outcomes, without appropriate policies, income and wealth inequality persist in emerging/developing economies.
- One reason for income inequality is mobility of capital. When capital is moving outside a country, it causes dislocation of labor and uncertain certain conditions, including permanent unemployment of specialized workers. Inequality is amplified. In contrast, inequality is reduced with direct investments in a country with more economic growth as wage increases reduce inequality.
- Labor migration has a positive effect on the economy as migrants contribute to the labor force, as younger workers often increase consumption, boost economic growth, and contribute to the domestic retirement system. Overall, migration (or immigration) contributes in a positive way to human capital formation.
- A higher minimum wage reduces income inequality. However, the link of minimum wages and inequality should be treated with caution. An increase in minimum wage generally increases unemployment in the short term, which in turn increases income inequality. Only in the longer term and with the right government policies is income inequality reduced.
- Free trade and globalization increase living standards around the world. To compensate for the negative effects of globalization,

namely inequality and unemployment, governments and policy makers often intervene and consider the trade-offs between two options, (a) slow globalization via tariffs and other trade restrictions. or (b) redistribute income to reduce inequality and improve employment.

These stylized facts, based on years of research and anecdotal evidence, offer a glimpse to executives about the difficulties in decision-making. Typically, executives embrace globalization by boosting company profits from lower prices of imports of intermediary components of goods they produce or services they offer. Higher trade openness across firms facilitates competition, investments, and increased productivity. In addition, companies can increase their competitiveness by developing value chains and outsourcing parts to other countries either by establishing subsidiaries, acquiring ownership in foreign companies, or contracting third parties, all leading to cost efficiencies.

Against this background, executives are confronted with the consequences of free capital and trade movements that include inequality and discontent for globalization. In the late 2010s and early 2020s, executives have been challenged in making decisions to create value for the companies they lead as issues of inequality and globalization have been central to political debates in advanced and developing country economics about the role of modern corporation in society.

THE FUTURE OF BUSINESS LEADERSHIP

What is the future of leadership when executives operate in a constantly turbulent environment with crises or anticipatory changes? A turbulent environment may provide opportunities for change through discoveries and innovation, but also presents challenges to core competences of the firm. Opportunities and threats are constant reminders of the extremes faced by executives during their tenures. Today's business leadership handles the polarities and differences while sometimes dealing with the contradictions between what needs to be done and what should be possibly done, theory versus practice, and the intellectual aspects of leading a firm versus practical realities that shape the direction of the business. While the intellectual framework provides the tools to understand how things should be, today's business leaders should be anchored around the ideas as to what can realistically be done in a world of extraordinary change.

The challenges that arise from the natural evolution of the world in which we live place additional demands on the complexity of decisions facing executives and create even more demands on business leaders than what have ever seen before. Our framework in decision-making helps leaders think through all these constraints to be dealt with almost every day. Sometimes they are conflicting and confusing. Our methodology provides a process and necessary foundation through which business leaders can confront challenges.

How you manage within this world of change becomes critical. Understanding change is key. Business leaders need to consider, among other things, what is changing from a societal standpoint, the new era of globalization, and what we have learned from the 2020 pandemic. Focus on the company's strategy and customers is necessary but not sufficient to address value creation. Attention to broader issues of digitization, demographics, environmental concerns, and inequality become increasingly important in decision-making. In this respect, the practice of capitalism may change as we move from a pure laissez- faire, investor-driven, Anglo-American capitalist model to a more constituency-oriented model centered around a stakeholders' value approach.

There is no doubt that the role of business leaders becomes more demanding as their work impacts the economy and society. People, their jobs, their families, their partnerships, the communities in which they live are very dependent on the ability of business leaders to create value. In addition, the context within which business activity is conducted today presents extraordinary trade-offs that impact the very same constituencies that business leaders try to impact, namely people, their families, and their communities. Business leadership is more required today than it has been in the last thirty years. Business leaders will need not only the intellectual framework but also the necessary skills, so they are grounded in practical applications.

In addition, we believe excellence in leadership will require a new CEO mindset that revolves around the following priorities:

* *Emphasis on dynamics, not mechanics.* The mechanics of decision-making are important as they determine the process in decision-making considering the idiosyncrasies of the firm's competences and human capital. Dynamics present unexpected changes in the context within which decisions are made. The external and the internal environments of the firm are always evolving, and the CEO's mindset should be focused on the dynamic forces that influence the context of decision-making.

* *Alignment of incentives.* Decisions at the top, to be executed, require the interactions of people across markets and within the organization. In an ideal world, those interactions are costless and straightforward. Unfortunately, diverse incentives and myopic behaviors on behalf of those involved in the implementation of decisions may derail outcomes and generate costs to the organization. It is necessary to align incentives through formal mechanisms (that is, compensation plans) or informal method (that is, culture shift).

* *Tolerance of ambiguity, not adherence to conformity.* While it is impossible to predict the future, it is widely accepted that business leadership will be practiced in an increasingly ambiguous environment with everchanging boundaries. Decision-making at the top will require reexamination of traditional and preconceived perceptions about the world where companies operate. Questions about changes in the business environment, which in the past were peripheral to the core operations of any firm, may become central in decision-making in the future. For example, the role of globalization in society, the ESG movement, the practice of capitalism as we know will add new dimensions to the context of decision-making. There is certainly no clarity yet on these and other issues. Nor will there be a time when the answers will be complete. Excellence in business leadership will require a mindset of tolerating ambiguity in a changing environment, entertaining contradictory points of view, and engaging in discussions that involve conflicting actions.

* *Stick-to-itiveness.* A good strategy with thoughtful execution provides results. Emphasis on dynamics, underdamping incentives and tolerance of ambiguities are pre-conditions for leadership that provides tangible results. However, results require discipline and

willingness not to give up every time there is an obstacle to strategy. Commitment and stick-to-itiveness to execution are paramount.

We believe business leaders will be challenged in the future to create value in an environment that will involve most likely a new model for capitalism. Regardless of the context, we believe our methodology for decision-making provides the framework to create value, no matter how value is defined. Our methodology advances the notion that business success leading to value creation is centered around five key drivers: (1) strategy formulation, (2) asset deployment, (3) a financial model that supports the strategy while it creates profits, (4) leadership, and (5) organizational culture. While these elements independently are well understood as components to a plan, their management is paramount for value creation and success. All these elements are interdependent; however, they should be considered in an integrated way. Conventional wisdom and theory suggest that strategy is the only element that defines the success of a business. We believe the contradiction is that in practice, strategy is an important facet but not the only determinant for success. While strategy provides a road map, it remains an aspirational plan unless it is supported by strong leadership, a robust asset deployment program, a financial model that aligns investments with profits, and an inspiring culture that allows the company to execute the strategy. In addition, leadership will require an understanding of the dynamics of the business environment, tolerance of ambiguity of conflicting and contradictory views, and alignment of interests among participants in decisions.

All these considerations represent a set of concepts that make a powerful perspective and implementable framework for managing a company. It is a methodology that entertains the idea that two possibly contradictory views, the theory and the practice, can provide answers to adapt to unique circumstances.

The 2020 Global Pandemic Crisis

During their careers, business leaders are confronted with frequent crises, but the 2020 pandemic will be a unique experience to all. The shutdown of the economy and disruptions in supply chains for many businesses have been unprecedented with unknown consequences. History suggests that crises have usually taken a long time to be fully understood. Without doubt the debate about the policy response to the 2020 coronavirus pandemic and its social, economic, and business implications is likely to continue for several years. Unlike academics who may debate the implications of a crisis for some time, executives are required to develop immediate plans for business continuity without knowing details of the long-term implications of the pandemic on market outlook and their firms' operations. Primarily, decision-making in the short term tests the ability of business leaders to recalibrate goals, restructure operations, and reinvent the company (3Rs). Most importantly, the disruptions during the pandemic have urged executives to rethink how they can create long-term value in the post-COVID-19 era.

Many believe changes are forthcoming with renewed expectations for economic growth and prosperity. In fact, the 2020 pandemic has accelerated or exacerbated several preexisting business and economic trends that include digitalization and its impact on how individuals, businesses, and governments operate; divergence of economic progression within and between countries; demographics as long-term preexisting shifts in population distributions change political and economic priorities; and finally, debt, both public (as government fiscal deficits balloon) and private.

As technologies and business models continue their rapid evolutions, companies are experiencing a steep change in the workforce skills they need to thrive and grow. Previous research has shown that as many as 375 million workers globally might have to change occupations in the next decade to meet companies' needs, and automation could free employees to spend as much as 30 percent of their time on new work.[142]

The pandemic has created many changes, but we single out the impact on (a) CEO's priorities (b) Technology (c) the role of the Board and (d) new business opportunities and (e) economics and vaccines. As we conclude this section, we firmly believe these changes, while unique in the COVID-19 era they represent typical discontinuities in the course of competitive dynamics in an industry. Our methodology offers a framework for decision making that integrates five elements, ie., strategy, asset deployment, financial model to support profits, leadership, and corporate culture. Focus in managing this process that integrates the five elements improves value and profitability.

CEO Leadership Shifting Priorities

The pandemic has been a test of determination, character, and ability to innovate for all business leaders. Anecdotal evidence suggest that CEOs are more than ever committed to steer their firms through the difficult period of reestablishing supply chains, repositioning their products in the marketplace, and recapturing revenues. Some CEOs also demonstrate societal sensitivities by donating their bonuses to charities linked to initiatives to fight COVID-19. Others voluntarily give up a portion of their salaries. Many CEOs also spend time on the front lines, innovating and experimenting with new services and digital deliveries as the disruptive forces of the pandemic offered opportunities to reevaluate strategy and operations. Finally, the pandemic has provided a forum for an improved dialogue between the CEO and employees about building new or enhancing existing capabilities for the firm.

---

[142] McKinsey Global Institute. *Jobs Lost, Jobs Gained: Workforce Transitions in a Time of Automation*, December 2017

Building capabilities is a business imperative and critical to helping companies execute their objectives in the future. CEOs have many more opportunities to capture business value through capability building and with careful planning to capitalize on potentially new growth in the future. It is will not be surprising that those developments, because of CEOs leadership during uncertain times, will yield stronger companies in the post–COVID-19 era. Finally, the pandemic revealed to outsiders the true strength or weakness of every firm as cash flows were stressed to extreme ranges, traditional supply chain relationships were tested, and customers preferences shifted. In this environment the CEOs leadership became important and once the crisis is over, everyone is likely to remember how CEOs acted during the pandemic. To pass this toughest leadership test, CEOs have been paying more attention to what they say and do.

New Frontiers in Technology

The pandemic initially produced some clear winners, such as big tech, health care, and online delivery services. It has also unveiled a transformational change in using technology as a vehicle of communicating, interacting, and making decisions. With remarkable and fast adjustments to working conditions, management teams worked closer together, and several trends have been accelerated in terms of behavioral interactions and decision making. While behavioral changes may not be permanent, we believe companies will continue to use technology to enable teamwork and collaboration. Also technology played a big role in the adoption of a new consumer behaviors that require interfacing with computers or mobile devices to request products or services. New companies have been developed, and existing embryonic firms have become robust enterprises during the crisis as consumer demand increased.

The most significant innovation with respect to technology, however, has centered around health. Technology has accelerated the development of vaccines and the health-care sector will continue to play big roles in the economy as working conditions will improve, and all experts point to a new boom in tech and health-care services with artificial intelligence breakthroughs and new applications of immunology and gene therapies.

The Role of the Board during the Crisis

The pandemic brought renewed interest on the role of the board during a crisis. During a crisis, a great board, first and foremost, understands the difference between CEO's role and the board's role. The leadership team should be given the space to handle the crisis, while the board should provide thoughtful support and advice as needed and focus more attention on enterprise risk. This is not the time to request immediate changes to a strategic plan, ask for accountability, or ask meaningless details from the CEO. A board understands that the leadership team perhaps has exhausted its capacity to manage the organization as priorities have shifted. Also, a helpful board should exercise good judgment to determine the immediate business priorities and steps required to reduce earnings gaps generated from the crisis while keeping an eye on key strategic priorities. Moreover, constructive boards understand the trade-offs between maintaining long-term objectives and delivering short-term performance.

One of the many important lessons learned during the 2020 Covid19 crisis is the need for any firm to maintain a business continuity plan and to organize quickly crisis response teams to provide not only to provide solutions to problems encountered, but also to handle changes required due to new business conditions.

Redirection and New Opportunities

The challenges of the 2020 pandemic created an enormous economic contraction in the short term, but it is expected to create an unprecedented economic boom in 2021 and beyond. The return of confidence and anticipated strong consumer demand is expected to create a healthy economic growth. Some of the trends that impact businesses include acceleration of productivity with digital transformation of processes, permanent changes in shopping behavior, changes in the work from home policies, rebalance in supply chains, and shift in distribution networks. Despite these discontinuities, a wave of innovation and discoveries will offer new challenges to business leaders. It will be difficult to predict the business transformations that will take place in the years ahead but some anticipated changes include a revolution in medicine and biopharma, with discovery of new diagnostic tools, medicines and vaccines; emergence of artificial intelligence which will help improve efficiencies; revolution in the way education is delivered to students; emphasis on concerns about the environment and climate change; and demographic challenges as population cohorts will be impacted differently in the years to come.

The pandemic created its own set of challenges for businesses and in many instances produced restructuring opportunities and a chance to refocus on plans and strategies. CEOs are challenged more in finding suitable solutions to problems and charging new strategies for the future.

The Geoeconomics of COVID-19

All indications suggest that COVID-19 will likely be a chronic pandemic. The nature of the virus (SARS-CoV-2) makes it more dangerous and harder to control. In addition, scientists believe that additional viruses are on the rise due to high human contact with the environment. The lack of global preparedness and cooperation has resulted in lack of communication, lack of social and political adhesion, and limited efforts for surveillance of genomics. It is predictable that as the COVID-19 virus replicates, it will eventually mutate. Mutations are random and can be deleterious or advantageous for the virus, the latter of which is happening more frequently and are known as variants of concern (VOCs). This may require continuous updates of vaccines.

Boards and management teams now realize that firm's performance, let along value creation, is dependent on vaccines, an unknown and unimaginable risk prior to the pandemic. The location of the firm is important as rich and developed countries have more doses contracted than needed, while developing and emerging countries have much less. In a world with different speeds of vaccination, the pace of economic recovery varies and will likely be faster in advanced countries compared to emerging or developing countries. Therefore, the firm's performance is dependent on speed of vaccinations, the geography of its customers or clients, and the location of the firm.

Health concerns and disruptions of business activity will not end with a massive undertaking of vaccinating people against COVID-19. Vaccines will have to be regularly updated to address new diseases and reduce variants of

COVID-19. This will create fiscal consequences of the chronic disease burden, debt and deficit obligations will be evaluated, and economic volatility may rise from sporadic lockdowns. All these conditions will lead to chronic business disruptions that were not anticipated from past health crises.

Leadership after the Crisis

The COVID-19 crisis has created a new environment where business leadership is expected to provide solutions arising for what we hope to be a short-lived phenomenon. However, business leaders will be challenged in the future to create value after of more than a year discontinuity of operations. We believe our decision-making methodology provides the framework to create value, regardless of the context. Our methodology advances the notion that business success leading to value creation is centered around five key considerations: (1) strategy formulation, (2) asset deployment, (3) a financial model that supports the strategy, (4) leadership, and (5) organizational culture. Each element should be examined from the lens of useful information and experiences learned during the COVID-19 world to address issues like the ones we discussed in this appendix. For example, shifting CEOs priorities or technology innovations that result from the pandemic should provide invaluable insights as the leadership team formulates a strategy and updates the firm's financial model to create profits.

We believe CEOs have been dealing already with each element of our framework and have developed plans to address the long-term and short-term impact of the crisis on business operations. However, we advocate the significance in managing a decision-making process that involves the integration of the five elements we have outlined in our book. Systemic crises that affect an entire economy or idiosyncratic disruptions that impact specific industry sectors are frequent events. What differentiates winners from losers is the way leaders address these discontinuities which affect the nature of competition and industry dynamics. Our contribution is to advance an organized and well-structured process of decision making that when it is internalized, improves value and profits. Our collective experience suggests that the probability of success in outcomes is measurably improved when CEOs follow our integrative framework.